AF556346

TEACHING SCIENCE SUCCESSFULLY

ENCYCLOPAEDIA OF TEACHING

Vol. I

TEACHING SCIENCE SUCCESSFULLY

By

Prof. Marlow Ediger
M.A., B.S.E., Ed.D.
Emeritus Professor of Education
Truman State University
201 West 22nd Street
North Newton KS 67117
United States of America

&

Prof. Digumarti Bhaskara Rao
M.Sc., M.A., M.A., M.Ed., Ph.D.
Principal
R.V.R. College of Education
D-43 (277) S.V.N. Colony
Guntur - 522 006 (India)

DISCOVERY PUBLISHING HOUSE PVT. LTD.
NEW DELHI-110 002

First Published - 2007

Reprinted - 2016

ISBN: 978-81-7141-600-4

Teaching Science Successfully

Published by:

DISCOVERY PUBLISHING HOUSE PVT. LTD.

4383/4B, Ansari Road, Darya Ganj

New Delhi-110 002 (India)

Phone: +91-11-23279245, 43596064-65

Fax: +91-11-23253475

E-mail: discoverypublishinghouse@gmail.com

sales@discoverypublishinggroup.com

web: www.discoverypublishinggroup.com

Printed at:

Infinity Imaging Systems

Delhi

PREFACE

Science education has become an integral part of school education. The quality of science teaching, so, is to be developed considerably so as to achieve its purposes and objectives, viz., to understand basic principles, to develop problem solving, analytical skills and ability to apply them to the problems of material environments and social living besides promoting the spirit of enquiry and experimentation. In this modern world dominated by science and technology, the science teaching must be effective and innovative, and beneficial to pupils.

This book meant for preservice and inservice science teachers contains a scope and sequence that will assist each teacher to provide for every pupil to achieve as optimally as possible. The content of this book integrates well with content from mathematics, social studies, literature and the language arts. An inter-disciplinary curriculum with science as the core is truly stressed. This book will be very much useful to those who wish to teach science innovatively and effectively.

Prof. Marlow Ediger,

Dr. D. Bhaskara Rao

1

Philosophy and Psychology of Teaching Science

Science teaching must reflect change within a curriculum that stresses assisting pupils to attain optimally. Objectives, learning opportunities, and appraisal procedures in science need to be relevant and updated to incorporate National and state standards. Units of Instruction in science should stress inquiry, motivate pupils, and encourage high levels of interest. Educational philosophies and psychologies used in teaching-learning situations by the teacher must guide pupils to develop an inward desire to learn.

PHILOSOPHY OF SCIENCE TEACHING

The science teacher needs to have a wide repertoire or means of assisting pupils to achieve optimally. There are diverse educational philosophies for teachers to use that encourage optimal learner achievement.

First, a problem solving approach may be used. Inquiry learning is highly salient here. Ideally, pupils with teacher guidance need to identify a problem within the framework of an ongoing science unit of study. The problem must be clearly stated. Learners might then brain storm possible answers to the problem. Value judgments should not be made on responses given by pupils. The consequences or results of each brainstormed answer must be evaluated after the brainstorming session has been completed. A variety of manipulative, pictorial, and abstract materials should be used here. Science experiments may be at the heart of testing each response or hypothesis. Responses are then modified changed, or refuted as a result of the tests. John Dewey and other experimentalists emphasised problem solving strongly in their philosophy of experimentalism. Committee endeavours and cooperative learning are stressed in the problem solving science curriculum.

Experimentalists believe the science curriculum should be as closely related to the real world of society as possible. School and society are not separate but integrated entities. To emphasise problem solving, the science teacher must provide a learning environment that is stimulating and arouses pupil interests. Hopefully, the interests of learners will lead to problem identification. The goal of the science teacher is to have learners select relevant problems. The teacher becomes a resource person, guide, and helper, rather than one who lectures and presents content deductively to pupils. Thus learners need assistance in brain storming, locating reference sources, and attaining hypotheses as means of inquiry learning.

With pupils being heavily involved in selecting problems and strategies to solve each problem, a psychological curriculum is in evidence since each learner is heavily involved in sequencing or ordering his/her own experiences. The learner himself/herself tends to order experiences in a problem solving approach of teaching, according to educational psychologists. Pertaining to John Dewey's philosophy of experimentalism, Meyer (1949) wrote the following:

All this, of course, depends in no small way upon thinking. For Dewey, however, thinking becomes significant only when applied to life's situations. It is, he has said, "as instrumentality used by man in adjusting himself to the practical situations in life." Or to phrase it more simply, human beings think in order to live. Because to this stimulus, which has its basis in biology and sociology, it is impossible—it is absurd—to interpret life in a systematic and abstract way. Since, moreover, Dewey holds that life is in constant flux, it is impossible to solve problems with any degree of finality for the problems of tomorrow will be different fro those of today.

As for the problem of knowledge, Dewey believes that knowledge is experience and that true experience is functional. What is this thing for? What is its use? Is a coal mine a physical deposit or does it have function? And if so, what is it? Such are the questions that help give meaning to one's experience; but such questions cannot be answered without antecedent action. Action must precede knowledge. Whatever knowledge we possess has resulted from our activities, our efforts to survive, to obtain food, shelter, and clothing. Only that which has been organised into our disposition so as to enable us to adapt our environment to our needs and to adapt our aims and desires to the situations in which we exist is really knowledge.

A second philosophy of education to stress is a subject centered science curriculum. Here, the science teacher must select and teach vital facts, concepts, and generalisations to pupils. Inquiry learning emphasising critical and creative thinking, explanations, and vital discussions are methods of instruction used to teacher learners. Intellectual development is a major objective of science instruction. Mind is real and needs challenging subject matter to encourage mental development. Cognitive objectives should be emphasised primarily. However, affective goals are also salient as they assist pupils to attain cognitive ends of science instruction. It is important to secure pupils interest in science, but each learner must also will to learn. Tasks in life are interesting as well as those that do not stress interest. Thus, the pupil must develop a will to achieve, attain, and develop well intellectually.

Subject centered approaches in teaching science emphasise the abstract instead of the concrete and semi-concrete facets of learning. The concrete (use of real objects, excursions, realia, and experiments), and the semi-concrete (illustrations, videotapes, videodiscs, computers with diverse capabilities, among other audio visual aids) should be used as learning opportunities to assist pupils to achieve the abstract. Thus objectives in teaching science need to stress the abstract in subject matter to be acquired as well as higher levels of cognition in ongoing units of study in science. The teacher largely determines which objectives and learning activities pupils are to pursue sequentially. Thus a logical science curriculum is being emphasised, according to educational psychologists. Ediger (1995) wrote:

Idealists are very academic and rigorous in the teaching of subject matter. They emphasise cognitive objectives much more so than affective (attitudinal) or psychomotor (use of muscles and eye-hand coordination) in teaching-learning situations. Meaning, understanding, and depth learning of subject matter are important to idealists. Vital subject matter, carefully selected, needs to be taught to students. The student in acquiring subject matter in ongoing lessons is to move form the finite (limited) to the Infinite Being. Ideas are important to attain in an idealist's curriculum. The ideal is also salient to achieve in terms of moral standards and values.

The teacher emphasising idealism as a philosophy of education stresses the selection of subject matter for student achievement which assists forming vital concepts and generalisations. Objectives of instruction need to reflect worthwhile concepts and generalisations. Depth teaching of specifics assists students to form and develop universal ideas. The use of behaviourally stated objectives for instruction would be frowned upon by the idealist teacher. Content would become too fragmented with the realist's position of testing and measuring reflecting measurably stated objectives. Rather, the idealist in emphasising an idea centered curriculum desires that students relate subject matter acquired so that intense learning transpires. Thus if students are studying causes of World War II, each cause would be studied thoroughly and not merely listed. Causes come in sequence and are complex to appraise. Viewing and analysing each cause takes time. After analysing, relating, or synthesising ideas take time in order to emphasise intensity, not survey teaching. Students are to be evaluated in progress as to how much vital subject mater has been acquired.

The use of the mind or intellect is salient for students to utilise in analysing and synthesising subject matter knowledge. Mental development is stressed as students learn, achieve, and develop.

Implications from idealism as a philosophy of education for the curriculum include the following:

1. intellectual, not attitudinal, nor psychomotor, goals come first in teaching-learning situations;
2. quality textbooks, workbooks, and selected audio-visual materials which aid in intellectual development should be used as learning activities to achieve stated goals for students;
3. evaluation techniques should stress appraisal of vital subject matter acquired by students;
4. depth teaching of subject matter is salient of guide learners to attain vital facts, concepts, and generalisations. Survey approaches are not acceptable;
5. the will of the student is needed to attain worthwhile subject matter. Interest of students, alone, is not adequate for students to achieve, attain, and develop well. Students must want to learn;
6. students need to achieve vital subject matter to prepare for the future life of an adult. Education is preparation for adult responsibilities, not present day situations in being a child;
7. learners need to develop from a finite (limited) being toward the Absolute or the Infinite (unlimited being). The Absolute may also be referred to as God;
8. a quality general education programme, consisting of vital content from major academic disciplines, is a must for all students.

A third philosophy of teaching emphasises pupils being

heavily involved in decision making in terms of choosing objectives, learning opportunities, as well as evaluation procedures. The science teacher needs to set up more stations with quality tasks than what any one pupil can complete. The pupil may then select sequential tasks to complete. Those tasks not having perceived purpose may be omitted by the learner. The teacher must choose relevant learning opportunities for pupils to select. Inquiry, problem solving, as well as critical and creative thinking tasks, are vital learning activities for pupils at each station. Careful consideration must be given to the worth of each station and task. The interests of pupils need to be cultivated in the science curriculum. The pupil is the chooser of which tasks to pursue and complete. The science teacher is a guide and stimulator but not a dispenser of information.

The attitudinal dimension is very important to develop within pupils when they select that which is vital to attain. Learners need to learn to make choices and decisions. Life itself consists of making choices within the framework of being open-ended and possessing freedom. In the science curriculum, pupils too need to make choices in which coercion is kept to a minimum A decision making philosophy stress the learner being responsible for choices and completions made. Decision making is a skill and an attitude that pupils should learn due to its tremendous value presently and in the future for pupils.

With pupils being heavily involved in choosing sequential tasks to complete, a psychological curriculum is then in evidence due to pupils sequencing their very own activities in the science curriculum.

Pertaining to existentialism and pupil choices in the curriculum, Ozman and Craver (1990) wrote:

It is interesting that most existentialists and phenomenological philosophers have had lengthy and rigorous educations... . Most of them taught at one time or another, usually in a university setting. They have been primarily concerned with the humanities and have written exclusively in the genre. Through the humanities the existentialists have tried to awaken modern individuals to the dangers of being swallowed by the megalopolis and runaway technology. This seems to have taken place because the humanities contain greater potential for introspection and the development of self-meaning than other studies.

The humanities loom large in an existentialists curriculum because they deal with the essential aspects of human existence such as the happy, the absurdities as well as meaning. In short, existentialists want to see humankind in its totality—the perverted well as the exalted, the mundane as well as the glorious, the despairing as well as the hopeful, and they feel that the humanitites and the arts do this better than the sciences. Existentialists, however. do not have any definite rules about what should comprise the curriculum. They believe that the student-in-situation making a choice should be the deciding factor.

Although existential phenomenologists have been interested in understanding the lived experience of the learner than in the specific content to be learned, some of them have given attention to curriculum organisation and content. The tendency, however, is to view curriculum from the standpoint of the learner rather than as a collection of discrete subject matter.

A fourth philosophy of education for science teachers to follow is a criterion referenced (CRT) procedure of instruction. Here the teacher needs to write measurably stated objectives for pupil attainment. These objectives are always written prior to teaching pupils. Each objective is written in as precise a manner as possible. Ideally there is no leeway in interpreting what will be taught when examining any one measurably stated objective. The science teacher can measure after instruction if a learner has or has not achieved a measurably stated objective. The CRT measures against the measurably stated objectives to ascertain pupil achievement.

Science teachers may even announce to pupils what they are to learn as a result of instruction. Learners then might possess security in terms of what they are expected to achieve as a result of teaching and learning. Learning activities selected by the teacher to assist pupils to achieve must be aligned with the measurably stated objectives. These activities must be selected on the basis of guiding each pupil to achieve objectives. A logical curriculum is in evidence if the teacher chooses sequential objectives for pupil attainment as well as learning opportunities that are sequentially arranged so that pupils can experience success in learning.

Since teachers determine the sequence of objectives and learning opportunities for pupils of pursue, a definite logical curriculum is being stressed by science teachers. The teacher then attempts to arrange the order of objectives and activities to guide optimal pupil achievement. Pertaining to realism, Bowyer (1970) wrote the following:

We have noted that there are different forms of naturalism and of idealism. The same is true of realism, which makes it difficult to define the realist point of view. One element that the various forms of realism do have in common is a rejection of the idealist theory of knowledge that the various qualities of experience depend upon a knower for their existence. Realists believe the universe is composed of real entities that exist in themselves. These entities can be known, and their existence is not dependent upon a knower or perceiver. Although realists can agree on this point, the do not all agree when they attempt to build a metaphysical system. Here, their views range from pluralism to dualism to monism.

The realist epistemological views include epistemenological monism where it is held that objects are presented in consciousness, and epistemological dualism where objects are thought to be represented. The monist defines mind as a relation between the organism and an object, while the dualists identify mind more closely with the organisms. Realists do have a tendency to view the world as the mechanism described by the physical sciences and they generally believe in determinism, in orderliness in the universe, and the objectivity of science. The unifying thesis of realism is that knowledge is thought to have a universal character and comes to man through his sensory capacity. The realists have a confidence in their assertions about reality and value which is most discerning to pragmatists.

RECENT PSYCHOLOGIES OF LEARNING

B.F. Skinner (1904-1990) was very instrumental in emphasising S-R theory of instruction. With S-R theory in teaching science, Skinner advocated programmed learning for pupils. Programmed learning can take place either in textbook or computer/software form. Here, pupils move forward very slowly from the simple to that which is gradually more complex. Pupils then respond to a logical sequence developed by the programmer. Thus the pupil reads a small amount of content, responds to a completion item, and checks his/her response with that provided by the programmer. If the pupil responded correctly, he/she moves on to the next sequential item. If the learner responded incorrectly, he/she tries a different response. If correct, the learner also moves on to the next sequential item. The sequence is the same each time with read, respond, and check. If the learner is correct, he/she is rewarded and reinforced for giving the correct answer to the completion item as provided by the programmer. Skinner believes that a programmer can always put in another item should the pupil taking the programme in the pilot study miss out in a sequential item. A quality programme should make for a ninety per cent correct pupil response per item for each in the pilot study. The pilot study involves conducting experiments to find out where weaknesses lie in the programme. If too many learners, miss an item, perhaps an additional step needs to be put in where these pupils responded incorrectly. Poorly written items are taken out or modified so that responses can be made based on clarity within that step of learning. I have observed selected well written programmes in science units of study which reflect the thinking of B.F. Skinner. Pertaining to programmed learning, Harris and Sipay (1985) wrote the following:

Programmed materials are designed so that the user (1) encounters a series of small steps on which success is very likely (2) is involved in the learning process through actively responding (3) receives immediate feedback as to the correctness of each response. In theory, programmed material should greatly facilitate individualised instruction because they allow each student to work almost independently with material suitable for his or her needs, proceeding at a pace commensurate with ability and interest.

Ediger (1997) wrote the following pertaining to programmed instruction:

The programmer decides upon the objectives for each programme. Also, the sequential activities and appraisal procedures are determined by the programmer. There is basically no input for pupils or from teachers in terms of objectives, learning activities, and evaluation procedures when utilising programmed materials.

Advantages given for using programmed learning include the following:

1. each learner may pace his/her own optimal speed of learning. No two pupils need to be at the same or similar level of achievement;
2. learners know immediately if they are right or wrong in responses made;
3. rarely do learners make mistakes in quality programmed materials. The error rate is five to ten per cent in field tested programmes;
4. reinforcement is possible in field tested programmed items. Thus an involved learner might experience rather continual progress;
5. sequential progress is made in small steps rather than covering content in terms of a large scope at a time.

Disadvantages given in emphasising programmed learning include:

1. programmed learning may not harmonise with learning styles of selected pupils;
2. step by step learning—read, respond, and check—does not harmonise with expectations of life in society. Life in society is not programmed;
3. programmed materials tend to deemphasise the utilisation of the concrete (reality), and semi-concrete (pictorial form) materials. Abstract content tends to be rather heavily emphasised in programmed materials;
4. selected pupils may not perceive interest and purpose in the programmer choosing objectives, learning activities, and evaluation procedures;
5. small sequential steps in learning may be too finite or limited to meet personal needs of gifted and talented learners.

The influence of programmed learning and the thinking of B.F. Skinner has had wide influence in educational thought. There still are programmed books available on many topics in book form as well as in computer packages. Perhaps, the strongest influence of Dr. Skinner is in the use of behaviourally stated objectives in teaching. These objectives are very precise and are written prior to instruction. A pupil as a result of instruction either does or does not achieve any single objective. Thus, it is possible to measure if a pupil has been successful in goal attainment. Leaning activities selected by the teacher align with the stated objectives. The evaluation procedures also are aligned with the measurably stated objectives. Objective results from pupils are in evidence from instruction, regardless of who does the evaluating. Relating B.F. Skinner's thinking and that of the behaviourally stated objectives movement, the following writing will assist in clarifying the two (Morris and Pai 1976):

As Skinner pointed out several times, the most important task of the teacher is to arrange the conditions under which desired learning can occur. Considering the fact that teachers are expected to bring about changes in extremely complex behaviour, they should be specialists in human behaviour. Effective and efficient manipulation of the muititude of variables affecting children's intellectual and social behaviours cannot be accomplished by trial and error alone, nor should such work be based solely on the personal experiences of the teacher, since this covers only a limited range of circumstances. Consequently, a scientific study of human behaviour is vital in the improvement of teaching, because it provides us with accurate and reliable knowledge about learning and leads us to the development of new instructional materials, methods, and techniques. Similarly, an empirical analysis of the teaching process is essential, for it clarifies the teacher's responsibility through a series of small and progressive approximations. Thus facilitating a more effective evaluation.

The measurably stated objectives movement, also called behaviourism as a psychology of learning, emphasises a rather closed system of instruction. The objectives are predetermined and may be announced to pupils for each end to be stressed, as the need progresses. The learning activities and the evaluation techniques harmonise or align. Many educators believe that this alignment optimalise learner achievement in teaching and learning situations.

With this close alignment, little room is left for pupils to raise questions that they deem to be relevant and vital.

HUMANISM IN THE SCIENCE CURRICULUM

Toward the other end of the continuum, humanism, as a psychology of learning stresses heavy pupil involvement in selecting objectives, learning opportunities, and appraisal procedures, the pupil here is the focal point of instruction. Learners are to involved in sequencing their own experiences; this emphasises a psychological science curriculum whereas the behaviourally stated objectives psychology advocated a logical sequence for pupils whereby the teacher orders objectives for pupil attainment. Pertaining to humanism and existentialism, Ediger (1996) wrote:

Existentialists believe that one exists and then purposes need to be found or developed. The individual self then determines his/her own goals in life. There are no absolutes or guidelines in life to choose what is right and what is good. Each person must select and make decisions. To avoid making decisions is to lack being human. The choice then is to go along with the crowd. However, to be human involves making decisions.

The only broad criterion for existentialists to follow in choosing is to make moral decisions in a complete atmosphere of freedom. Others should definitely not decide one's destiny. One did not ask to be born and yet each person must make authentic decisions.

Moral decisions are difficult to make. An environment of awe exists in making authentic decisions.

Which objectives, learning activities, and evaluation procedures should be inherent in an existentialist curriculum? Existentialists believe in each person choosing objectives. In the school setting, the goals may be selected by learners with teacher guidance within the framework of an open-ended curriculum. The teacher needs to select ends, means, and evaluation procedures which stress the importance of pupils becoming increasingly responsible for personal freedom. The teacher should definitely not be a policeman. Rather, teachers realise their role as providing for an open environment in order that the learner may select sequential experiences... .

Each decision made in life involves personal decisions in reaching a goal or goals... . Each person makes or breaks himself or herself. No other person or being is responsible for consequences of decisions made. Blaming others for what happened in life is meaningless, according to existentialists. Each person needs to learn to accept responsibilities for thoughts, deeds, and actions.

The humanist existentialist science curriculum may be implemented in several ways. One approach is to use learning centers in the school/classroom setting. We have observed the following learning centers pertaining to the science unit "The Changing Surface of the Earth," from which pupils may select sequential tasks to complete:

1. a reading center;
2. an art center;
3. a drama center;
4. a writing center;
5. an audio-visual center;
6. a computer and software center;
7. a music center;
8. a model making center;
9. a problem solving center;
10. an experiment center.

Each pupil in a classroom may select which center and which task to work on. There are more tasks at each center than what any one child can complete. Learners may then choose what to work on and what to omit in a humanistic science curriculum. The individual pupil determines sequence or order of which tasks to pursue and which to omit. Purpose for learning then reside within the pupil. Examples of which materials will be at a learning center and the kinds of tasks or learning activities that will be in evidence may be illustrated with the first center mentioned above—a reading center. Here, a variety of library books on the unit title and on diverse reading levels need to be in evidence. A pupil chooses a book to read and may complete as many of the following tasks at this center as individual purpose dictates:

1. write a summary covering content read;
2. make a model of inherent subject matter read, such as a model volcano;
3. draw a picture of folding and faulting;
4. write an additional page for the library book read;
5. identify a problem dealing with changes on the earth's surface and use various reference sources to locate information for solving the problem.

Pupils individually make choices sequentially as to what to learn and the means of learning. Tasks can relate to choosing to work by the self or with others. If too many work at one center, the teacher may make a rule as to the optimal number of pupils that may work at any one center. The science teacher here is a guide or motivator of pupils to stay on task and complete satisfactorily what has been selected as learning activities. The pupil may even plan with the teacher what to work on if greater purpose is perceived in working on something else than what is at any of the centers.

Humanists advocate that pupils reveal authentic behaviour, not facades, to be authentic, the pupil needs to reveal more of the real self. Trust in communicating with others is important. Humans have tremendous worth and value. Being authentic and trusting others in a positive relationship is relevant to humanists.

Many studies currently made stress the importance of multiple intelligences. Sternberg (1997) emphasises that in a Yale University study, intelligence has analytical, creative, and practical aspects. He presets the following model for science in four categories:

Memory—name the four types of bacteria;

Analysis—analyse the means the immune system uses to fight bacterial infections;

Creativity—suggest ways to cope with the increasing immunity bacteria are showing to antibiotic drugs;

Practicality—suggest three steps that individuals might take to reduce the likelihood of bacterial infection.

In any lesson and unit of study, the science teacher may emphasise these four categories of instruction. Pupils need to achieve at higher levels of cognition than the memory level. Learners will then reveal in different ways what has been learned in the analysis, creativity, and practicality levels. Intelligence then is not a single score nor a single way of indicating what has been learned. Sternberg (1997) goes on to say:

By exposing students to instruction emphasising each type of ability, we enable them to capitalise on their strengths while developing and improving new skills. This approach is also important because students need to learn that the world cannot always provide them with activities that suit their preferences. At the same time, if students are never presented with activities that suit them, they will never experience a sense of success and accomplishment. As a result, they may tune out and never achieve their full potential... .

Success in today's job market often requires creativity, flexibility, and a readiness to see things in new ways. Furthermore, students who graduate with A's but cannot apply what they have learned may find themselves failing on the job.

Creativity, in particular, has become even more important over time, just as other abilities have become less valuable. For example, with the advent of computers and calculators, both penmanship and arithmetic skills have diminished in importance. Some standardised ability tests, such as the SAT, even allow students to use calculators. With the increasing availability of massive, rapid data retrieval systems, the ability to memorise information will become even less important... .

This is not to say that that memory and analytical abilities are not important. Students need to learn and remember the core content of the curriculum, and they need to be able to analyse—to think critically about—the material. But the importance of these abilities should not be allowed to obfuscate what else is important.

In a pluralistic society, we cannot afford to have a monolithic conception of intelligence and schooling, it's simply a waste of talent. And as I unexpectedly found in my study, it's no random waste. The more we teach and assess students based on a broader set of abilities, the more racially, ethnically, and socio-economically diverse our achievers will be. We can easily change our closed system—and we should. We must take a more balanced approach to education to reach all of our students.

Sternberg believes strongly that pupils individually are not permitted to indicate what has been learned in diverse ways. It is true that pupils so often are asked to show achievement through testing, generally through pupils taking multiple choice tests. Thus verbal approaches are used to ascertain what pupils individually have learned. This is limiting in that there are many other means of revealing achievement. Howard Gardner (1995) has determined there are at least seven intelligences, according to his research; these are verbal-linguistic, interpersonal, intrapersonal, musical, spatial, bodily-kinesthetic, and logical mathematics. Pupils may show similar strengths, but not necessarily in the same ways or to the same extent over time. With multiple intelligences, pupils learn in diverse ways and are interested in different subject matter in the academic arena. Learners then reveal their strengths and weaknesses in what has been learned in a variety of ways, not one way only such as in verbal testing using multiple choice items. Thus, the pupil who is strong in the verbal arena will reveal differently what has been learned as compared to the one endowed with musical intelligence. Too frequently, the emphasis has been upon verbal approaches to assessing pupil achievement and yet there are numerous other ways to indicate intelligence, as Gardner has indicated in multiple intelligences theory. Hatch (1997) wrote:

> Such a view of intelligence is reflected in programmes and practices that seek to determine which areas young children show the greatest strengths. Children who do well on tasks in a particular area—story telling or reporting, athletics or dance, drawing or building—are broadly labeled as having strengths in linguistics, bodily-kinesthetic, or spatial realms, respectively.
>
> Such an approach, however, implies that children have a reservoir of talent in a variety of activities, shown consistently over a period of time. It suggests that there are more intelligences,

but does not necessarily call into question assumptions about the nature, display, and development of intelligence.

Conclusion

Science teachers need to develop a philosophy and psychology of instruction that optimalise learner attainment. Pupils differ from each other in many ways including methods and procedures of acquiring relevant facts, concepts, and generalisations. A careful study and implementation of a worthwhile philosophy and psychology of learning might well assist each pupil to learn as much as possible.

To stress science as inquiry in harmony with National Standards, the writer emphasises what he believes to be best from each school of thought discussed above. These are:

1. a problem solving science curriculum in which pupils with teacher guidance identify and solve relevant lifelike problems;
2. a subject centered science curriculum emphasising pupils attaining higher levels of cognition in achieving salient facts, concepts, and generalisations;
3. pupil selection from among alternatives of takes perceived to be purposeful. Tasks at different stations should reflect science as inquiry;
4. measurably stated objectives which reflect National Standards in a predetermined science curriculum. Precise objectives are then selected prior to instruction for learner attainment. A carefully designed science curriculum may then be in evidence. The content obtained should be inherent in science as inquiry teaching and learning.

Pertaining to the psychology of learning in science, pupils should achieve quality sequence. Interest, purpose, and meaning are important concepts to stress in teaching science in ongoing lesson plans and units of study.

With multiple intelligences theory, pupils do learn in different ways and through diverse methods of instruction. Learners individually do possess their favourite means of learning and achieving. There are numerous methods of revealing what has been learned.

The science teacher then needs to have pupils participate in a variety of learning opportunities and have them indicate achievement using diverse procedures to provide for different learning styles possessed. The following learning opportunities are available for pupils in the science curriculum:

1. hands on approaches in learning;
2. experiments and demonstrations;
3. field trips and excursions;
4. problems solving experiences;
5. reading from basal texts, library books, and science encyclopaedias;
6. viewing video tapes, video disks, films, and filmstrips;
7. discussing, interviewing, dramatizing, and pantomiming;
8. writing poems, plays, outlines, summaries, diary entries, log entries, journal entries, and stories;
9. making dioramas, collages, bulletin board displays, murals, models, and equipment for science experiments;
10. using technology such as computer packages, the word processor, internet and world wide web, and calculators.

References

Bowyer, Carlton (1970), *Philosophical Perspectives for Education.* Glenview, Illinois: Scott, Foresman and Company, page 17.

Ediger, Marlow (1995), *Philosophy in Curriculum Development.* Kirksville, Missouri: Simpson Publishing Company, pages 22 and 23.

Ediger, Marlow (1997), *The Modern Elementary School.* Kirksville, Missouri: Simpson Publishing Company, pages 110 and 111.

Ediger, Marlow (1996), *Essays in School Administration.*. Kirksville, Missouri: Simpson Publishing Company, pages 58 and 59.

Ediger, Marlow and D. Bhaskara Rao (2000), *Teaching Mathematics Successfully.* New Delhi, India: Discovery Publishing House.

Gardner, Howard (1995), "Reflections on Multiple Intelligences: Myths and Messages,' *Phi Delta Kappan* 77,3:200-203, 206-209.

Harris, Albert J., and Edward R. Sipay (1985), *How to increase Reading Ability.* White Plains, New York: Longman, Page 71.

Hatch, Thomas (1997), "Getting Specific about Multiple Intelligences," *Educational Leadership*, 54, 6:26.

Meyer, Adolph (1949), *The Development of Education in the Twentieth Century*, Englewood Cliffs, New Jersey: Prentice-Hall, Inc., pages 42-43.

Morris, Van Cleve, and Young Pai (1976), *Philosophy and the American School.* Boston: Houghton Mifflin Company, page 340.

Ozman, Howard A., and Samuel M. Craver (1990), *Philosophical Foundations of Education* Columbus, Ohio: Merrill Publishing Company, page 257.

Rao, Digumarti Bhaskara (2000), *Teacher and Education.* Guntur, India: Nagarjuna Publishers (in Telugu language).

Sternberg, Robert J. (1997), "What Does It Mean to be Smart? *Educational Leadership*, 22-24.

Vijaya Bharathi, D. and D. Bhaskara Rao (2000), *Educational Philosophies of Swami Vivekanand and John Dewey.* New Delhi, India: APH Publishing Corporation.

2

Scope and Sequence in Science

The science curriculum needs continuous study. There are changes in science content that has been discovered by scientists and needs incorporation. For example, surrounding the planet Saturn are ringlets that just a few years ago appeared to be a solid core of rings around this planet. Facts, concepts, and generalisations in science need to be accurate and taught in an understandable manner to pupils. The science teacher then needs to keep up with the latest information in science. Subject matter here does not stand still, but modifications and new idea come to us from the world of science.

In addition to new subject matter being available for science teaching, modified and innovative approaches in teaching and learning are in the offing. The science teacher needs to keep abreast of methods of teaching and learning that will assist pupils to learn more optimally. Society seemingly wants higher achievement from pupils, and thus science teachers need to find the best approaches possible that help pupils learn as much as possible.

Inservice education to stimulate quality teaching should be in the offing. Thus, improved objectives in the science curriculum might be available to teachers in teaching/learning situations. These objectives have been carefully scrutinised to provide relevant goals for pupil attainment. Methods of instruction should highlight what is salient to stress in ongoing lessons and units of study.

The total set of objectives for pupil achievement need to be challenging, yet attainable. They need to stimulate interest in learning, but emphasise that which is salient and important, not trivia. Major concepts and generalisations should then be stressed in the ongoing curriculum. A variety of interesting procedures need to be used to guide pupil acquisition of these goals.

Learning opportunities need to possess tendencies to motivate pupils to persevere and accomplish. These activities are varied and provide for pupils of different achievement levels so that each may learn as much as possible. Learning opportunities help pupils to attain the stated science objectives. They are ordered in a manner that assist pupils to achieve, develop, and grow in science learnings.

A quality programme of evaluation needs to be in the offing so that pupils may reveal what has been acquired and achieved. Diverse techniques of evaluation need to be used to truly determine what pupils have achieved in ongoing lessons and units in science.

Teachers, school administrators, parents, and the lay public should have a clear understanding as to what the goals of science instruction are as well as of pupil achievement gained in the science curriculum.

SCOPE IN THE SCIENCE CURRICULUM

Teachers and school administrators need to give ample time to study the scope of the science curriculum. Scope refers to the breadth of objectives that need to be emphasised within each science unit of study. A subject centered approach has been used to determine scope. Thus, those involved in developing science units of study use diverse reference materials to ascertain what should be taught. Science textbooks, university science professors, state mandated science objectives, courses of study, curriculum guides, internet science units of study presented therein, teachers, principals, national school science study groups, among others, may provide information on the scope of the science curriculum in terms of relevant subject matter. The academic disciplines, such as the earth sciences, the physical sciences chemistry, and the biological sciences, may be analysed to secure vital subject matter ideas. Salient content from these sources then may be stated as objectives for pupils to achieve. Subject matter chosen needs to be:

1. significant for learners;
2. useful in dealing with problems in society, such as solving environmental dilemmas;
3. important for an educated person to know, such as current events that deal with the natural environment;
4. attainable for pupils in ongoing activities and experiences;
5. challenging to motivate pupil learning;
6. planned to provide opportunities for pupils to organise and classify content acquired;
7. flexible to encourage pupil input into each science lesson, including question raised by learners, as well as emphasising pupil/teacher planning;
8. vital in stressing key, structural ideas in ongoing units of study;
9. evaluated using voluntary national standards and objectives;
10. appraised rather continuously to keep abreast with current trends in teaching science.

By following the above named guidelines in teaching science, the teacher may offer a curriculum which will be beneficial to learners, presently as well as in the future. There is much science subject matter for pupils to learn. Thus, it is imperative to determine the scope carefully and meticulously. If the scope of science instruction pertains only to pupils' acquiring relevant subject matter, narrowness in breadth of objectives for pupils to attain is indeed then in evidence. Certainly there are vital skills in science that are equally important to emphasise in ongoing science lessons and units of study. Modes of inquiry that scientists use should be incorporated into teaching and learning situations. With skills processes inherent in acquiring subject matter in science, the scope of the curriculum should include the following for pupil achievement:

1. being a good observer. The learner then does not jump to hasty conclusions in a science experiment, but observes carefully what actually does transpire;
2. identifying questions and problems,. In context, or as the need arises, the pupil identifies gaps in knowledge which require necessary information;
3. communicating ideas clearly. In a discussion setting, the learner presents ideas orally that possess meaning and clarity. Being able to communicate effectively is a must in studying scientific phenomena;
4. measuring accurately in the scientific world is important. Science tends to stress numerical data, such as in measuring force, distance, velocity, acceleration, average speed, among others, in the physical sciences;
5. classifying knowledge to bring order and meaning from a mass amount of information. Thus, vertebrates may be classified in terms of fish, amphibians, reptiles, birds, and mammals;
6. achieving reliable inferences. Not always is knowledge and data presented clear cut and precise, thus requiring pupils to develop inferences. For example, in reading United States population figures covering the years 1890 to 2000 from a table in terms of ten year intervals, a pupil needs to be able to infer what has transpired in time. Reading between the lines is necessary here;
7. thinking scientifically. Here, the pupil needs to be objectives and remove all biases in thinking. Wherever

the truth may lead in scientific investigations, the pupil is willing to follow evidence and analysed reliable information;

8. using reliable reference sources. These include quality experiments and demonstrations, objectives conclusions reached by qualified individuals and groups, reputable textbooks, science encyclopaedias, significant internet and world wide web sources of scientific information, CD ROMS, trade books, video-tapes, films, filmstrips, illustrations, drawings, diagrams, excursions, as well as concrete, semi-concrete, and abstract materials of instruction, in general;

9. being open-minded. In science, pupils need to invite verifiable facts, concepts, and generalisations for discussion in problem solving. Testing ideas in problem solving, using experiments and demonstrations, is salient in the science curriculum. Opposite of open-mindedness is the closed mind which does not accept evidence, even though it is trustworthy. Appreciating the methods of science in obtaining trustworthy information is vital for all children;

10. exhibiting curiosity in wanting to learn. Young children, in particular, desire to know more about the natural environment. They appear to have much interest in all facets of nature. Animal life, specifically, draws the wonder and awe of young children. As pupils progress through the different years of schooling, the science teacher has a challenge in securing the interests of and motivating pupils to attain vital science objectives.

ATTITUDINAL OBJECTIVES IN SCIENCE

In addition to knowledge and skills objectives, the teacher needs to stress attitudinal ends of instruction. Good attitudes help pupils in wanting to learn more science. This means that having positive attitudes toward science guides pupils to achieve knowledge and skills objectives in depth. These attitudinal, or affective objectives, goals make it possible for the learner to like learning in science in its diverse manifestations. In supervising and observing student teachers/cooperating teachers in the public schools, in talking with school administrators, and in conducting research, we have compiled the following pertaining to attitudinal goals that are relevant for pupil attainment:

1. wanting intrinsically to learn science. This inward desire to learn is perhaps the most important factors in learner achievement in ongoing lessons and units in science. There are pupils who inwardly achieve, grow, and develop in science. On their own as well as in class, their attitudes toward science and science methodology is certainly highly commendable. These are children that teachers enjoy having in science classes due to their inherent sincerity in wishing to learn more in science. Pupils can present models for others to emulate in the science curriculum. Regardless of a pupil's present status pertaining to science knowledge and skills, all need to be assisted to achieve intrinsic positive attitudes toward achieving science objectives;

2. possessing an adequate self concept. Positive feelings about the self and toward others is necessary for pupils to feel that they can achieve well in ongoing lessons and units of study in science. Helping each pupil to feel successful is one of the best ways for the teacher to guide learners to have confidence in themselves to achieve relevant objectives;

3. desiring recognition for doing well in science. By recognising contributions of pupils, the teacher might well be providing for meeting a vital need of pupils. Meeting recognition needs might well invigorate pupils to achieve more optimally in science. Contributions in science may be made by any pupil regardless of ability and capacity levels and this needs encouragement for all learners;

4. feelings of belonging to a committee or group is salient. Being left out from decision-making in science activities makes for negative attitudes. Seemingly, people are social beings and desire to be accepted by others. The

science teacher need to emphasise wholesome attitudes toward each other when learners are engaged in collaborative endeavours. Standards need to be established and set for group work. Evaluation of learner achievement in realising these goals need periodic attention. Definite strivings in attaining objectives pertaining to improving human relations in group endeavours are a must. More optimal achievement in committee work should be an end result of pupils accepting each other when meeting belonging needs;

5. developing individual satisfaction in science activities and experiences. Human beings work individually and collaboratively in society. Both are important to stress as goals of instruction in science. Thus, there need to be ample opportunities for pupils to work individually in lessons and units of study. Working individually is a learning style and selected pupils achieve more optimally working by the self. Hands on experiences may involve the individual in conducting a science experiment;

6. appreciating the contributions of science in making for a better world in health and technology. Through a study in diverse science units, learners might understand what has been accomplished by scientists to make for a more enjoyable world of work. Pupils, too, should learn to appreciate, for example, how selected diseases have been wiped out/minimised due to contributions from scientists. These deadly diseases include polio, small pox, diphtheria, tuberculosis, and mumps;

7. valuing science subject matter and skills as a means of solving problems in society as well as in school. The scientific method may be used in the identification and solutions to problem areas. Values in life provide guidance and direction to roles and responsibilities that need to be stressed in the personal dimension as well as at the work place. Values also provide assistance in becoming a good citizen and to contributions made toward furthering a better society for all;

8. achieving a desire to engage in lifelong learning. Subject matter and methods of scientific endeavours can provide interest for learning throughout one's life-span as well as continuous development in being an educated person. Things are not learned once and for all time, but knowledge, skills, and attitudes change in time and space. Individuals need to think of learning, not as being final and fixed, but subject to modification and revision. Much knowledge and many skills arrive rather continuously and these need to evaluated and assessed in terms of accuracy and reliability. What results should become a part of the person in an information age;
9. wanting to incorporate the latest worthwhile technology is certainly a must. Technology changes so rapidly. For example, a computer can be updated less that six months after it has been purchased! Daily updated entrees appear on the internet pertaining to science news as well as from other academic branches of knowledge. Individuals live in a world of change. Acceptance of change in technology and using what appears therein for the good of the individual and for society are vital goals;
10. showing care and concern for the self and for others is an ultimate goal that cuts across all academic disciples and citizenship duties and responsibilities in the societal arena. Interdisciplinary learnings are important for pupils in a world society that moves across borders and geographical regions.

SCOPE AND PERFORMANCE OBJECTIVES IN SCIENCE

Teachers and supervisors need to determine which objectives should pertain to a single unit in science instruction. Additional units in science will also need to incorporate carefully selected objectives when ascertaining scope, or what should be taught. For pupils to achieve more optimally in the science curriculum, intensive study of vital objectives by teachers and supervisors needs to be given. These ends determine what pupils might well learn in teaching and learning situations. The total number of objectives stressed within a science unit of study determine the scope for that singular unit.

Generally, after careful study, the chosen objectives are written in performance terms. Performance objectives are clear and direct and assist and teacher to ascertain specifically what pupils are to learn. The following are examples of how learners may reveal what has been learned and stated in terms of performance objectives for pupils to achieve in a science unit on 'The Changing Surface of the Earth.':

1. explain causes of soil erosion and indicate major methods used to prevent or minimise these occurrences;
2. develop a controlled science experiment to show erosion with the experimental container of soil having a grass covering as compared to the control container having no protective covering when equal amounts of water are poured on each, as well as each container having the same tilt or slope;
3. collect different types of soil, such as loam, sand, and alkali: record differences in plant growth on each type after seeding seeds of the same quality and kind;
4. report orally on happenings to soil when drouth, floods, obnoxious weeds, and harmful insects are in evidence;
5. cassette record content on a self selected library book read on conserving natural resources;
6. make a mural on earthquakes, folding and faulting, mud slides, avalanches, and glacial action;
7. collectively within a committee, complete a collage on harmful insects and weeds in the production of farm crops and livestock;
8. do a research project on the positive and negative effects in the use of pesticides and herbicides;
9. report via video-tape on the necessity of maintaining a clean source of drinking water as well as clean rivers, streams, and lakes;

10. debate land use for establishing and maintaining places for wild life refuge as compared to land use for developing shopping malls, urban sprawl housing areas, and places of business in the economic arena.

The above named performance objectives, in total, provide for the scope of the science unit entitled 'The Changing Surface of the Earth'.

SEQUENCE IN THE SCIENCE CURRICULUM

Sequence is an important concept to stress when arranging the order of objectives and learning opportunities for pupils to pursue within each science unit as well as among the different units taught. Quality sequence is necessary so that pupils individually may achieve as optimally as possible. If the sequence is of poor quality, learners then cannot attain as much as their abilities permit. Why? Objectives and learning opportunities that are too complex for pupil attainment and engagement might well make for feelings of failure in pupils. Whereas, objectives and learning opportunities that lack challenge for pupils may represent that which is boring. Learner enthusiasm is then dampened. Good sequence stresses that each pupil may feel challenge and the new learnings are based upon what has been taught/learned. A seamless web of achievement may then be in evidence.

A logical sequence may be developed. Here, the science teacher chooses and orders objectives for pupil achievement. The logic or reasoning used for sequencing the science objectives resides within the teacher. The teacher, through education, training, and experience should know which arrangement to use in ordering the objectives from the easier to those that are gradually more complex in ascending order of difficulty. He/she studies and understands pupils in the classroom in knowing what background information is possessed. The background information is then used to choose objectives whereby pupils may be successful in their achievement. If an inadequate sequence was developed, the teacher may always:

1. fill in needed subject matter in which the steps in a sequence were too great, resulting in learners not attaching meaning to what is being presented;

2. review with pupils previously presented subject matter or skills so that the new learnings are understandable and meaningful;
3. move to more complex objectives if pupils indicate that the content and abilities being taught are too easy;
4. change the order of chosen objectives or learning opportunities if the wrong order had initially been chosen, as revealed from learner interaction and engagement;
5. develop new objectives if pupils reveal a lack of interest or purpose in science achievement (Richardson and Britsch, 1997, 17).

With a logical sequence the teacher is the decision maker. Toward the other end of the continuum, a psychological sequence may be developed. Here, Pupils with teacher guidance sequence their own objectives and learning opportunities emphasised in thematic or unit teaching. Learning centers stress the following:

1. the teacher works out a series of learning centers in the classroom. Perhaps, eight different centers or stations should be in the offing. Each center has concrete, semi-concrete, and abstract materials of instruction that relate directly to objectives in a science unit. Also, pupils with teacher guidance might plan these eight centers and the materials of instruction for each. In either case, there should be task cards at each center. On the task card are listed learning opportunities. Pupils may then select from all the centers which tasks to complete and which to omit so that a pupil centered sequence is truly there. Decision-making is left up to the learner. In other words, each pupil sequence his/her own order of learning opportunities to achieve viable objectives. The following is an example of tasks at one learning center in a classroom:

   a. locate information from reference sources at this center to write a report on the functions of the mouth and salivary glands, the esophagus, stomach and liver, gall bladder and pancreas, as well as the large and small intestines. Use the word processor to write the final report for this long term project;

b. watch the video-tape on 'Common Diseases in the Community.' Make an illustrated chart and indicate preventative measures that may be taken to minimise each of the following problems: the common cold, pneumonia, tooth decay, measles, indigestion, tuberculosis, allergy symptoms, skin cancer, and aids;

c. listen to a tape recorded presentation by a local dentist and develop an illustrated movie set on dental hygiene;

d. develop a bulletin board display on 'Creating a Healthy Environment.' Collect and/or draw pictures for the sequential display of illustrations with written content underneath each;

e. display pictures in the classroom on 'The Basic Food Groups Healthy Living.' Have pupils bring pictures to the classroom that fit under each of these basic food groups. Discuss why these foods belong under the category of 'basic'.

The other centers should have equally fascinating experiences that motivate pupil choice in science achievement. With learning centers, pupils individually decide the order of tasks to pursue. There are an adequate number of learning opportunities so that learners individually may omit that which is not perceived purposeful/meaningful and yet persevere fully/sequentially in each endeavour.

Additional psychological sequences in science learning might well include the use of the contract system. Here, the pupil with teacher guidance determines what he/she wishes to learn in an ongoing science unit or theme. The objectives and learning opportunities in science are clearly spelled out in the contract and, if agreed upon, signed by both the pupil and the teacher. The due date for fulfilling the contract is also written down. The motivator here is the learner himself/herself in ascertaining what to learn in a psychological sequence.

Another procedure in stressing a psychological sequence is to emphasise pupil/teacher planning of certain facets of the science unit. Here, pupil interests, questions, and concerns become paramount. For example, the pupil might be quite interested in current events pertaining to science and identify problems such as the following to pursue in the new science unit of study:

1. What causes hurricanes and tornadoes?
2. What are 'lows' and 'highs' when listening to a weather forecast?
3. How does a 'dewpont' reading relate to fallen dew or frost on the ground?
4. Why are selected animals on the endangered species list?
5. How does a barometer work in showing air pressure?

The more pupil input there is in a science lesson or unit of study, the more likely a psychological sequence is being stressed in the curriculum. The learner then perceives order in learning when using his/her own ideas in the science curriculum.

Conclusion

Scope and sequence in the science curriculum are two vital concepts for teachers and supervisors to consider in developing the science curriculum, the teacher needs to consider the breadth of knowledge, skills, and attitudes to develop within pupils as objectives of instruction. A narrower scope would eliminate selected objectives due to time, teaching materials, and other valid reasons. A broader scope would encompass more objectives due to being more beneficial for pupils to attain additional goals, such as an integrated curriculum and having pupils engage in more depth study.

Each science unit needs to be adequate in scope to provide pupils

1. with vital knowledge, skills, and attitudes;

2. with opportunities to experience a variety of learning materials, using activities and experiences stressing the methods of science;
3. with a design that emphasises the integrated science curriculum to incorporate reading and the language arts, social studies, mathematics, vocational experiences, art music, and physical education. Multiple Intelligences Theory suggests that teachers have pupils indicate what has been learned through the intelligence(s) possessed (Gardner, 1993);
4. with the psychology of learning stressed from educational psychology such as pupil interest, meaning, and purpose in ongoing units of study;
5. with a caring curriculum and democracy as a way of life stressed in each ongoing lesson.

Quality sequence in science should emphasise

1. an order of objectives and learning opportunities stressed whereby each pupil might experience challenge within the new lessons being based on prior readiness experiences;
2. a logical and/or psychological order whichever benefits an individual pupil to an optimal degree;
3. learner success in ongoing lessons and units of study in science;
4. pupils perceiving connections between and among the diverse science units encountered;
5. experiments and demonstrations as the heart of the science curriculum, in a sequential placement.

Teaching science in the school setting should reflect the quality standards developed by the National Science Teachers Association (NSTA, 1997). Each school system engaged in the teaching of science needs to give these national standards careful attention when improving teaching and learning situations, involving objectives, learning opportunities, and evaluation procedures.

References

Bhaskara Rao, Digumarti and Digumarti Pushpa Latha (1993), *Achievement in Science.* New Delhi, India: Discovery Publishing House.

Ediger, Marlow (1997), *Teaching Science in the Elementary School.* Kirksville, Missouri: Simpson Publishing Company, 1-17.

Ediger, Marlow (1997), 'Impro...g the Science Curriculum, *Experiments in Education*, 25(3), 55-63. Published by the SITU Council of Education Research, in India.

Ediger, Marlow (1995), 'Philosophy of Teaching Science,' *School Science,* 33 (3), 1-2. Published by the National Council for Educational Research and Training, in India.

Ediger, Marlow (1996), 'Personalised Science Instruction,' *Prism*, 5(1), 25-27, The Professional Magazine of Newfoundland and Labrador Teacher's Association, in Canada.

Ediger, Marlow (1994), 'The Unexpected in Science,' *Investigating*, 10 (3), 24-25. Published by the Australian Science Teacher's Association.

Ediger, Marlow (1999), 'Attitudinal Objectives in the Chemistry Curriculum,' *New England Association of Chemistry Teacher's Association Journal*, 17 (2), 15-22.

Ediger, Marlow, and D. Bhaskara Rao (1996), *Science Curriculum.* New Delhi, India: Discovery Publishing House, Chapter Six.

Ediger, Marlow (1999), 'Innovative Reading Science Content,' Talk given at the Hoosier Association of Science Teachers, Inc, Annual Convention, February 18, Indianapolis, Indiana.

Ediger, Marlow (1995), 'Designing Science Units of Study,' *School Science*, 33 (1), 14-15.

Ediger, Marlow (1997), *The Modern Elementary School.* Kirksville, Missouri: Simpson Publishing Company, 110-111.

Ediger, Marlow (1995), 'Demonstration Teaching in the Schools, *Education*, 114 (3), 371-374.

Ediger, Marlow (1995), 'Early Field Experiences in Teacher Education,' *College Student Journal*, 28 (3), 302-306.

Gardner, Howard (1993), Multiple Intelligences: Theory into Practice. New York: Basic Books.

National Science Teachers Association (1997), *National Science Educational Standards.* Arlington, Virginia: NSTA.

Rao, D. Bhaskara, and Marlow Ediger (1996), *Scientific Attitudes vis-a-vis Scientific Aptitude.* New Delhi, India: Discovery Publishing House, Chapter One.

Richardson, Daniel P., and Susan Britsch (1997), 'Children's Science Journals' Tools for Teaching, Learning and Assessment,' *Science and Children*, 34 (5), 17.

Rao, Digumarti Bhaskara (1999), *Teaching of Science.* Guntur, India: Nagarjuna Publishers (in Telugu language).

3

ATTITUDINAL OBJECTIVES IN SCIENCE

Science teachers need to stress three kinds of objectives in teaching and learning. The first kind, cognitive, does receive major emphasis by teachers. Cognitive goals stress pupils achieving well in acquiring vital facts in ongoing lessons and units of study. There are selected educators in science who tend to downplay the importance of vital facts that learners are to achieve. Perhaps the problem here is more of what is done with the facts as compared to saying that pupils achieving factual information is evil. Facts are the building blocks of developing concepts. Concepts are broader than facts and may contain many facts in each concept. Consider the following fact: there are three major kinds of rock-igneous, metamorphic, and sedimentary. We believe this is a valuable fact for pupils to achieve in a unit on 'Rocks and Minerals.' The term 'igneous' is a concept. Many facts are contained therein, such as

1. Igneous rock comes from the interior of the earth where temperature readings are very high;

2. Molten rock is made of magma and lava.;
3. The molten rock comes through fissures in the earth.

In addition to vital facts and concepts, pupils should also acquire major generalisations. Generalisations in science relate several concepts into a declarative sentence. The following is a generalisation:

Common forms of igneous rock are granite used for tombstones, pumice used in building materials, and obsidian used in making decorative items. The concepts here are igneous rock, granite, tombstones, pumice, building materials, obsidian, and decorative items.

In addition to facts, concepts, and generalisations, pupils also need to be able to think critically. When pupils, for example, make comparisons among igneous, metamorphic, and sedimentary rocks, critical thinking is involved. When pupils brainstorm the many uses of rock and think of unique uses also, then creative thought is in evidence. Going one notch higher in cognitive objectives, if pupils engage problem solving, they need to identify a problem, gather information in answer to the question or problem, an test the information in a utilitarian situation. The following are examples of identified problems:

1. Why does the interior of the earth continually become hotter the further one goes inside the surface?
2. What causes volcanic eruptions?

Cognitive objectives are salient or pupils to achieve in ongoing lessons and units of study. Thus there is much knowledge that a pupil needs to acquire as well as use the knowledge in a practical way in society. Related to cognitive objectives are affective ends for pupil attainment.

AFFECTIVE OBJECTIVES IN SCIENCE

Affective objectives involve attitudes, feelings, emotions, and beliefs. There are several relatively new programmes in science education that stress the emotions and their consequences for individuals. We have noticed several of our student teachers and cooperating teachers, called a teaching team, whom we supervised in the public schools who stress much pupil involvement in the science curriculum. These teachers emphasise rather heavy pupil involvement in curriculum development. In several situations these teaching teams had worked out a set of learning center whereby pupils individually could choose which tasks to pursue and which to omit in an ongoing science unit of study. Learners might then sequence their very own experiences in the ongoing science unit of study. We will describe one set of centers one of us observed in which the unit of study in science was entitled. 'The Changing Surface of the Earth.' The following learning centers were then in evidence:

1. a soil erosion center;
2. folding and faults in and on the earth's surface;
3. flood damage in an area center;
4. contours, strip cropping, terracing, and planted grass/ trees to avoid erosion;
5. wind and water erosion;
6. the weathering process, including freezing and thawing;
7. pollution of the natural environment;
8. saving forest regions;
9. mining for rocks and minerals in a responsible manner;
10. use of natural resources responsibly.

Each center had concrete (real objects and items), semiconcrete (audiovisual aids), and abstract materials of instruction (cassettes, reading materials, written work, discussions and other oral communication activities). There were four to five tasks per learning center for pupils to select to work on. For example, center #2 above had the following tasks on a task card:

1. By using reference material at this center, find causes for both folding and faulting;
2. Using the modeling materials, make a model of folding and of faulting in and on the planet earth;

3. Prepare an oral report on folding and faulting to be presented to the entire class;
4. Make drawings of folding and faulting for display on walls in the hallway;
5. What happens to lives and property when severe faults cause problems?

Pupils at these learning centers make many decisions, such as which tasks to pursue sequentially. Teachers are guides and encourage as well as assist pupils to achieve continually. The pupil then chooses which tasks to complete and which to omit. The choices are made based on purposes possessed by each pupil. Then too, there are ample opportunities for pupils to work collaboratively if they so desire. There are activity centered tasks as well as those that require or stress more of abstract endeavours. The learning style of individual pupils are involved in making decisions. The teacher does not dictate nor lecture what pupils are to learn. The interests of pupils are salient in learner centered instruction. Thus the attitudinal dimension of the learner is paramount in an affective centered science curriculum. The feelings and emotions are involved here in decisions made. The pupil also assists in evaluating his/her own progress in products and processes of learning.

EMOTIONAL INTELLIGENCE

There are an increasing number of educators who advocate the feeling dimension in learning. Pool (1997) summarises key ideas presented by Dan Goleman (1995) who wrote Emotional Intelligence and speaks frequently at educational conventions; these main ideas follow. According to Goleman, there are five dimensions of emotional intelligence, First if self awareness. Here, pupil realise increasingly so that there are personal strengths and weaknesses and use these to become decisive in decision making. Understanding their very own feelings is important so that action options are more prevalent. Self confidence is very important in order to make choices and act to make decisions.

Second, pupils need to learn to handle their emotions. Impulsive behaviour may make for incorrect decisions. Learners need to develop more of a wait approach so that options may be scrutinised in terms of advantages and disadvantages. The consequences of each choice need to be assessed. Being impulsive might well lead to improper ends in life. Third, learners need to feel motivated in achieving definite goals. Hope is involved in having these goals in life. The motivation then comes from diverse goals that an individual aims for. Optimism is necessary to achieve and reach objectives one has in mind. Fourth, empathy is very important for pupils to develop. Feelings of empathy make possible to sympathize with others. Empathy is learned. Thus one learns to assist others in positive ways or be brutal to others. Compassion for others is important. Fifth, the development of social skills enables a pupil to help others in every day situations in life. Politeness and friendliness enable a person to interact well with others in society on a daily basis.

Emotional intelligence harmonises well with an affective science curriculum. Thus with pupil/teacher planning of the curriculum, self awareness is developed increasingly so when pupils select the order of learning activities in science. Strengths in decision making should be an end result. When pupils learn to handle emotions, there is persistence and effort put forth in learning. The immediate goal is not what is necessarily good such as in impulsive behaviour. Rather the pupil needs to evaluate the pros and cons in making choices Motivation is necessary in order that goals are achieved by pupils in science. With the absence of goals, energy levels for learning go downhill.

Feelings of empathy make it possible for pupils individually to get along well with others. In school and in society, it is necessary to have good human relations so that achievement and group efforts are possible. Human beings are feeling individuals, not automatons. Social skills need learning by pupils so that a friendly and considerate environment is available for all to achieve more optimally. Committee endeavours in ongoing lessons and units of study in science provide many opportunities for pupils to develop social skills.

Pertaining to humanism as a psychology of education, Woolfolk and Nicolich (1990) wrote:

Humanistic interpretations of motivation emphasise personal

freedom, choice, self-determination, and striving for personal growth, or as A.H. Maslow (1954) called it, self-actualisation. With these emphases, the humanistic psychologists tend to be in harmony with many of the constructivist approaches. Perhaps most important is the fact that both views stress intrinsic motivation.

Shepherd and Ragan (1982) outline a summary of A.H. Maslow's (1954) hierarchy of human needs or goals as follows:

1. Physiological—a need to survive;
   - A. Homeostasis—a balance of internal bodily functions,
   - B. Appetites—need for nurture—food, sleep, air, elimination...
2. Safety—freedom from damage and threat;
   - A. Routines and Rules (know and accept),
   - B. Consistency and security...
3. Belongingness—need for love and affection...;
   - A. Intimate relations with other people,
   - B. To be accepted, wanted, and cherished...
4. Esteem—status, recognition, competence, importance, independence;
   - A. Personal—need for strength, mastery,
   - B. Group—reputation, status, dominance, appreciation...
5. Self-Actualisation;
   - A. To satisfy potential—you must be what you can be...

In our own experiences as teacher educators, we believe affective and cognitive objectives interact. It is difficult to separate the two categories of goals. Thus when we speak at conventions for teacher education and write for publication, we stress that quality emotions and feelings assist pupils to achieve at a more optimal rate in the cognitive domain. Our observations of pupils in the public schools indicate that individuals who are hostile, negative, have short attention spans, and mistreat others in the classroom have a difficult time to achieve what their potential is, much more so than other pupils in the class setting. Thus quality attitudes in the affective dimension assist learners to achieve more optimally in the cognitive area.

Humanists desire openended or general objectives, rather than measurably written or behaviourally stated objectives for pupils to achieve. Why? Not all pupils, by any means, learn the same things due to choices and decisions made by pupils in ongoing units of study (see learning centers above for examples). If teachers determine objectives for all pupils to achieve in science units of study, there is no room for learners to select and omit selected learning opportunities, based on learner perceived purposes. If pupils select sequential objectives to achieve, within a flexible framework, a psychological sequence is involved as compared to a logical order whereby the teacher arranges the order of objectives for pupil attainment. Sequence resides within the learner, not within the minds of teachers or textbooks in science. Formal means of teaching here are eliminated and replaced with learner choices and decisions as to what to learn and what to omit. The feeling, affective dimension is definitely involved in making choices and decisions.

A pupil centered curriculum might be emphasised, in part, through individualised reading in science. Thus instead of using basal textbooks in science units, pupils may choose to read library books that related directly to the unit title being studied. In a unit on 'The Changing Surface of the Earth,' an adequate number of library books on different reading levels need to be available for pupil choice. We have observed this approach to be very successful in ongoing lessons and units of study. Pupils then relate what was read from a library book read to the ensuing discussion. There appears to be much discussion and excitement when this approach is used in teaching science. Pupils might then notice different points of view expressed which can lead to analysis and evaluation of subject matter read.

In addition to pupils choosing sequential library books to read and relating the content to ongoing discussions, the science teacher might also have conference with individual pupils or several pupils who have read the same library book where multiple copies of a boo were available. Here, the teacher might observe pupil enthusiasm, interest, and quality of comprehension. The science teacher can always diagnose strengths and weaknesses shown by pupils in the conference setting. What has been diagnosed as weaknesses might then be remediated through additional learning activities. Pupil choices in the science curriculum might be made in whole or in part. The latter might be stressed in individualised reading in science which then substitutes for the basal textbook in ongoing units of study.

DEMOCRACY IN THE SCIENCE CURRICULUM

Democracy as a way of life emphasises that pupils respect each other's ideas and contributions. Ridiculing and minimising others has no role to play in democratic situations. Pupils should achieve more optimally when democracy as a way of life is practiced. Fenstermacher (1996) wrote:

> We hear a great deal about readying the next generation of workers for global competition... about world class standards for what is learned in school. We hear almost nothing about building civic participation or building and maintaining democratic communities, whether these be neighbourhoods or governments at the local, state, or federal levels. The advancement of democratic ideals and institutions goes largely unmentioned, taken for granted or insufficiently important to rank up there with such world shaking events as or playing Avis to Japan's Hertz.

Pupils discussing current events items in science provide excellent opportunities for learners to practice tenets of democratic living within a committee endeavour. In one of may classroom observations, student teachers and cooperating teachers orientated learners in the classroom to bring from the home setting current events items pertaining to natural disasters. These natural disasters included tornadoes, hail, volcanic eruptions, floods, strong winds, heavy snow, and ice storms, among others. New items could deal with different times of the year. The clippings were brought to class for discussion within a committee endeavour. A large world map was placed at the center of a bulletin board.

Yarn was used to connect the happening from the news clipping with the place of occurrence, located on the world map.

We have observed numerous student teachers and cooperating teachers whom we have supervised stressing democracy in the classroom with cooperative learning endeavours. These teachers have developed standards with pupils in terms of how a committee should function. The following were developed as standards for a committee, with teacher guidance, to work by in discussing current events in science:

1. respect each other and the thinking of others;
2. listen carefully to the thinking of committee members as ideas are being presented;
3. have all pupils participate in discussing current events in science within the committee;
4. let leadership emerge as the discussion moves forward
5. ask questions if comments made are not clear;
6. do not interrupt when others are participating.

These criteria were posted in the classroom and reviewed with learners prior to each committee working in the area of discussing current events in science. After committee work, members with teacher guidance evaluated how well the group had followed each criteria. It appears that reviewing with pupils the meaning of each standard and appraising if individual standards are being met is helpful to learners. Pupils can be taught democratic tenets as a way of life. Pupil achievement hinges on being able to accept others more fully and not real animosity or ill will toward others. Positive attitudes toward others enhances the individual to achieve more optimally in the cognitive domain as well as make for better feelings about the self. Pupils seemingly quarrel less and assist each other more when healthy self concepts and emotional well being are in evidence.

Conclusion

The emotions, feelings, and values are important parts of an individual's well being and achievement in life. Science teachers should emphasise an adequate number of objectives stressing the affective domain. Actually, the affective domain cannot be separated from the cognitive. If pupils possess quality attitudes, the chances are the rest will be achieved well in life as much as the individual is capable.

Reference

Bhaskara Rao, Digumarti and Digumarti Pushpa Latha (1993), *Achievement in Biology*. New Delhi, India: Discovery Publishing House.

Ediger, Marlow (1996), *Elementary Education.* Kirksville, Missouri: Simpson Publishing Company, 134.

Ediger, Marlow (1997), *Teaching Science in the Elementary School.* Kirksville, Missouri: Simpson Publishing Company, 10-12.

Ediger, Marlow (1997), *Teaching Reading and the Language Arts in the Elementary School.* (Kirksville, Missouri: Simpson Publishing Company, 32.

Ediger, Marlow and D. Bhaskara Rao (2000), *Teaching Reading Successfully.* New Delhi, India: Discovery Publishing House.

Fenstermacher, Gary D. (1995), 'The absence of democratic and educational ideals from contemporary educational reform initiatives,' *Educational Horizons*, 73:70.

Goleman, Daniel (1995), *Emotional Intelligence.* New York: Bantam Books.

Maslow, A. H. (1954), *Motivation and Personality.* New York: Harper and Row.

Pool, Carolyn R. (1997), 'Up With Emotional Health', *Educational Leadership.* 54, 8:12-14.

Shepherd, Gene D., and William B. Ragan (1982), *Modern Elementary Curriculum.* New York: Holt, Rinehart and Winston, 15.

Woolfolk, Anita, and Lorraine McCune Nicolich (1990), *Educational Psychologies for Teachers.* Englewood Cliffs, New Jersey: Prentice—Hall, Inc, 321.

4

Problems in Teaching Science

The science teacher has highly important tasks in implementing vital trends in the curriculum. In a rapidly changing society, the science curriculum needs to be assessed and updated where necessary. Changes should not be made for the sake of doing so, but rather due to meeting personal needs of pupils in a world of science. Pupils tend to be curious and interested in science as young learners. Sometimes, this curiosity and interest wears down as pupils progress through diverse levels of schooling. The teacher then has major responsibilities in helping pupils to be attentive in achieving vital objectives in ongoing lessons and units of study.

Thematic units provide a focal point for pupils to be actively involved in attaining objectives. Learning opportunities should guide learners to attain the objectives of instruction. These learning opportunities need to challenge pupils, but not be unduly complex whereby optimal achievement is not possible.

OBJECTIVES IN SCIENCE

Objectives for pupil attainment should stress vital knowledge goals as one of three types of objectives. Securing knowledge emphasises pupils acquiring facts, concepts, main ideas, and generalisations. A second type stresses application ends. Here, a pupil is assisted to apply what has been achieved in terms of knowledge objectives. Ample opportunities need to be given for pupils collaboratively and individually to use what has been attained in the knowledge domain. With use, less forgetting occurs and, then too, learners might perceive value in learning that which is beneficial.

To be useful as objectives in science instruction, pupils need to have ample chances to engage in solving real problems identified in context. These problems require deliberation and thought in their solving, including the use of critical and creative thinking. Problem solving as well as critical and creative thinking, no doubt, will always be important in school and in society. Many trends and emphases in science teaching may come and go, but these three application skills are indeed worthy to stress presently as well as in the future.

A third kind of objectives to stress continuously is good attitudes of pupils towards the science curriculum. Mental health goals emphasise pupils achieving well in the affective dimension. Wholesome attitudes toward the self and others as well as toward acquiring knowledge and application skills in science are indeed worthy for all.

SEQUENCING SCIENCE OBJECTIVES

Sequencing objectives for pupil achievement is an important facet of teaching. The ordered objectives, then, should be arranged so that pupils experience new knowledge and skills based upon previously acquired learnings. A seamless web of achievement might then be in the offing. A logical sequence emphasises the teacher arranging the objectives so that success in pupil learning is increasingly possible. With a psychological sequence, the science teacher assists pupils to identify questions, problems and solutions they deem to be relevant. A combination of these two approaches is probably the most feasible and acceptable. Pupils differ on the kind of sequence they feel is the most worthwhile. Success in learning is salient for each pupil. Readiness for learning and achieving of new objectives depends much upon what the pupil has already learned and blends in with the new objectives of instruction. The learner should be guided to access what has been learned as well as relate his/her own experiences with the objectives to be realised.

SCIENCE LEARNING OPPORTUNITIES

To achieve objectives, pupils need learning opportunities which capture and maintain learner attention. Unless pupil interest is being accessed, the chances are learning will not accrue as it should. Thus, to establish set, the science teacher needs to provide initiating experiences which engage the learner actively. It is important for pupils to attend to what is being presented for more optimal learning to occur.

Learning opportunities should contain concrete materials (objects, items, realia, excursions, and hands on approaches), semiconcrete materials in teaching science (illustrations, videotapes, CD ROMS, films, filmstrips, drawings, diagrams, graphs, charts, software packages, and multi-media presentations in general), and abstract (Reading, writing, listening, and speaking) experiences.

The materials of instruction may well provide content for science experiments and demonstrations which should be the heart of the science curriculum. Methods of teaching may also include problem solving, inductive and deductive activities, projects, pupil/teacher planning in ongoing lessons and units of study, unit teaching and thematic approaches, teacher directed experiences, peer teaching and collaborative endeavours, learning centers and constructivism as a philosophy of instruction, as well as sustained silent reading involving pupil choice of trade books in science.

ORGANISATIONS OF THE SCIENCE CURRICULUM

Too frequently in the science curriculum, there are recommendations to use one approach in organising the science curriculum. We recommend multiple approaches of organising the science curriculum to provide for individual differences of and in pupil achievement. The separate subjects approach stresses using only one science academic discipline in ongoing units of study. There are times when only a single subject matter area should be taught. Why Depth learning is important in assisting pupils to acquire vital concepts and generalisations. This procedure tends to fragment learnings for pupils, if used exclusively. An other approach is to correlate two academic disciplines in science. An improved chance is then in the offing for pupils to perceive relationships in knowledge so that comprehension and retention are more likely to occur. In many situations, all science academic disciplines, as these are relevant, need to be implemented in teaching and learning in an integrated science curriculum. Pupils then have more chances to perceive how knowledge may be integrated. They may sense fusion of ideas and attach increased meaning to content in science experiences.

Going beyond the separate subjects, correlated, and integrated approaches to organise the curriculum, a teacher may stress interdisciplinary procedures. In inter-disciplinary procedures, the language arts (diverse reading materials and various purposes for writing, oral communication criteria in speaking experiences, and standards for quality listening), mathematics as the language of science, and social studies (the history of science, geographical influences on science, as well as economics, political science, anthropology, and sociology) may provide content for ongoing lessons and units of study as they are deemed significant to aid pupil interest and meaning in learning. Vital knowledge and skills need to be chosen to stress as objectives of instruction. Pupils need to be assisted to achieve these significant ends.

THE PSYCHOLOGY OF INSTRUCTION

To do better with increased engagement in learning opportunities, pupils need to experience principles of learning from educational psychology (Ediger, 1998, 203-208). there are selected principles which do pay off well when used in teaching science. First, the science teacher needs to secure the interests of pupils in ongoing lessons and units of study. Here, learning opportunities need to be chosen which will interest learners. The manner of presentation should be such that the pupil has an inward desire to learn and achieve. Pupils need to ask questions pertaining to curiosities felt in these experiences. The questions identified might well become problems areas to be solved. A learning center containing items and objects stressing the new unit in science might well serve as an area of engagement in learning for pupils. The teacher needs to allow ample time for pupils to become fascinated with the items and objects at the learning center. Once problems have been identified, committees may be formed in using a variety of materials to work toward solutions. A committee of four members may serve on each committee. Ideally, learners should volunteer to serve on the committee of their choice. If a special committee needs to be formed to meet interest needs of pupils, this should be emphasised with implementation. Individual problem areas also need to be considered. Needs of each pupil should be met in ongoing science units of study.

Meaning must be stressed as a second vital principle of learning in teaching pupils. For meaning to occur, pupils need to understand that which is being taught. Comprehension on different cognitive levels should be emphasised in each science lesson. If pupils do not attach meaning to what has been learned, the chances are the subject matter and skills being taught will soon be forgotten.

A third principle of learning emphasises pupils perceiving purpose in learning. To sense purpose, the pupil needs to feel that there are valid reasons for achieving and developing. Thus, each pupil with purpose perceives one or more important reasons for active engagement in ongoing learning opportunities.

Fourth, individual differences need to be provided for in the science curriculum. To provide for individual differences, the teacher needs to provide for the learning styles of learners (Dunn and Dunn, 1979). Some pupils, for example, like to work on individual endeavours while others prefer committee work. Multiple Intelligences Theory stresses pupils using their unique intelligence(s) to indicate what has been learned (Gardner, 1993). Here, the following means are available to have learners indicate achievement: scientific, verbal/linguistic, logical/mathematical, visual/spatial, musical, bodily/kinesthetic, interpersonal, and intrapersonal.

Fifth, pupils need to become motivated individuals in studying science. To motivate, the teacher should show enthusiasm for reading science content as well as doing scientific endeavours. The high energy level for teaching science should then be reflected in pupil interest and achievement.

Learners individually should also be assisted to develop a good self concept for learning. Thus, the teacher needs to help each pupil to be successful in making progress in the science curriculum. Success in achieving objectives in science is a must! Recognition needs of individuals also must be met. Each pupil should be identified for doing well in facets of science regardless of ability levels. It behooves the teacher to observe where esteem needs should be rewarded in ongoing lessons.

ASSESSMENT OF PUPIL ACHIEVEMENT

A variety of assessment techniques need to be used to appraise achievement in science. Teacher observation of learner progress in context is important. Better sequence in pupil learning might well be an end result when the teacher uses quality standards to assess when observational methods are used. In addition, the following, among others, need to be used to assess and improve the science curriculum for pupils:

1. portfolios and pupil journal writing;
2. diary entries and logs written individually or collaboratively by learners;
3. pupil participation in discussions;
4. project methods of instruction and evaluating their processes and products;
5. art work, written reports, and dramatic experiences as each relates directly to a science lesson or unit of study;
6. tutorial results from software packages, using micro-computers.

The following may be used diagnostically with positive attempts made to remedy vital deficiencies:

1. teacher written tests;
2. standardised, norm referenced tests;
3. criterion referenced tests.

Conclusion

The science teacher has vital responsibilities in providing the best science curriculum possible to guide optimal pupil progress. The objectives need to represent salient knowledge, skills, and attitudes for learner attainment. Proper sequence of the objectives assists pupils to achieve in a more optimal manner. The learning opportunities need to help pupils achieve the desired ends. Principles of learning from educational psychology used in teaching provide for motivated learners. Quality assessment techniques need to be used to appraise what pupils have learned. What has not been learned needs diagnosis and remediation with excellent learning opportunities.

References

Bhaskara Rao, Digumarti, ed. (2000), *International Encyclopaedia of Science and Technology Education*, 11 Vols. New Delhi, India: Discovery Publishing House.

Dunn, Rita, and Kenneth Dunn (1979), 'Learning Styles/Teaching Styles,' *Educational Leadership*, 36 (4), 238-244.

Ediger, Marlow (1997), *Teaching Science in the Elementary School*. Kirksville, Missouri: Simpson Publishing Company, Chapter Six.

Ediger, Marlow (1998), 'Change and the School Administrator,' *Education*, 118 (4), 541-548.

Ediger, Marlow and D. Bhaskara Rao (1996), *Science Curriculum*. New Delhi, India: Discovery Publishing House, Chapter Four.

Ediger, Marlow (1996), 'Evaluation of Pupil Achievement,' *Education Magazine*, Published by the Qatar National Commission for Education—The Middle East.

Ediger, Marlow (1998), 'Sequence in Primary Grade Mathematics', *Journal of Instructional Psychology*, 26 (3), 203-208.

Gardner, Howard (1993), *Multiple Intelligences: Theory into Practice*. New York: Basic Books.

Rao, D. Bhaskara, and Marlow Ediger (1996), *Scientific Attitude Vis-A-Vis Scientific Aptitude*. New Delhi, India: Discovery Publishing House, Chapter Two.

Rathaiah, L., D. Bhaskara Rao and P.K. Rao (1997). *Correlates of Achievement*. New Delhi, India: Discovery Publishing House.

Veena Kumari, B. and D. Bhaskara Rao (2000), *Psycho-social Correlates of Achievement*. New Delhi, India: Discovery Publishing House.

5

IMPROVING THE TEACHING OF SCIENCE

Science teachers need to stay abreast of recent trends in teaching science. They need to study, analyse, and appraise new developments in the teaching of science. We will indicate selected trends and discuss related comments. Each School might then appraise their very own science curriculum to make necessary changes. The science curriculum needs to be brought up to date frequently. Modification of the present science curriculum is necessary so that pupils achieve as much as possible in each unit of study.

RECOMMENDED TRENDS IN TEACHING SCIENCE

First, the science teacher needs to develop thematic units of study which provide for individual differences. In the science unit, there needs to be a carefully thought through set of objectives. These objectives should emphasise vital subject matter, skills, and attitudinal objectives. Subject matter for the objectives section should be based upon structural ideas identified by university professors in science, public school teachers, and school administrators. Structural ideas represent key concepts and generalisations in each unit of study. These concepts and generalisations represent important and relevant content in science. The skills objectives section should stress, among others, critical thought whereby pupils separate the accurate from the inaccurate, the relevant from the irrelevant as well as the important from the unimportant ideas in science content.

Generally with critical thinking, the content chosen will fit into the solving of problems in science. Pupils with teacher guidance need to identify problems in ongoing units of study in science. Each problem is adequately delimited and salient. Information is then needed to secure content as an answer to the problem(s) identified. Creative thinking, as a further skill, is necessary so that pupils come up with unique, novel solutions to problem areas. Tried and true solutions may not work. Therefore originality in pupil skills is needed so that problems are identified and solved. After adequate data has been secured, the pupil needs to test the solution in a lifelike situation. Should the solution work, the hypothesis (tentative answer to the problem) is accepted. If the answer to the problem does not work, a new solution needs to be found with further collecting of information.

In addition to subject matter and skills objectives, a third kind of objective for the science teacher to stress is attitudinal objectives. Attitudinal objectives include developing pupil interest in science, establishing diverse purposes for learning, wanting to learn more science, and wishing to use science content in everyday life.

A second trend in teaching science emphasises relating subject matter acquired in ongoing lessons and units of study. If pupils learn to correlate and integrate subject matter, the chances are less forgetting will occur. Why? A pupils who thinks of content being related will find that one idea recalled triggers other ideas to the level of consciousness. The process is continuous in that each idea recalled will assist in the recollection of others. Thus, the areas of biology, chemistry, geology, astronomy, physics, and geology may be taught as being interrelated.

Third, inservice education is necessary so that teachers keep abreast of modern methods of instruction. The workshop and faculty meeting approaches need to stress what teachers deem to be of help in the instructional arena. Teachers need to have much input into the development of inservice education programmes. Ideas gleaned from inservice education need to be applied in teaching and learning situations. Feedback to participants need to be given at the inservice education meeting so that others may try new ideas in teaching to assist each pupil to achieve as optimally as possible.

Fourth, teachers need to appraise pupils more so within the actual engagement of learning, rather than external factors. What are these external situations? Testing in their diverse dimensions tend to be outside the actual specific act of learning. Rather, evaluating a pupil within the framework of being involved in performing science experiments in ongoing lessons and units of study stresses the constructivist philosophy. With constructivism as a philosophy of evaluation, the pupil is evaluated with in the framework of teaching and learning, not outside of it. Thus, within science experiments, demonstrations, viewing audio-visual materials, reading science content, giving a book report, making a diagram, constructing a graph, and doing an art project related to the thematic unit being studied, pupils reveal achievement and progress. Evaluation may then be continuous. Diagnosis and remediation are possible in constructivism as a philosophy of evaluation.

Fifth, pupils need to indicate progress to teachers, parents, and school administrators through the development of the portfolio. A portfolio contains a collection of relevant materials of pupil achievement in ongoing units of study. A representative sampling of pupil work needs to be a part of the portfolio. To organise the portfolio properly, the pupil with teacher guidance needs to select those products and processes that reveal learner progress. A table of contents is needed as well as a selection of listed worthwhile objectives to achieve. The objectives need to guide pupil achievement in selecting what goes into a portfolio. Items for a portfolio might include written work, art products, construction endeavours, snapshots of pupil work, videotapes of collaborative endeavours, and drawings, as well as statistical data in the form of graphs and tables. The completed portfolio may be shown to parents and others who are responsibly involved in evaluating pupil achievement. The philosophy of constructivism is involved in that pupil work reflects what was done within different ongoing lessons and units of study. What about test results? By all means, these should be a part of the portfolio contents. However, they are a part of the portfolio and should not dominate the contents therein. The portfolio should not become unwieldy, but represents what a pupil has completed in terms of being a representative sampling.

Sixth, there should be ample input into thematic science units of study from the pupil. The pupil needs to be actively engaged in learning and therefore needs to have input in terms of objectives, learning activities, and evaluation procedures to be stressed in the science unit of study. For this kind of pupil input, we would suggest a set of learning centers as being the heart of the thematic unit of study in science.

With learning centers as the heart of the thematic science unit of study, pupils individually may choose which center and which tasks to pursue sequentially. The tasks need to have learner appeal and inherent interest. The learner might then order his/her own tasks to pursue as learning opportunities. Ideally, there should be more tasks than what a pupil can complete so that omissions can be made. Time on task is very important for each pupil so leanrers achieve as much as possible. A psychological sequence is involved when pupils individually choose the order of their very own tasks to complete.

The learning centers may also be used for enrichment activities. Here, a more limited number of learning centers are available for pupils to choose from, but these tasks are used to supplement pupils' work from other kinds of learning activities not found at the learning centers. When spare time is available, a pupil may work at the enrichment centers to achieve additional objectives in the thematic science unit of study. The teacher then selects most of the objectives, learning opportunities, and evaluation procedures in the regular science curriculum with a logical sequence being in evidence. Why is this a logical sequence? The science teacher orders which activities come first, second, third, and so on in teaching and learning These activities are selected on the basis of being meaningful and purposeful to involved learners.

Seventh, the psychology of pupil learning needs to be selected based on how pupils individually and collaboratively may achieve as much as possible. Behaviourism stresses stating objectives in science in measurable terms prior to instruction. The teacher develops and orders the objectives for pupils to attain. Learning activities are chosen by the teacher on the basis of having pupils achieve the objectives. With precise objectives of instruction, a pupil either does or does not achieve the stated objectives as a result of instruction. If a pupil fails to attain an objective, he/she may experience a different teaching strategy. Criterion referenced tests (CRTS) are a major way to determine pupil achievement. These tests are aligned with the stated objectives so that validity and reliability in testing is in evidence.

In addition to behaviourism as a psychology of learning being emphasised in teaching, a somewhat opposite approach stresses pupil/teacher planning of objectives, learning opportunities, and evaluation procedures. Here, the pupil may have opportunities to plan with the teacher the objectives of instruction as well as the learning opportunities to achieve the objectives. Evaluation procedures to ascertain what has been learned might also be planned cooperatively with the science teacher. Planning together involving the pupil with teacher assistance is a difficult method of instruction. However, the end result is that pupils have a better chance of experiencing unit teaching that meets personal needs and interests.

In between points of view may be stressed in ongoing units of study such as having some teacher determined facets of the science curriculum, such as in behaviourism, as well as emphasising pupil input into the curriculum, such as in the pupil teacher planning model of unit teaching in science. What determines which plan to implement in teaching pupils?

1. Under which conditions does the pupil do best in learning?
2. Under which plan are pupil's needs and interests met best?

3. Under which plan of instruction does the teacher do the best job of professional teaching?
4. Under which plan might the psychological needs of pupils and teachers be met best?
5. Under which conditions can the methods of science be taught so that pupils experience excitement and optimal achievement in a positive learning environment?

Eighth, the philosophy of education needs to be considered in designing the science curriculum. There are diverse philosophies which assist pupils to achieve more optimally. A problem solving philosophy certainly does harmonise well with objectives to be stressed in science. Science educators seemingly agree that problem solving should be at or near the apex of objectives for pupils to achieve in ongoing lessons and units of thematic study. To be involved in problem solving, pupils also need to think critically when data is gathered in answer to the problem. Creative thought is needed when unique solutions are necessary for answers to problem solving.

A second philosophy stresses an idea centered science curriculum. Here, the teacher guides pupils to achieve objectives in science which stress the abstract in concept development and achievement of generalisations. The abstract is prized more highly in teaching science as compared to the concrete and semi-concrete learning activities. However, the concrete and semi-concrete are valued as learning experiences that assist pupils to achieve abstractions in science lessons and units of study.

A third philosophy stresses pupils attaining measurable results in the science curriculum. Thus, a pupil can pinpoint an exact level of achievement in science such as the fiftieth percentile or being one standard deviation above the mean. With quality tests that are valid and reliable, the teacher may pinpoint the exact achievement level of the involved learner. Here, the precise objectives are stated prior to instruction. The learning opportunities guide pupils to achieve each measurably stated objectives in ongoing science lessons and units of study. Test results indicate how well a pupil is doing in science.

A fourth philosophy of education in teaching science emphasises a decision making model. Here, the learner is actively involved in planning the objectives, learning activities, and evaluation procedures in teaching and learning. The pupil with teacher assistance is to be a responsible person in selecting what to learn in the science curriculum. What is learned in science units may stress problem solving, an idea centered approach, and/or achieving measurably stated objectives. The decision making model emphasises pupils being accountable for goal attainment in the science curriculum In deciding upon which philosophy of science teaching to stress, the teacher will need to appraise his/her strengths in the instructional arena as well as appraise learner progress involving to teaching and learning in the science curriculum. The choice(s) zero in upon pupils needing to attain as optimally as possible in science instruction.

PRINCIPLES OF LEARNING

There are specific principles of learning that are recommended to be used to teaching pupils on science. These principles of learning are advocated by educational psychologists in the teaching arena:

1. set establishment is important. If pupils are to learn and achieve, their attention must be secured in ongoing learning experiences. A definite strategy needs to be formulated by the science teacher to obtain pupil attention for teaching and learning situations. Pupils who do not attend to the ongoing lesson do not attain as much as they should;

2. pupils need to possess reasons for achieving stated objectives in science. The science teacher may use an inductive approach in guiding pupils to establish reasons for learning. Here, the teacher asks questions of learners in class on why it is salient to master what is contained in the stated objectives. Or a deductive procedure may be emphasised in that the teacher might explain to pupils why it is important to learn that which is contained in the listed objectives on the chalkboard or overheard projector. Teachers advocating

extrinsic rewards may announce prizes/awards for pupils who attain a certain precise level of achievement in science. Pupils need to be clear on what to learn so that the prize/award is obtained;

3. pupils need to perceive relationships of the new subject matter to be taught with the previous content emphasised and mastered. Quality sequence is an end result;
4. time on task is relevant. Here, pupils perceive as worthwhile that which is being presented as learning opportunities to achieve objectives;
5. motivation for learning is in evidence in that each pupil is revealing a higher energy level for accomplishment in sequential units of study in science;
6. learners attach meaning to content presented. Understanding and comprehension of ideas gleaned make for meaningful learning.

NATIONAL SCIENCE EDUCATION STANDARDS

Voluntary standards for science teachers to emphasise in teaching have been developed and published in the volume National Science Education Standards (NSES). There are excellent objectives here for teachers to stress in teaching and learning situations. 'The Science as Inquiry Standards' section states the following (NSES, 1996):

Scientific inquiry refers to the diverse ways in which scientists study the natural world and propose explanations based on evidence derived from their work. Inquiry also refers to the activities of students in which they develop knowledge and understanding of scientific ideas as well as an understanding of how scientists study the natural world...

The Teaching Standard for all K-4 students emphasise the following, as an example:

In guiding and facilitating science instruction, teachers should:

1. Focus and support inquiries while interacting with students;
2. Orchestrate discourse among students about scientific ideas;
3. Challenge students to accept and share responsibility for their own learning;
4. Recognise and respond to diversity and encourage all students to participate fully in science learning;
5. Encourage and model the skills of scientific inquiry, as well as the curiosity, openness to new ideas and data, and skepticism that characterises science.

Conclusion

The science teacher needs to use diverse ingredients in teaching and learning which guide optimal progress. The structure of knowledge, the psychology of learning, the philosophy of education, and vital principles of learning need to be used to determine and organise a purposeful set of sequential units in science instruction. Subject matter, skills, and attitudinal objectives must reflect careful planning by the science teacher. Learning opportunities should guide pupils to achieve objectives. Evaluation of achievement needs to indicate the kinds of progress made by pupils in ongoing lessons and units of study. Diverse evaluation procedures need to be used to acquire information pertaining to each pupil's progress in science. The information obtained should be used to plan further sequential units of instruction.

References

Ediger, Marlow (1997), *Teaching Science in the Elementary School.* Kirksville, Missouri: Simpson Publishing Company, pp. 1-7.

Ediger, Marlow (1994), 'Shared Leadership in the Curriculum,' *Education Magazine*. Qatar National Commission for Education, (23): 110, pp. 11-15.

Ediger, Marlow (1996), *Elementary Education*. Kirksville, Missouri: Simpson Publishing Company, pp. 10-24

Ediger, Marlow (1995), *Philosophy in Curriculum Development*. Kirksville, Missouri: Simpson Publishing Company, p. 1-18.

National Science Education Standards (1996), published by the National Research Council. Washington, DC: National Academy Press.

Marja, Talvi and Digumarti Bhaskara Rao, eds. (1996), *Educational Leadership and Social Changes*. New Delhi, India: Discovery Publishing House.

6

QUALITY IN THE SCIENCE CURRICULUM

Each person lives in a world of science. The natural environment affects all of us. It operates in terms of scientific theories, principles, and laws. Pupils in the public school setting need to achieve relevant goals in science. These goals should be attainable, meaningful, and possess purpose for the learner. *The Show Me Standards* (1996) list the following science objectives for pupil achievement in Missouri schools:

In science, students in Missouri public schools will acquire a solid foundation which includes knowledge of

1. properties and principles of matter and energy;
2. properties and principles of force and motion;
3. characteristics and interactions of living organisms;
4. changes in eco-systems and interactions of organisms with their environment;
5. processes (such as plate movement, water cycle, air

flow) and interactions of Earth's biosphere, atmosphere, lithosphere, and hydrosphere;

6. composition and structure of the universe and the motions of objects within it;
7. processes of scientific inquiry (such as formulating and testing hypotheses);
8. impact of science, technology and human activity on resources and the environment.

Each of the above named objectives should be emphasised within a related, designated unit of study. The objectives might also be written more precisely, If desired so that it can be measured if a pupil has/has not achieve each stated end of instruction. There are states in the United States that mandate measurably stated objectives. Other states have a more open-ended approach in allowing leeway in writing objectives. We recommend that objectives not be written so precisely that facts only are emphasised on tests to appraise pupil achievement. The following objective stresses memorising facts: the pupil will list in writing the names of ten arthropods. Then too, objectives can be so broadly stated that they become meaningless such as 'The pupil will learn science.' This objectives certainly lacks clarity in terms of what will be taught and evaluated to determine pupil achievement.

To improve the quality of life for each person, a problem solving approach should be emphasised in ongoing lessons and units in science. With problem solving, change occurs from what is to what should be in science.

Diverse schools of philosophical thought will be discussed and how each might relate to improve the science curriculum.

REALISM IN THE SCIENCE CURRICULUM

A science teacher who is a realist emphasises that one can know the real world, in whole or in part, as it truly is. The mind then does not modify or change what is being perceived. Tillman, Berofsky, and O' Connor (1971) wrote, "Most people when they think about the objects of perception, would say that they perceive a world of objects which is external to them and which exists independently of their perception of it. This view is called realism.'

Since the external world is perceived the way it is in actuality, specific objective of instruction can be determined by scientists and science educators for pupils to achieve. Each objective must be relevant and is a part of the whole that can be known by the learner. Thus in geology, biology, chemistry, physics, and astronomy, among other academic disciplines, measurably stated objectives of instruction need to be emphasised in teaching and learning in the science curriculum. With quality learning opportunities selected by the science teacher, pupils either achieve or do not achieve the specific objective(s) as a result of instruction. Measuring pupil achievement in learning stresses what pupils have learned what was stated in each objectives. Realists desire observable results in learning from pupils. The results are verifiable regardless of which teacher is appraising learner progress. The verification principle is very important to teachers of science who adhere to realism as a philosophy of instruction.

Skinner (1979) was a leading advocate in stressing precise objectives for pupil attainment. Reinforcement is emphasised to reward correct/good responses in learning. Observable, measurable results are obtained from what pupils have achieved. Guesswork is not involved, but per cents, standard deviations, quartile deviations, grade equivalents, and percentile ranks emphasise how well each pupil is doing in the area of science instruction. Numerical results of pupil achievement in science is wanted by the realist teacher. Scores from tests; objective evaluations of science experiments and demonstrations performed by pupils; ratings given to learner performance as well as responses to questions, oral reports, portfolios and related papers written in which interobserver reliability is in evidence, present data as to how well pupils are achieving. These procedures qualify as objective means of appraising learner progress.

Mager (1972) stressed the importance of writing objectives so they are operationalised. Objectives are then specific and clear to teachers, pupils, and other interested persons. Learning opportunities may be chosen and aligned with the stated objectives. Appraisal procedures used to determine pupil achievement are also aligned with the objectives. Quality validity and reliability are then in the offing. A pupil reveals if he/she attained or did not attain a stated objective. The realist science teacher wishes to know if pupils individually are or are not achieving objectives of instruction. The results may then be reported to parents in a very precise way.

Prior to instruction, the teachers may announce to pupils which objectives will be emphasised in the science lesson or unit. The pupil knows exactly what will be expected in terms of knowledge or skills to be obtained. The involved pupil should have more confidence in learning when realising what the instructor's expectations are. The science teacher might desire to arrange the objectives in an ascending order of complexity. A logical sequence follows since the teacher sequences objectives in science for the pupil to achieve.

Advantages given for emphasising realism as a philosophy of instruction are the following:

1. teachers may realise how successful they are in teaching since results form pupil learning are clear and observable;
2. objectives, learning activities, and evaluation procedures are interrelated in that the learning activities and the evaluation procedures must harmonise with the stated objectives. Thus, for example, it becomes easier to choose learning activities than otherwise would be the case due to the harmony needed between these activities and the stated objectives;
3. effective schools research states that pupils achieve better if there is a clear relationship between the learning activities and the evaluation procedures with that of the objectives of science instruction (Edmonds, 1982).

Disadvantages given for emphasising realism as a philosophy of education stress the fragmented knowledge that pupils may learn since each objective achieved emphasises parts of a whole.

The teacher controls the science curriculum since he/she determines the objectives, learning opportunities, and evaluation procedures; pupils are not involved here in decision making. The products of instruction in science are emphasised, leaving little room for processes such as abstract thinking which is rather difficult to measure.

Examples of precise objectives for pupils to achieve in science are the following:

1. The pupil will write a paragraph indicating seven animals involved in a food chain;
2. The pupil will make a drawing showing ten animals in a forest food web and their interactions;
3. The pupil will list in writing the names of five parasites and their respective hosts;
4. The pupil will define each of the following: producers, consumers, decomposers, symbiosis, and an aquatic—land community.

EXPERIMENTALISM IN THE SCIENCE CURRICULUM

Experimentalists stress a problem solving approach in the curriculum. They emphasise that individuals cannot know the real world as it truly is. Individuals , however, obtain experiences of this reality. With experiences, changes occur in one's thinking and believing. A changing world makes for problematic situations. Problems need identification and solutions sought. In the science curriculum, pupils with teacher guidance select a problem within an ongoing lesson or unit of study. The problem needs to be adequately delimited so that meaning and understanding is involved. An hypothesis is developed directly related to the stated problem. Information from a variety of sources is used by learners to arrive at a tentative solution. Experimentalists believe all knowledge to be tentative, not absolute. The result might well involve changing and modifying the original hypotheses. The new hypothesis is then tried out in a concrete situation (Geiger, 1955). Problem solving may be used in all curriculum areas and in life itself. Knowledge here is used to solve problems and is not an end in and of itself. The practical and the utilitarian are emphasised within the framework of problem solving: knowledge secured from a variety of sources has an application dimension. Knowledge then is useful to solve problems in changing world, science included.

Experimentalists emphasise that school and society are one, not separate entities. Since groups in society select and solve problems, pupils in committees also need to be involved in cooperative learning stressing problem solving. School and society are one, not separate entities. Dewey (1915) is still very widely recognised as a leading advocate of experimentalism in teaching and learning. In integrating the learner with the self as well as with the societal arena, he advocated four characteristics of pupils which have wide implications for the teaching of science. These are that pupils posses the social impulse in that they desire to work together with others in the curriculum; the constructive impulse in which learners like to learn by doing, not being passive individuals; the investigative and experimentation inclination whereby pupils desire to learn by discovery rather than being told and lectured; and the creative or expressive impulse, rather than have rigid formal expectations for achievement.

Advantages given in emphasising experimentalism as a philosophy of teaching science are the following:

1. pupil interest in science becomes paramount when they with teacher assistance identify problem areas. Interest in learning makes for effort in achieving;
2. very young pupils in early primary grades may be involved in problem solving experiences;
3. problem solving is useful in all curriculum areas and in life itself when problems are selected and solutions sought.

Disadvantages of using experimentalism as a philosophy of education include problem selection being too difficult as well as problem solving may not be a favourite style and way of learning for a few pupils. Also motivation may be lacking for some pupils to identify and solve problems.

The following are examples of possible problems for pupils to solve:.

1. How do animals adapt to their natural environment?
2. How do cells differ in size and shape to fulfill their unique functions? How are cells similar in features possessed?
3. How do unicellular and multicellular organisms differ from each other?
4. Which life processes do all living things perform?

Pertaining to John Dewey's philosophy of experimentalism, Meyer (1949) wrote:

All of this, of course, depends upon in no small way on thinking. For Dewey, however, thinking becomes significant only when applied to life situations. It is, he has said, 'an instrumentality used by man in adjusting himself to the practical situations in life.' Or to phrase it more simply, human beings think in order to live. Because of this stimulus, which has its basis in biology and sociology, it is impossible—it is absurd—to interpret life in a systematic and abstract way. Since, moreover, Dewey holds that life is in constant flux, it is impossible to solve problems with any degree of finally for the problems of tomorrow will be different from those of today.

As for the problem of knowledge, Dewey believes that knowledge and true experience is functional. What is this thing for? What is its use? Is a coal mine a physical deposit or does it have function? and if so, what is it? Such are the questions that help to give meaning to one's experience; but such questions cannot be answered without antecedent action. Action must precede knowledge. Whatever knowledge we possess has resulted from our activities, our efforts to survive, to obtain food, shelter, and clothing. Only that which has been organised into our disposition so as to enable us to adapt to our environment to meet our needs and to adapt our aims and desires to the situation in which we exit is really knowledge.

IDEALISM IN THE SCIENCE CURRICULUM

Idealists believe that one can receive ideas about the real world only. Thus one cannot know the real world as it truly is independent of the observer. Mental development in idealism becomes of utmost importance since an idea centered world is in evidence. Mind is real and needs development. As a leading idealist still quoted widely presently, Horne (1932) stressed the importance of the use of reason and rational thought in arriving at truth. Concepts and generalisations or universals such as justice, truth, goodness, ethics, and beauty have always existed and can be discovered by human beings. These universals are a priori, to an idealist, in that they have existed prior to human experience.

A subject centered curriculum in science is of paramount importance. In science lessons and units of study, pupils should achieve vital concepts, and generalisations. Depth teaching is needed to cultivate the intellect in guiding pupils achievement in science. A multimedia approach in leaning is needed to assist pupils to achieve abstract ideas in science. The abstract to an idealist is superior to the concrete and semiconcrete in learning. The concrete and semiconcrete facets of learning in science are salient to the degree that learners attain the abstract such as vital facts, concepts, and generalisations in ongoing lessons and units of study. Since reading and writing, in particular, stress abstract learnings, they should not be minimised in the science curriculum.

To emphasise a subject centered curriculum as idealists recommend, an academically inclined teacher needs to teach in a scholarly way so that objectives stressing intellectual goals are attained by pupils. Blanchard (1964) wrote:

> The aim of thought from its very beginning, we saw, was at understanding. To understand anything meant to apprehend it in a system that rendered it necessary. The ideal of complete understanding would be achieved only when the system that rendered it necessary was not a system that itself was fragmentary and therefore contingent, but one that was all—inclusive and so organised internally that every part was linked to every other by intelligible necessity.

Advantages given for emphasising idealism as a philosophy of teaching science include the following:

1. pupils are to achieve significant subject matter. Idealism emphasises the acquisition of vital content in science that pupils need to attain. Uses made of knowledge in science need to emphasise what is just too all, what is truthful, what is good in its application, what will truly stress ethical dimensions, and that which has beauty in its esthetical areas;

2. many pupils may be motivated to learn when an academic approach to learn science is stressed. This might be especially appealing to the gifted and talented learners in science. All pupils need motivation to achieve and learn in science;

3. the abstract in idealism is preferred to the concrete and semiconcrete; relevant concepts, and generalisations, and other universals emphasise abstract goals in science teaching. Idealist advocate wholeness in knowledge, not fragmentation. Knowledge is related in all of its manifestations.

Disadvantages given for idealism as a philosophy in teaching and learning include minimising a hands on approach in learning science since the focal point of teaching is to have pupils develop well intellectually; placing emphasis upon universals much more so than specifics—the latter is salient in pupils arriving at conclusions such as in science experiments; and integrating of knowledge to the point where science as a discipline is not as clearly defined as it might be. Idealists tend to stress that which goes beyond the five senses. Thus metaphysics and the a priori are salient to an idealist.

Quality sequence in science might be slighted when abstract phases of learning are more prized more highly than the concrete and semiconcrete. Most educators presently recommend a sequence of concrete, semiconcrete, to the abstract in teaching-learning situations. Quite similar in sequence, Bruner (1968) advocated using manipulative materials such as objects and items; followed by iconic materials such as audio-visual materials which are one step removed from the manipulative phase; and then symbolic activities which stresses the abstract including reading and writing.

Objective in science, according to idealism as a philosophy of education, might well stress the following universal topics:

1. monerans such as bacteria and blue green algae. Monerans are prokaryotes in that they have no true nucleus. They consist of producers, consumers, and decomposers. A few move around whereas others are stationary;

2. protists, such as paramecium, euglenas, diatoms, and cribaria. Protists are unicellular and have a true nucleus. With a true nucleus, protists are eukaryotes, and are producers as well as consumers;

3. fungi, such as mushrooms and bread molds. Most fungi are multicellular. Since fungi do not contain chlorophyll, most are decomposers with a few being consumers;

4. plants, such as mosses, liverworts, ferns, and seed plants. Plants are eukaryotes and producers. Plants do not move from one place to another.

Pertaining to idealism, Bigge (1982) wrote:

The heart of idealism is the belief that basic reality consists of ideas, thoughts, minds, or substantive selves, not physical matter. Since priority is given to minds, minds have bodies, but bodies do not have minds. Idealism carries with its view the idea of subsistence (the superexistence) of God, who also is basically mind or self. The universe is an expression of intelligence and will; its order is due to an eternal, spiritual reality. For idealists, people are good-active substantive minds; they are absolutely real selves endowed with free will or genuine moral choice. This philosophy has ancient roots; it dates back to Socrates (469-399 BC) and Plato (427-347 BC).

Idealism really is idea-ism. The source of this title is based on Platonic thought. For Plato, ideas only are genuinely real; they consisted of immaterial essences. That which people perceive is a shadow of reality; each thing that they perceive gets its existence from its Thingness; an idea. A book is a book because of its being more or less an imperfect replica of Bookness. A woman is a woman because she is a replica of Womanness. Plato's assumed world of 'eternal verities' consisted of the True, the Good, and the Beautiful.

We can trace the development of idealism by listing some of the leading philosophers who have contributed to this position and stating a leading idea that each has contributed to this philosophy. Socrates believed that children are born with knowledge already in their minds, but they needed help to recall this innate knowledge. Plato contributed to the idea of ideas, which are the universal forms of all existing things and are the essence of reality. St. Augustine (350-430) held a dualistic (mind-body) force of goodness.

EXISTENTIALISM AND THE SCIENCE CURRICULUM

Existentialists believe that one exists first and then finds his/her purposes in life; there are no standards to guide human beings other than those developed by the human race. Most existentialists advocate that people are condemned to be free with no a priori standards in life. Individuals then make or break themselves due to the kind of society wanted. Each person chooses and makes choices continually. To be human is to choose. If a person permits the self to have someone else makes one's own decisions, then the individual ceases to be human.

Combs (1972) stresses that the way individuals perceive a situation will assist in determining how the individual will behave. Perception is unique to the individual. Each person decides upon what is true, judges what is good, and decides upon plans of action. The science curriculum then must provide opportunities for pupils individually to decide what to learn, that is the objectives of instruction. The pupil needs to be heavily involved in selecting learning opportunities as well as methods of determining progress. The teacher is a guide and encourages pupil learning. The teacher, however, does not lecture nor determine the science curriculum for the individual pupil. A learning centers approach in teaching science may then be emphasised. Here, there are an adequate number of centers with quality tasks for learners at each center. There needs to be more tasks than what a pupil can complete so that individual sequential choices may truly be made. A psychological, not logical, science curriculum is then in evidence. Each pupil may select tasks based on personal needs, interests, and purposes. The choice to be made is up to the individual pupil. If tasks do not meet personal needs of the involved learner, he/she might plan with the teacher what has merit and value to the pupil. A contract system might also be implemented in which the pupil with teacher guidance selects tasks to put into a contract for completion. The leaner himself/herself is responsible for choices made. The individual perceives what is good and has quality. Knowledge is subjective, not objective to the existentialist. For example, in a values clarification session, the pupil determines what is moral in terms of uses made of science and technology; the teacher has a difficult position as a stimulator and of one who encourages pupil learning. Being humane in an absurd environment is a major goal for pupil achievement in existentialist thought and thinking.

Within an existentialist science curriculum, through pupil/teacher planning a learner may select topics such as the following to pursue:

1. How do pesticides and herbicides help or hinder the natural environment? This question pertains to curbing insects and weed growth for the raising of farm crops versus possible contamination of soil and water;
2. How does one deal with animals in a humane way? This question stresses what to do with surplus dogs and cats roaming an area, as well as using animals for food and for scientific experiments;
3. How can the natural environment be used for development so that adequate numbers of jobs are available for workers versus the destruction of natural habitats for wildlife?
4. How can the needs of individuals be met as well as those in the societal arenas? This raises the question of the individual versus the larger group in a community, state, nation, and the world.

Alston and Brandt (1978) write the following direct quote of Jean Paul Sartre, a late leading existentialist:

Man is nothing else but what he makes of himself. Such is the first principle of existentialism. It is also what is called subjectivity, the name we are labeled with when charges are brought against us. But what do we mean by this, if not that man has a greater dignity than a stone or table? For we mean that man fist exists, that is, that man first of all is the being who hurls himself into the future and who is conscious of imagining himself being in the future. Man is at the start a plan which is aware of itself, rather than a patch of moss, a piece of garbage, or a cauliflower; nothing exists prior to this plan; there is nothing in heaven; man will be what he will have planned to be. Not what he will want to be. Because by the word 'will' we generally mean a conscious decision, which is subsequent to what we have made for ourselves. I may want to belong to a political party, write a book, get married; but all that is only a manifestation of an earlier, more spontaneous choice that is called 'will'. But if existence really precedes essence, man is responsible for what he is. Thus, existentialism's first move is too make every man aware of what he is and to make the full responsibility of his existence rest upon him. And when we say that a man is responsible for individually, but that he is responsible for all men.

THE PSYCHOLOGY OF EDUCATION

Principles of learning from the psychology of learning give direction to the science teacher in teaching-learning situations in ongoing lessons and units of study. Ediger (1994) lists the following criteria upon which educational psychologists agree should be followed by teachers:

1. meaningful learning experiences should be provided pupils in the curriculum;
2. interesting content and skills should be offered in lessons and units of study;
3. purpose needs to be established within pupils for learning;
4. quality sequence for pupil learning is a must;
5. rational balance among knowledge, skills, and attitudinal objectives is important in the instructional arena.

Conclusion

Science teachers need to select tenets form the philosophy of education which stress pupils attaining vital content, abilities, and attitudes. In reviewing the different philosophies of education discussed in this paper, the following is salient from each philosophy:

1. clarity in objectives of science instruction, carefully selected, as recommended by realists. However, it is important to avoid fragmenting knowledge obtained by pupils;
2. problem solving procedures as recommended by 50 experimentalists. Life in society emphasises the importance of being able to solve personal and social problems;
3. major concepts and generalisations, as universals in science, advocated by idealists;
4. decision making opportunities in science as recommended by existentialists. Each person needs to learn to make decisions.

We believe that a problem solving philosophy encompasses the other three philosophies. We recommended problem solving as a major philosophy of education to emphasise in teaching science due to its relevance in the curriculum and in life itself. Problems abound and need solutions. Knowledge acquired then is instrumental or useful in problems to be solved which are selected by pupils with teacher guidance.

Ediger and Rao (1996) wrote the following in summarising different psychologies of teaching:

Comparisons were made among the following models in teaching science:

1. problem solving with teacher guidance;
2. behaviourism with its pre-determined precise objectives for student attainment;
3. humanism and its emphasis upon students selecting sequential activities from among alternatives;

4. the structure of knowledge with key concepts and generalisations identified by academicians in their respective areas of specialisation. Science teachers assist students to achieve these structural ideas inductively using methods and procedures of scientists in a science laboratory setting;
5. stimulus—response learning of students in which a specific response is associated with a precise stimulus.

The writers advocate a problem solving approach be utilised in teaching science. From a stimulating learning environment in science, students with teacher guidance identify and solve vital problems. Problem solving skills are useful in all academic areas, as well as in the societal arena. Behaviourism, humanism, the structure of knowledge, and stimulus—response learning may be emphasised within the framework of problem solving situations. Subject matter in science may then be utilised in the problem solving science curriculum.

References

Alston, William P., and Richard W. Brandt (1978), *The Problems of Philosophy*, third edition. Boston: Allyn and Bacon, Inc. pages 257-258.

Bigge, Morris (1982), *Educational Philosophies for Teachers*. Columbus, Ohio: Charles E. Merril Publishing Company, pages 25-26.

Blanchard, Brand (1964). *The Nature of Thought*. New York: Humanities Press, 492-517.

Bruner, Jerome (1968), *Toward A Theory of Instruction*. Cambridge, Massachusetts: Harvard University Press.

Combs, Arthur (1972), *Educational Objectives: Beyond Behavioural Objectives*. Washington, DC: Association for Supervision and Curriculum Development.

Dewey, John (1915), *School and Society*, Chicago: University of Chicago Press.

Ediger, Marlow (1999), 'Teacher Education and the Public Schools', *The Progress of Education*. 73 (12), 278-279, published in India.

Ediger, Marlow (1998), 'Objectives in the Science Curriculum,' *Spectrum*. 24 (2), 24-27.

Ediger, Marlow (1995), 'Demonstration Teaching in the Schools'. *Education*, 114, 371-372.

Ediger, Marlow (1994), Mathematics, Problem Solving, and the Young Learner. *The Primary Teacher*, 19, 34-37.

Ediger, Marlow (1997), 'Excellence in the Science Curriculum', ERIC # Ed 406144.

Ediger, Marlow. Early Field Experiences in Teacher Education. *College Student Journal*. 28, 302-306.

Ediger, Marlow, and D. Bhaskara Rao. *Science Curriculum*. New Delhi, India: Discovery Publishing House, page 117.

Ediger, Marlow and Digumarti Bhaskara Rao (2000), *Teaching Mathematics Successfully*. New Delhi, India: Discovery Publishing House.

Edmonds, Ron (1982), Programmes of School Improvement: An Overview. *Educational Leadership*. December, Volume 4.

Geiger, George W. (1955), An Experimentalists Approach to Education. *Modern Philosophies and Education*. Chicago, Illinois: National Society for the Study of Education, 54, 137-174.

Horne, Herman Harrell (1932), *The Democratic Philosophy of Education*. New York: The Macmillan Company, 325-340.

Mager, Robert F. (1972), *Goal Analysis*. Belmont, California: Fearon Publishers.

Missouri Department of Elementary and Secondary Education (1996), *Show Me Standards*. Jefferson City, Missouri.

Meyer, Adolph E. (1949), *The Development of Education in the Twentieth Century*. Englewood Cliffs, New Jersey: Prentice-Hall, Inc., pages 42-43.

Skinner, B.F. (1979), *Beyond Freedom and Dignity*. New York: Alfred Knopf, Inc.

Tillman, Frank A., and others (1971), *Introductory Philosophy*. New York: Harper and Row, page 550.

7

Current Events in School Science

Pupils desire to experience relevant content in science. The content then needs to be based on the interests and needs of learners. Who determines these interests and needs? The pupil should be in the best position to determine what is relevant. He/she decides what is useful and has application values. One way of approaching the problem of ascertaining relevancy is for the teacher to develop and provide learning stations for pupils whereby each pupil may select that task or learning activity which has the greatest value when engaging in sequential learning experiences. There should be enough tasks at the different stations so that learners may omit what does not possess perceived relevancy and yet have plenty of work to do.

A second approach in teaching is to use teacher-pupil planning within the framework of a thematic unit of study. The science teacher then plans with the pupil that which the latter wishes to learn. There may be large class, collaborative experiences within committees, as well as individual study activities. Thus, the teacher assists pupils to determined objectives, learning opportunities, and evaluation procedures that possess relevancy.

A third approach in deciding upon relevant topics or pupils to pursue in the science curriculum is for teachers, principles, and supervisors to study, analyse, and accept thematic units of study involving consensus thinking. This might well incorporate state mandated objectives as well as the National Science Teachers Association standards for learners to achieve in the science curriculum. Clearly written objectives, quality learning opportunities for pupils to attain the objectives, as well as valid/ reliable evaluation procedures to ascertain if pupils have attained the stated objectives of instruction must then be in the offing.

We would like to suggest a fourth approach which emphasises a current events procedure. Pupils may hear new items in the home setting pertaining to what is happening currently in the natural environment. Current events indicate that the happening is occurring at the present time and is of concern to many people.

CURRENT EVENTS IN SCIENCE

What is transpiring presently has many natural phenomena for pupil study. At this writing, there are devastating floods in Oregon and to some extent in Washington. Annual floods occur in different areas around the world. People lose homes, lives, cards, furniture, and other property in flood waters. Floods carry much energy with the damage that these high waters can do. Learners then find floods to be natural phenomenon that occur frequently. It is a very worthy topic and theme to study if human being wish to do something to deter the devastating happenings that result from floods. Newspapers TV and radio news reports, newsmagazines, newspapers written for pupils such as *My Weekly Reader*. Video tapes, multiple series basal texts, science encyclopaedias, computer packages, internet, and video disks, among other materials of instruction, might well provide appropriate content for pupils to use in problem solving such as:

1. identifying and answering questions involving 'What causes floods to occur?'

2. securing information in problem solving activities;
3. developing a hypothesis or tentative answer to the question/problem;
4. testing the hypothesis when reading and acquiring information to approve or refute the hypothesis;
5. revising the hypothesis if necessary as a result of the test.

When studying about floods, pupils should also learn what human beings do to try to alleviate the suffering that occurs from these problematic situations. Social studies here becomes a part of the science curriculum. An integrated, inter-disciplinary curriculum results. Pupils then need to learn about the work of the Red Cross, relief organisations which provide cleanup crews with no costs involved, as well as state, county, and federal efforts working toward remedying problems involving flooding.

A second natural disaster which occurred two weeks ago, at this writing, was freezing rain in the south-eastern states of the US. North Carolina, an entire state, dismissed schools and business workdays for one day due to electric wires being down, roads being slick and unsafe, and tree limbs blocking areas for driving. Freezing rain which damages electrical lines and makes roads slick occurs when the temperature reading goes below thirty-two degrees Fahrenheit and moisture falls in the form of rain. The costs of freezing rain might well run into the billions of dollars and cause many accidents and deaths from slick road surfaces.

Pupils need to learn about causes for freezing rain. They should learn about hazards that occur and why. Safety should be discussed and taught when freezing rain comes about. Goals of instruction pertaining to the phenomenon of freezing rain should be relevant and important for pupils. Learners need to have opportunities to work individually and collaboratively in problems identified pertaining to learning about freezing rain. A variety of materials need to be used by pupils in finding answers to problems. Depth teaching should be in emphasis. Intensive learning about freezing rain and its consequences should be an end result.

Sequence in learning may follow a logical approach whereby the science teacher sequences or orders the learning opportunities for pupils. At other times a psychological sequence may be followed in that learners with teacher guidance may order experiences and activities. Methods of teaching should involve induction, deduction, guided instruction by the teacher, as well as pupils with teacher guidance planning the ongoing lessons and units of study pertaining to natural disasters.

Three years ago at this writing, California had a series of earthquakes with its accompanying after shocks. China, Japan, Russia, the Ukraine, and Iran, among other nations on the planet earth, experience rather frequent problems pertaining to earthquakes as a natural phenomena. Property and road damage can be high indeed depending upon the severity of the quake as measured by the Richter scale. Destruction to buildings might well depend, in part, upon how these were built and which materials were used. Pertaining to earthquakes online, Butler, et. al: (1996) wrote:

Earthquakes provide a perfect inter-disciplinary teaching opportunity to involve students in highly motivational real-world experiences. Access to information regarding earthquakes is available from several sources on the internet, but the primary source is the National Earthquake Information Service (NEIS) in Golden, Colorado. This service is provided by the US Geological Survey... . The site gives near-real-time international information on earthquakes. For each earthquake, the following data are provided: the time in Universal Time, the latitude and longitude of the epicenter, the depth in kilometers to the focus, the magnitude, and the general location.

To implement the earthquake project, access to a computer with a modem, a printer, and an Internet account is necessary. In addition to the hardware, the real ingredient necessary for a successful project is a group of motivated teachers. In our district this mix of material and personnel was located at Canton Middle School, Las Vegas, Nevada. The lead teacher was a science teacher, who was supported by a geography teacher and a mathematics teacher.

The science teacher, who has the internet connection in

the classroom, introduced students to the internet. On the first day of the programme, one student from each class period was trained to use the computer and modem to access NEIS's earthquake reporting site. The following day, students who had been trained each trained another student... . In the weeks that followed, each student became a trainee and a trainer in turn... .

A large Mercator projection map of the Earth was posted on a bulletin board in the science classroom. Each day as information was gathered, groups of students located the epicenter of each earthquake reported on the map using pushpins colour coded according to earthquake magnitude... .

Objectives for instruction should be developed cooperatively by teachers with supervisor assistance. Careful evaluation of each objective is a must. The learning activities for pupils to attain vital objectives need to be conducive to helping pupils attain as optimally as possible. Pupil interests, needs, purposes, and attitudes need proper provision so that quality achievement in these areas are in evidence. Appraisal procedures to determine pupil attainment of goals need to be varied so that each facet of achievement is evaluated. Teacher developed, norm referenced, as well as criterion referenced tests may be used to ascertain pupil achievement of vital objectives. Anecdotal records, journal writing, teacher observation, pupil self evaluation, learner products of instruction, class participation, videotapes, and snapshots of learner achievement. Thus a variety of procedures should be used in determine how much pupils have learned pertaining to natural disasters on the planet earth.

Four years ago, several of the plain states were hit by tornadoes. One tornado in central Kansas uprooted evergreen trees ten feet tall and eleven inches in diameter. A half mile away, a newly built study brick house had just been completed as a dream house for a retired couple. This durable structure was completely demolished by the 150 miles per hour winds in the tornado. Houses in the path of the tornado that remained standing were damaged to the point where they were later torn down. The path of the tornado could be followed easily in terms of where devastating destruction had occurred. Farm houses and barns, directly adjacent, were unharmed. There is tremendous energy in the force of tornadoes.

Pupils with teacher guidance then need to:

1. identify relevant problems areas to solve;
2. choose subject matter content which supplies needed answers;
3. select from the acquired subject matter that which provides tentative answers to the question;
4. check the accuracy of the answer (s) through additional study;
5. notice additional problem areas pertaining to tornadoes that would be relevant to solve.

Cyclones and hurricanes may be incorporated into the study of tornadoes. Pupils also need to view each natural disaster in terms of what human beings can do to minimise its destructive forces as well as what can be done to alleviate human suffering.

Lightning strikes buildings and kills human beings, perhaps not to the extent that the previously discussed natural disasters do. A barn or shed filled with hay bales and farm implements may be struck by a bolt of lightning causing the property to be completely destroyed. Millions of dollars worth of labour and property burn ferociously, even with fire departments out in full force in rural areas. It is costly to remove the remains such as bulldozers dozing the concrete floors and slabs, from the destroyed buildings, to be hauled away by trucks. Trash from the burning property needs to be disposed of using bulldozers to load the contents onto trucks. Thus the hauling away of trash after lightning has hit a building is labour intensive and expensive.

The science teacher needs to identify key structural ideas that pupils should achieve pertaining to lightning and its affects on people and the environment. Forests, among other areas, can be damaged much due to being hit by lightning. This is easy to observe when travelling through any wooded area, small or large.

Drouth, as another natural disaster, keeps farm crops from producing or makes water scarce for livestock and other rural needs. Farmers and ranchers can be bankrupted when drouth hits an area. Livestock has to be sold cheaply since no one can afford to care for these animals when feed costs become very high due to scarcity and greed. It has an opposite affect as compared to farm crops being destroyed due to floods or excessive rain. Drouth has as a consequence a lack of water in cities for watering the lawn or washing the car, luxuries perhaps.

When farm land has drouth and strong winds are in evidence, erosion of soil can well be an end result. Erosion of top soil is difficult to restore. The farmer can minimise erosion through terracing, strip cropping, as well as growing grass and trees on farm land. All of these measures to control soil erosion are costly and tend to bring in minimal farm income. For example, quality hay, baled from excellent grassland, will not provide the income to farmers as compared to cultivated land where wheat, corn and soybeans are grown. Generally an inch of eroded top soil takes 100 to 500 years to rejuvenate.

Pertaining to drouth as a natural disaster, we recommend the following questions and issues for pupils to pursue using a variety of learning opportunities:

1. How can a balance be established between farmers making a living from farming as compared to using proper methods of preventing soil erosion?
2. Should there be federal and state government payments to farmers to prevent soil erosion, wetlands protection, as well as other means of protecting soil in the natural environment?
3. How can the natural environment best be protected, especially in the area of soil protection?

The use of pesticides and herbicides has become increasingly common to control harmful insects and weeds. If pesticides were not used, the chances are that our food supply would be greatly reduced due to sharing more and more of it with insects and other pests. Apple damage from moths can indeed be extensive. The corn borer, as well as smut, can greatly minimise yields in corn production. The Colorado potato beetle, in larva stage, can strip an otherwise good crop of potatoes in matter of two to three days. A hoard of grasshoppers can cause extensive damage, in a few days, to growing soybean plants. The reasons for using pesticides is quite obvious. Farmers may experience huge financial losses from insects and other pests in a short time of hours or a few days.

Weeds also can do much damage to farm crops in a few days. Cockleburs, for example, can crowd out soybean plants, in a week, from securing needed moisture and sunlight Herbicides when used may completely destroy all cockleburs in a matter of hours. Gardeners realise that foxtail weeds might well take all the moisture away from growing garden crops. How to minimise weed damage in the growing of farm crops as well as to prevent damage to ornamental plants can indeed be a problem. Pesticides and herbicides can control insect populations and weed growth. Increasingly, there are more resistant strains of insects and weeds to pesticides and herbicides. When DDT first came out in 1944, there was much optimism about its future in controlling files, mosquitoes, and other pests that hinder livestock production. DDT initially was very successful in curbing flies, insects, and other pests, particularly in livestock production. It did not take long, twenty years in general, when there were insects that became increasingly resistant to DDT. DDT also had its affects upon pollution of land, water supplies, and bodies of water until its use was banned.

One of the authors recently attended a science teachers convention in which a speaker stated how beneficial earthworms are to soil such as in providing natural fertilizer from body wastes, aeration of the soil, and richness of the soil. The speaker perceived the situation from one perception only and that was the negative effects of using pesticides and herbicides which kill many, many earthworms. The earthworm certainly provides soil with its numerous benefits to be sure. However, the income factor for farmers is also involved in that pests and weeds destroy domesticated plants. A highly complex problem is involved. With adequate background information, pupils with teacher guidance may brainstorm possible solutions to the dilemma of using agricultural chemicals to destroy pests and weds as compared to using other procedures to minimise yield damage to farm crops. Other procedures might include the use of insects which feed upon pests that destroy farm crops. To control weeds, brightly coloured flowers which attract pests have been used by gardeners, thus protecting valuable garden crops for human consumption. However, efforts so far in controlling pests and weeds have been only successful in a minor way.

To vary procedures of instruction mentioned in this manuscript, a learning stations approach may be used in the curriculum on natural disasters. An adequate number of stations need to be in the offing. Each station has concrete, semiconcrete, and abstract learning activities from which learners may choose sequentially to pursue. There are more tasks at the different stations than what any one learner can complete. Those tasks not possessing perceived purpose by the pupil may be omitted. The pupil is the chooser. The teacher assists and helps each pupil to accomplish as much as possible. The tasks at each station should be meaningful, interesting, emphasise a balance between individual and group endeavours, as well as possess challenge. Learners sequence or order their very own activities and experiences. An activity centered curriculum in science is an end result.

Ediger and Rao (1996) stress the important of having a variety of learning opportunities in teaching science for the following reasons:

1. pupils have different learning styles;
2. different levels of achievement in science exist within any class of pupils;
3. not all pupils, of course, benefit equally from the same activity;
4. teachers have different teaching styles;
5. selected learning activities capture the interests of pupils more than do other kinds of experiences;
6. individuals desire new experiences;
7. monotony in activities hinders pupils in developing motivation toward learning.

PHILOSOPHY OF SCIENCE EDUCATION

A study of diverse philosophies of education might well assist teachers to make quality decisions pertaining to current events in the science curriculum. Ediger (1995) wrote:

Diverse philosophical schools of thought in science are in evidence to develop and implement lessons plans and units in science. Experimentalism emphasises the use of problem solving experiences for pupil. Flexible steps in problems solving involve:

1. Identifying the problem;
2. Gathering data to solve the identified problem;
3. Developing a hypothesis, directly based to the obtained data and in answer to the problem;
4. Testing the hypothesis;
5. Revising the hypothesis, if evidence warrants.

Experimentalism emphasises that real live problems be identified by pupils. The problems come directly from society. In society, earth quakes, hurricanes, tornadoes, volcanic eruptions, among other natural phenomena occur. Out of these scenes and situations, problems arise and are identified, such as 'What makes for the happening of earthquakes?' Information needs to be gathered to answer the problem or question. An answer, tentative in nature, is then developed. The answer, a hypothesis, is then checked against further content, secured form a variety of reference sources. Modification of the original answer or hypotheses may then be needed.

Idealism, as a philosophy of education, emphasises an idea centered curriculum. Science then becomes a part of the general education curriculum. A subject centered, not an activity centered philosophy, is then in evidence. Diverse academic disciplines such as zoology, botany, physics, astronomy, biology, chemistry, and geology provide subject matter for ongoing units of study. Textbooks, workbooks, worksheets, and a few selected audio-visual aids provide content for pupils. Universal ideas or generalisations in science units need to be achieved by pupils. The teacher needs to be a true academician and scholar to stimulate pupil learning.

Realism, as a third philosophy of education, advocates the use of precise, measurable objectives. Realist believe the real world can be known in whole or part as it truly is. What pupils achieve in each science unit can be measured. The real world of natural phenomena can be stated in precise, measurable objectives. A variety of concrete learning activities, in particular, should be provided for pupils to attain the precise ends. Semi-concrete as well as abstract experiences also should be in the offing. After instruction, it is observable and measurable if an objective has been achieved by pupils.

Existentialism, as a fourth philosophy of education, emphasises the learner, himself or herself, being heavily involved in deciding what (the objectives) to learn, as well as the means (learning activities) in ongoing science units of study. Thus, a learning centers philosophy may be emphasised. More centers and tasks for learners to pursue are in evidence than what can be completed. Each pupil may then sequentially choose which tasks to complete, as well as which to omit. Pupils individually are involved in making these decisions. The teacher develops the centers for learner interaction. Better yet, pupil/teacher planning may be used to develop the centers and their inherent tasks.

In supervising student teachers and cooperating teachers in the public schools, we have observed the following current events items in science emphasised in each of the above named philosophies:

1. **Experimentalism:** In an ongoing lesson, pupils identified problems such as (a) Why did Iran experience a major earthquake this past weekend? (b) How is the strength of earthquakes measured?

2. **Idealism:** A teacher determined topic for discussion with pupil involvement stressing in an ongoing unit (a) the causes of hurricanes and their after affects (b) the differences between hurricanes and tornadoes.

3. **Realism:** The science teacher stating prior to implementing the lesson on the following two precise objectives pupils are to achieve: (a) The pupils will list

in writing three causes of major floods in the environment. (b) The pupil will write a fifty word paragraph on ways of preventing flood damage.

4. **Existentialism:** Pupils choosing what to study in a unit through teacher/learner planning. These areas, for example, might include (a) What may be done to help people care for each other when a natural disaster such as a cyclone occurs. (b) How might the United States annual budget be changed so that the needs of people are met in times of emergency when destruction from natural forces occur?

Our recommendations here are that current events in science emphasise problem solving. Experimentalism then should hold sway. Thus subject matter acquired when stressing idealism, content achieved from attaining measurably stated objectives (realism), and pupil/teacher planning procedures (existentialism) may all be used to identify and solve problems. Why is problem solving important? In life's situations, people face problems which need identification and necessary solutions. Each solution appears to be tentative and will need revisions as evidence indicates. In everyday situations then, individuals and groups experience problems continually which need some kind of answer.

There are current events papers written especially for the grade level pupils are in presently. These present items pertaining to natural disasters, among other human related factors.

Newspapers written for pupils have an intended audience and that is the learner himself/herself. Many problems in word recognition have been taken care of when a child centered paper has been written, but to provide for individual needs, selected learners will still need assistance in identifying unknown words. A few pupils will also need guidance in understanding the meaning of important words. Current events papers can have much appeal to learners providing that the teacher assists pupils in achieving background information prior to reading these weekly/monthly newspapers.

To assist pupil learning in discussions after having read the current events items, the following guidelines need to be stressed by teachers:

1. Each pupil needs to stay on the topic being discussed and not digress to other information;
2. Learners must respect the thinking of each discussion participant;
3. It is important to listen carefully to the ideas of others in the group;
4. All should be actively engaged in the discussion, but no one dominate the interactions;
5. Content presented should be evaluated in an atmosphere of respect and trust;
6. Participants need to speak clearly and accurately, in terms of concepts, generalisations, main ideas, and facts presented;
7. Valid and reliable conclusions should be drawn from each discussion;
8. Chairpersons may be chosen by the teacher with rotation procedures. Leadership might also emerge within a group without a chairperson.

Group/committee endeavours may follow listening to a radio news broadcast on natural catastrophies in the environment. These may be cassette recorded by the teacher in the home setting so that only relevant information is played to pupils. The teacher may also video-tape, with a VCR, vital current events items from TV broadcasts in the home setting. These may be played in the classroom with proper readiness provided by the science teacher. Daily newspaper items as well as weekly news items from reputable magazines might well provide relevant information on natural disasters and means used to prevent these occurrences from doing damage. The latest data sources should also be heavily used and involved in the science curriculum such as internet and computer packages. To achieve optimally in science current events, pupils need to experiences quality reference sources using a hands-on approach.

ORGANISATION OF THE SCIENCE CURRENT EVENTS CURRICULUM

There are several approaches that may be used by the teacher to organise the current events programme in science. First, the teacher may take time at the beginning of each class session to discuss news articles that pupils have brought in for discussion. Thus, a pupil might, for example, have brought in a news items about an avalanche that caused much destruction in a village in Switzerland. The temperature readings there were much warmer for that season than usual causing the snow and ice to melt above on the mountains. The result was a massive amount of snow and ice that came crashing down onto houses in the village. Or a pupil brought to the class a news clipping about the flooding of the Ohio River causing home evacuations and much property damage due to the mighty force of the rushing flood waters. A third pupil brought into the classroom and reported on a volcanic eruption in the Philippines. These happenings occurred simultaneously. There are enough natural disasters occurring which could provide an entire unit in science for pupils to study. These occurrences may be placed around a world map with a coloured piece of yarn connecting the place of the geographical location with the news clipping. Geography and the science curriculum are then correlated and taught as being related. Several of our student teachers and their cooperating teachers whom we have supervised in the public schools believe very strongly in bringing in humanitarian efforts used to alleviate the resulting human suffering from natural disasters. Historical efforts in assisting the unfortunate during times of natural disasters bring in a study of history integrated with the science curriculum. With the above examples given an entire science unit may be taught entitled 'Natural Disasters and Their Consequences.'

A second approach in organising the science current events curriculum is to discuss with pupils news items as they relate to the ongoing unit of study. Thus, if pupils for example, are studying a unit on 'Preserving Wildlife,' current events items may emphasise sanctuaries for bald eagles, an endangered species. Also recently, wolves from Alaska were released into a designated area in the state of Wyoming. Wolves formerly had a niche in that state but had become extinct until a new pack from Alaska was released in Wyoming. An issue that can provide for higher levels of cognition which might be discussed here is the point of view of cattle ranchers in Wyoming versus those of wildlife advocates in restoring an area to its original state. We have observed pupils with teacher guidance doing much research from a variety of reference sources to understand opposing sides in a dispute. Intrinsic motivation seems to be in evidence here.

A third approach in organising the current events is to stress the separate subject curriculum. Here, pupils are encouraged to bring news items to class if they relate to the ongoing unit in science or not. There are excellent reasons for emphasising the separate subjects procedure in organising the current events programme in science. Thus, there are vital news happenings in the world of science that have no relationship to the ongoing unit of study being taught. Then too, there are not an adequate number of science news items that relate so that an entire unit may be taught. At the same time, the isolated news item brought to class is highly relevant and should receive adequate attention in class as soon as possible. We have observed in different classrooms which have a quality programme of science in the news and yet the items are not related to the present unit being taught. We would like to offer the following suggestions for implementing a good current events programme. These suggestions are the following:

1. pupils should volunteer to bring into the classroom setting news items pertaining to science. If there is a lack of voluntary participation, the science teacher may require pupils to collect and have well in mind relevant news items pertaining to science;
2. the teacher(s) need to reward pupil participation by praising positive efforts;
3. learners should understand and attach meaning to news items presented to classmates;
4. each news item needs to be evaluated using critical and creative thinking as well as problem solving procedures. To think critically, pupils need to separate facts from opinions, fantasy from reality, as well as

detect bias. With creative thinking, pupils come up with new, novel ideas when predicting what might happen in the future based on knowledge. Unique ideas are needed in any endeavour since creativity is necessary in response to problem areas. Too frequently, the tried and true are stressed and this may not work in a new situation involving problem solving;

5. pupils should be encouraged to use what has been learned. If knowledge is not used, it might be forgotten. Also, use made of what has been learned makes for relevance in the current events science curriculum.

There are many uses that can be made of any vital current events items studied. The following have been observed in different classrooms and appear to work well:

1. pupils in a committee collaboratively working on a mural to portray content learned. Thus three or four pupils worked on a mural four feet by five feet in dimension. Planning together what to show using a variety of art media stress a problem solving approach. Thus each pupil showed one of the following: plate tectonics in art form; a hurricane with its destructive path; a fault with different layers of rock; and sheet gully erosion;

2. three pupils in a committee made a model volcano using wadded newspaper for the core with a potted empty meat can for the opening at the top of the model volcano. The outside of the volcano was finished with a plaster of paris mix to make for a realistic portrayal. The plaster of paris dries quickly and pupils need to work quickly to give the model an identifiable lifelike appearance. Tempera paint may be used to give the model a natural like appearance in its final form. Ammonium dichromate crystals may be put into the empty potted meat can. These crystals, obtained from a scientific supply company, should then be ignited. A model volcanic eruption occurs. There needs to be ample ventilation in the classroom when doing this experiment;

3. pupils developing and presenting a simulated radio newscast on recent natural disasters, locally and nationally. Careful writing and editing of the news is important. A pupil playing the role of the reporter may read the news to the class as would be done in regular newscasts on the radio;
4. three pupils in a committee researching and completing a written report on natural disasters in farming. The science teacher assists these learners to secure relevant information on drouth, hail, and excessive rainfall. Oral reports to classmates on each of these disasters may reveal to pupils what happens when there is a lack of moisture for growing crops, when hail destroys farm crops in a minute or two, and when fields are too wet for seeding or for harvesting;
5. pupils may plan and play roles of famous scientists when studying this science unit. Much background information is needed to develop the creative dramatics activity. Thus, individual pupils may play roles of well known scientists such as Louis Pasteur, Galileo, and Anton Leuvenhook. The presentation may be given to classmates and pupils in other classrooms, as well as to parents invited to the classroom.

The above five examples of how to put knowledge of current events in science to use by pupils are given as models. There are numerous other ideas that can be used by teachers to have pupils apply what has been learned. Shepardson and Britsch (1997) favour pupil journal writing as an excellent means of having pupils apply what has been learned:

Children's observations are essential for learning, but unfortunately they are often downplayed in the science teaching process. It is from science observations that the child begins to construct scientific understandings. Children may, however, have difficulties in observing differences, erroneously recording deductions as observations. To assess the quality of these observations, teachers can analyse journals for the following indicators:

1. actual observations versus deductions;
2. level of detail (qualitative and quantitative);
3. notations of similarities and differences;
4. comparisons between phenomena in terms of position (spatial) and time (change);
5. and accurate, careful descriptions...

To assess the quality of children's observations, specific scoring rubrics need to be developed based on the nature of the activity and the importance of the children's observations in the teaching/learning process.

Conclusion

There are numerous natural disasters which need to be emphasised in the science curriculum. A key concept here is ıelevancy when choosing which news items to pursue. An interdisciplinary curriculum incorporates social studies, mathematics, and language arts. Pupils need assistance to understand that knowledge is related. Retention of subject matter learned improves when pupils can perceive that current events is related to diverse academic disciplines. Ample opportunities should be provided for pupil to work collaboratively with others in the school setting. Problem solving and learner decision making need to be stressed since life itself consists of solving problems and choosing from among alternatives to make decisions. Relevant objectives, learning opportunities, and appraisal, procedures should be in the offing for all pupils in units pertaining to natural disasters in the environment. A good current events curriculum in science is a must.

Pertaining to current events, Schuncke (1988) wrote:

There are four basic questions that should be considered in a current events discussion:

1. What does the news items say? Here, your job is to determine that the children are aware of the basic message contained in the news item. You'll want to

insure that they know the facts surrounding an event, the who, what, when, where, why, and possibly how;

2. What does it mean? Knowing the facts...does not necessarily mean that the children understand it. Therefore, you will next need to determine their level of comprehension, how they interpret the item, and what inferences they can make about it. You'll want to make certain they have, at least, a basic understanding of what's going on;
3. Why is it important? The question, or a related one, should be used to help children probe the effect of an event—on the children themselves, on others, and on the world;
4. How does it relate to me? Here children can be assisted to examine their roles as citizens—of a community, state, nation, and world—to determine if the importance of an event requires some action on their part. Often the question can lead to decision making, valuing, and social action in their part.

References

Bhaskara Rao, D. (2001), *Educational Psychology.*

Butler, Gene, et.al. (1996), 'Earthquakes Online,' *The Science Teacher,* Vol. 63, No. 9, pages 31-32.

Ediger, Marlow (1999), 'Affective Objectives in the Science Curriculum' *Exchange,* 22 (2) 24-28, published by The Pennsylvania Science Teachers Association.

Ediger, Marlow (1992), 'Creativity in Science,' ERIC # ED 342641.

Ediger, Marlow, and D. Bhaskara Rao (1996), *Science Curriculum.* New Delhi: Discovery Publishing House, pages 40-41.

Ediger, Marlow and D. Bhaskara Rao (2001), *Teaching Social Studies Successfully.* New Delhi, India: Discovery Publishing House.

Ediger, Marlow (1995), 'Designing Science Units of Study,' *School Science,* Vol. 33, No. 1, pages 14-15.

Edigar, Marlow (1998), 'Computers in the Science Curriculum,' *School Science*. 36 (4), 62-71.

Ediger, Marlow (1997), 'Excellence in the Science Curriculum,' ERIC # ED 406144.

Schuncke, George M., *Elementary Social Studies*. New York: The Macmillan Publishing, page 72.

Shepardson, Daniel P., and Susan J. Britsch (1997), 'Children's Science Journals: Tools for Teaching, Learning and Assessing,' *Science and Children*, Vol. 34, No. 5, page 17.

8

Learning Opportunities for Pupils in Science

There are numerous quality learning opportunities that may be provided for learners in ongoing science lessons and units of study. These opportunities need to provide for individual differences in the classroom, such as pupils with diverse levels of achievement. Each learner needs to achieve optimally. The science teacher needs to provide activities and experiences for pupils that are:

1. purposeful to have pupils perceive reasons for participating actively;
2. interesting in that the attention of pupils is secured so each may learn, achieve, and grow;
3. meaningful so that pupils individually may make sense of and comprehend that which is taught;
4. goal centered in order to achieve motivated individuals.

5. reflective in nature so that pupils individually ponder over what has been taught.

Learning opportunities chosen need to guide pupils to achieve objectives in ongoing lessons and units of study. Thematic units help pupils to focus upon the centrality of what is being emphasised and stressed in the science curriculum. A variety of leaning opportunities need to be in the offing so that multiple intelligences theory (Gardner, 1993) is in the offing. Thus, the following are intelligences for pupils to reveal what has been learned in science thematic units:

1. scientific—emphasising objective thought pertaining to the natural environment;
2. verbal/linguistic—stressing the use of reading, writing, speaking, and listening. The latter four skills are indeed relevant in science teaching;
3. logical/mathematics—indicating numeral and logical thinking abilities. Mathematics tends to be the language of science in that numerals are applied to quantities and qualities in science;
4. musical—revealing talents in lyrics and musical notation. Science content acquired may be written in terms of musical content by selected learners. Then too, music has vibration, pitch, stress, accent, and other items pertaining to the quality of sound that relates directly to the world of science;
5. bodily/kinesthetic—possessing neuromuscular skills, relevant in handling and using science equipment, as well as in a hands on approaches in learning;
6. interpersonal—pertaining to achieving well in committee and group endeavours when pupils work collaboratively in science;
7. intrapersonal—being able to achieve at a high level in individual tasks and responsibilities, such as in the project method of learning;
8. visual/spatial—abilities in art work, architecture, and

geometry. Here, pupils may make and develop art products, collages, murals, dioramas, movie sets, and video-tapes of group or individual work. Creative and formal dramatics when studying the lives of famous scientists may also be pictured in video or snapshot forms.

USING EXPERIMENTS AND DEMONSTRATIONS

Experiments and demonstrations should be the heart of the science curriculum. Scientists in a laboratory setting conduct research in controlled settings; pupils should also be involved in these kinds of learning opportunities, among other activities, directly related to an ongoing unit in science in the classroom setting.

In a thematic unit on air pressure, learners with teacher guidance may be actively involved in performing the following experiments:

1. using the classroom aquarium, a glass tumbler may be used together with a piece of tissue paper. Pupils may hypothesise what happens to the dry tissue paper when the glass tumbler is placed upside down inside the aquarium which is filled with water. Pupils should feel that the tissue paper is completely dry and give hypotheses freely. Each pupil's response needs to be accepted, respected, and written down on a transparency using the overhead projector. Unless, this experiment has been conducted previously or remembered as to its outcomes, learners are fascinated with the results! Selected experiments should be performed/demonstrated again due to their relevance to what is being studied;

2. the egg in the bottle is a good experiments to show the force of air pressure. By taking a gallon glass milk jug and placing a piece of tissue paper at the bottom, pupils may watch as a hard boiled egg with the shell taken off is placed at the opening of the container. Learners then might hypothesise what will happen as the tissue paper is lit at the bottom of the gallon glass

milk jug and the boiled egg placed snugly at the opening. Pupils are to be helped in thinking scientifically and logically. Pupils are fascinated to notice the loud noise made as the boiled egg is 'pushed' through the narrow opening of the milk jug. With the tissue paper using the oxygen at the bottom of the jug and the air pressure at the top pushing the egg through the narrow opening, pupils understand what the concept of 'air pressure' means. Learners through research may also learn that at sea level there are fourteen pounds of air pressure per square inch;

3. pupils need to observe a tumbler filled with tap water placed on a table for all to observe clearly. Next, with pupils observing, the science teacher should place an ice cube inside the tumbler. Pupils will notice a thin film of water on the surface of the glass tumbler. Learners then should hypothesise as to why this happened. Recorded hypotheses should be checked against a reputable sources of information, such as from a science textbook, science encyclopaedia, and/or internet source;

4. the water level in an aquarium may be marked with pupils closely watching where the recorded line is located. A day later, the total water in the aquarium should be marked and compared with the previous day's level. Successive day's markings may also be observed and noticed. Occurrences may be hypothesised for their happenings. Each hypothesis needs to be discussed in an atmosphere of respect. Pupils have given the following hypotheses for the successive lower water levels:

   a. the fish drank the water;

   b. the aquarium leaks;

   c. water was dipped out of the aquarium;

   d. fish needed the water to keep their skin soft;

   e. the water evaporated.

5. a large cube of ice may be placed in a glass clear plastic dish. Learners may hypothesise what the state of matter is when referring to an ice cube. As the solid turns to water, pupils need to hypothesise what the state of matter is then called. The liquid is then placed on a hot plate and pupils notice what happens when the water changes to steam. The causes for the physical changes need to be understood meaningfully by pupils when a solid changes to a liquid and then to a gas through evaporation. These three states of matter become a structural set of ideas for pupils to attach meaning and understanding. In many cases, matter can change from a solid to a liquid and then to a gas. Exceptions may be noticed later in sequence.

There are many experiments and demonstrations that may be conducted and performed in any science unit of study. The teacher needs to have qualified resource personnel, science textbooks and teacher education texts available as a ready source of information pertaining to using experimentation as a leading approach to learning in ongoing science units of study. Criteria to follow in using science experiments and demonstrations are the following:

1. make certain that pupils can observe the activity as well as the results clearly within each experiment;
2. have pupils, if possible, participate in planning and doing the science experiences;
3. be certain safety is stressed in each experiment and demonstration;
4. emphasise that the learning opportunity assists pupils to achieve worthwhile goals in ongoing science lessons and units of study;
5. relate the learning opportunity to a problem identified by learners;
6. do something with the findings, such as pupils' writing up the sequential steps in doing the experiment. Variety needs to be stressed as follow up activities;

7. stress sequence in learning opportunities so that pupils may build upon what has been learned previously;
8. obtain the attention of pupils;
9. invite questions from pupils before, during, and after each experiment;
10. identify additional problems within the ongoing experiment or demonstration.

USING VIDEO-TAPES IN TEACHING SCIENCE

The science teacher and the school librarian should have access to videotapes housed in the library Videos should be rented and purchased from school moneys with adequately financing. The video tapes are directly related to the objectives of instruction within a science unit of study. A strategy needs to be developed whereby the teacher successfully initiates the videotape by stimulating learner interest, developing necessary background information so that each pupil may understand its contents, achieving sequential learnings with the previous learning opportunity, and having follow up experiences pertaining to the video-tape.

Video-tape content makes it possible for pupils to experience the semi-concrete in a meaningful way. It integrates with what a learner already knows. Scaffolding is an important concept for the science teacher to use in teaching. Scaffolding pertains to the zone of proximal distance. The zone of proximal distance may be thought of as the gap between where a pupil is presently in goal achievement and what is left to learn to satisfactorily achieve the desired end. The science teacher may use the video-tape, or other learning opportunity to discuss subject matter with pupils to close this gap.

Pupils need to posses readiness to benefit from the video-tape. Readiness experiences include those that motivate learners in wanting to learn from the videotape, such as securing information in answer to questions and problems selected prior to implementing the showing of the video-tape. Which content might a videotape emphasise pertaining to a thematic unit in science?

1. celestial location and celestial distance of stars in the night sky;
2. origin and brightness of stars;
3. temperature of stars as well as the life of a star;
4. the Milky Way Galaxy, as well a the life of a galaxy;
5. the geocentric versus the heliocentric model of the solar system;
6. the planets, asteroids, comets, meteors, and meteorites.

The science teacher needs to choose a videotape that is on the understanding level of pupils and does not contain too many concepts. An excessive number of concepts covered in a videotape can make for a lack of meaningful learning. Vital concepts chosen need to be taught in depth such as # 1 above 'celestial location.' With depth teaching, pupils experience many examples and a variety of learning opportunities on content pertaining to one concept such as 'celestial location.' Survey teaching must be avoided. Survey teaching stresses shallow learning of each concept by pupils.

USING SLIDES, FILMSTRIPS, AND TRANSPARENCIES

As compared to videotapes—slides, filmstrips, and transparencies contain no movement and motion in their inherent presentations. The science teacher, too, may use all the time needed on one frame in the slide or filmstrip, as well as the transparency. For example, in a sequential series of frames or transparencies, pupils with teacher direction may learn about each of the following, using as much time as is needed for meaningful concept learning:

1. air mass, arid, and climate;
2. cold front and continental air mass;
3. cyclone, hail, and hurricane;
4. polar air mass, precipitation, and stationary front;
5. tornado, tropical air mass, and typhoon.

There are concepts that are easier to understand due to being more concrete in nature and less abstract. Selected learners may also possess more background information on some concepts as compared to others. There are concepts, too, that are used more often in every day conversation as compared to others. Science teachers need to appraise rather continuously if a pupil understands a concept, rather than trying to memorise subject matter only. For example, a pupil may reveal understandings pertaining to air mass (number one above) if he/she can

1. give numerous examples;
2. explain the meaning of this concept;
3. make a drawing to indicate meaning;
4. use illustrations to explain and reveal comprehension;
5. raise related questions pertaining to the concept being studied.

USING FILMS IN TEACHING SCIENCE

Films have motion as do videotapes. There are selected pupils who learn more from an audiovisual aid that has inherent motion and movement as compared to those that do not. Generally, films are older devices in use as compared to videotapes. Still, many schools have films that have quality up-to-date content to be used in teaching science. In observing a student teacher and cooperating teacher teach, the following content was contained in a filmstrip:

1. continental shelf and continental slope;
2. an aquifer and an artesian well;
3. long shore current and ocean currents;
4. a sea and a pond in terms of surface water;
5. a water table.

For each of the above, the illustrations and explanations were very clear. Learners were very attentive when observing the contents in the film. This was indicated by excellent questions which were raised after the presentation. Thus for example, pupils indicated clarification when receiving additional comments on the differences between a sea and a pond as related to surface water, item number 4 above.

USING DAILY NEWSPAPERS AND NEWSMAGAZINES IN TEACHING SCIENCE

A good current events programme can do much to guide pupils to stay abreast with present day happenings in the world of science (for children's magazines see 'Current Science' and 'Ranger Rick' (addresses in the Reference section). For example, we are looking at additional finding in a newspaper pertaining to the dinosaur debate. Children find dinosaurs to be fascinating and pay considerable attention to the following debated items by scientists:

1. were all or some dinosaurs warm or cold blooded?
2. what caused the age of dinosaurs to become extinct?

Learners are eager to search for information, from a variety of reference sources, to locate necessary data in relationship to each of the above named questions. Pupils have then learned to use the following concepts pertaining to the age of dinosaurs in ongoing discussions:

1. Mesozoic era, as well as its subdivisions—triassic, jurassic, cretaceous in terms of time frames;
2. Meat eaters (carnivorous) versus plant eaters (herbivorous);
3. tyrannosaurus rex, stegasaurus, brontosaurus, diplodocus, triceratops, and duck billed dinosaurs, among others;
4. fossils, paleontologists, carbon dating, climatic changes, and meteorites;
5. mastodons and woolly mammoths—these animals were located in reference sources as a by product of pursing information on dinosaurs.

In looking at the above five numbered items, it is salient to notice that pupils can learn to use and attach meaning to very complex terms if interest is there in the learning opportunities. Interest tends to lead to motivation whereby pupils hardly look at their watches to notice the amount of time left for a lesson to end. Then too, learner can learn to read difficult words if the desire is there to do so.

When coming back to science being in the news, it appears that any issue of a newspaper or newsmagazine contains content pertaining to the scientific world, such as earthquakes, hurricanes, tornadoes, floods, mud slides, avalanches, drought, hail, blizzards, and snow storms. A teachable moment might well be when learners ask for the causes of any of these events, such as earthquakes. The teacher might then guide pupils to attach meaning as to why this phenomenon occurs.

When supervising student teachers and cooperating teachers in the public schools, we have observed radios and television being used to keep children abreast on current events that deal with science, such as viewing a sequential lift off for a relevant space feat on television. Pupils exhibit much curiosity in happenings such as these and have an inward desire to learn more about the following: space probes, space satellites, space shuttles, space stations, space labs, the Hubble telescope, the Voyager, the Magellan, and the Galileo.

For each news item to be read, make certain that each pupil has related necessary subject matter in his/her possession to understand that which is to be read and discussed in terms of scientific happenings. Assist learners with identifying unknown words in the reading selection. Ask questions in sequence which guides pupils to move from factual subject matter to that or critical and creative thought, as well as problem identification.

USING TECHNOLOGY IN TEACHING SCIENCE

The science teacher needs to be well versed with what exists in computer technology and teaching materials in order to provide for individual differences in the classroom. The school librarian also must be highly knowledgeable about what is available in computer and software materials. The following kinds of software need to be available that harmonise with ongoing science lessons and/or units of study:

1. tutorials that present new subject matter to learners;
2. simulation which provides lifelike situations involving problem solving;
3. drill and practice whereby pupils have opportunities to review and summarise what has been learned in an ongoing unit of study;
4. gaming which gives learners an opportunity to enjoy play activities that stress science subject matter;
5. diagnosis and remediation whereby the software programme detects an error and assists pupils to overcome the identified weakness.

Things for science teachers to notice when implementing technology into the science curriculum are the following:

1. Does the software assist pupils to achieve vital objectives of instruction?
2. Are the programmes sequential in nature whereby each package has new content within, that relates directly to the previous step of learning subject matter?
3. Do pupils feel they are actively engaged in each software programme?
4. Do pupils feel successful in learning?
5. Are pupils able to use what has been learned in new situations involving other kinds of learning opportunities?

Programmed learning moves forward very slowly in a step by step sequence. Thus, a learner reads a very small amount of content, such as a short paragraph, responds to a multiple choice item, and receives immediate feedback on what has been learned. The immediate feedback is there to guide pupils to avoid making errors in obtaining subject matter. Commercial software generally has been tried out in pilot studies in order to remedy weak sequences in the programme. Some programmes claim a ninety-five per cent correct rate of responses as given by pupils. Being right 95% of the time is quite a record. Usually, software programmes do not stress critical and creative thinking as well as problem solving. Simulation programmes would come closest to stressing these kinds of objectives in science.

All pupils in sequence should learn to use the word processor. With using the word processor, the following learnings may be typed into the computer:

1. steps followed and conclusions found in doing a science experiment or demonstration;
2. an outline of an oral report to be given to learners in the classroom;
3. journal writing that pertains to completed science lessons;
4. diary entries kept on a day to day basis on learning opportunities pursued in class;
5. logs which summarise the diary entries, on a weekly or monthly basis;
6. summaries of science content read, directly related to the ongoing unit of study;
7. poems and stories written from science content studied;
8. letters written to order free science materials of instruction.;
9. science subject matter acquired to be shared with pen pals. E-mail messages may also be sent;
10. experience charts may be typed to indicate specific activities and opportunities focused upon.

When using technology in the curriculum, much emphasis may be placed upon pupils engaging in doing research for a science project. Along with traditional quality methods of gathering data from print discourse and audio-visual materials, technology may stress using internet sources, CD ROMS, applicable software, World Wide Web, and the word processor. Information desired may be retrieved quickly and accurately for a research study.

USING CASSETTE RECORDERS IN THE SCIENCE CURRICULUM

There are numerous uses that may be made, as learning opportunities, of cassette recorders in science teaching. Cassette recording of subject matter from basal texts can be wisely used by pupils who do not read well. The recording may be listened to by slow readers as they read along in their textbook. These learners then comprehend better and become improved readers as a result of having the subject matter read. Selected library books may also be cassette recorded for pupils having difficulty in word recognition and comprehension. These readers may also enjoy reading content to achieve objectives as well as improve reading skills and possess increased knowledge. Additional ways to use cassette recording ongoing science units and lessons are the following:

1. having a committee record peer interactions in meeting quality standards for doing collaborative work;
2. recording a creative or formal dramatics activity in the classroom;
3. engaging pupils in giving individual or committee book reports;
4. explaining a collage, a montage, a bulletin board display, and/or a diorama as each relate to a thematic science unit of study;
5. evaluating involved processes in doing a classroom science newspaper.

Science teachers should continually find new and better methods of instruction to guide increased levels of pupils achievement. Additional methods of teaching are found in time and newer procedures are in the offing in changing school and societal arena. Using Basals, Library Books, and Writing Activities in Teaching Science

A carefully chosen science textbook can do much to improve the curriculum if

1. it becomes a part of, but does not dominate the science curriculum;
2. it guides pupils to achieve vital objectives of instruction;
3. it can be used to initiate, develop, and culminate a science unit of study;
4. it supplements experiments and demonstrations as a knowledge source of pupils;
5. it helps pupils in developing a rich science vocabulary;
6. it assists pupils to increase reading and writing skills, necessary to communicate ideas clearly and effectively in thematic science units;
7. it is used as a source for objectives, learning opportunities, and appraisal procedures from the teacher's manual section;
8. it varies learning opportunities in order to stimulate and motivate pupil interest in science;
9. it makes for increased meaning and understanding in the science curriculum;
10. it increases pupil skills in word recognition and comprehension.

There is much that the science teacher may do to help pupils in word recognition and comprehension of subject matter. Thus, in word recognition, the science teacher may assist pupils in using phonics to unlock unknown words, in developing syllabication skills, in attaining context clues to determine new words in reading, in recognising a given set of useful sight words in science, and in application of background knowledge to subject matter being read.

To comprehend science subject matter being read, the teacher may assist pupils in reading for vital facts, concepts, main ideas, and generalisations. Learners also need to analyse subject mater read, synthesise ideas, evaluate content acquired, and use what has been learned in a new situation.

Library books may be used to enrich, to extend information, to develop ideas in greater depth, to achieve objectives in science, to develop interest in a topic, to use spare time wisely, and to enjoy the world of scientific endeavours.

Pupils, basically, should select their very own library books to read. The titles and topics in science should be broad in scope so that a learner may locate what is truly on his/her reading level (not the frustration level) as well as provide for the respective interests possessed by learners. Library books may be used to provide content for an oral/written report in a science unit of study, as a basis for small or large group unit discussion, as a method of instruction whereby the teacher reads stimulating sections aloud to pupils, and as a way for learners to appreciate quality literature in science.

Reading and writing are complementary in science in that each skill assists further competency in the other. There are many quality writing experiences for pupils in ongoing science lessons and units of study. Among others, the following salient writing activities:

1. diary entries and logs to record specific activities engaged in within sequential lessons in science;
2. journal writing to indicate content learned and that which is left to learn in unit teaching;
3. summarise and conclusions of content read from basal texts;
4. book reports and formal dramatisations written from that contained in relevant sections of library books;
5. steps involved in performing a science experiment and/ or demonstration;

6. creative writings such as poetry or prose directly related to subject matter being studied in science;
7. letters written to order free and inexpensive science materials (See entry—Environmental Protection Agency Public Information Center and Library—in References section when writing for free and inexpensive science materials.

USING AND MAKING CHARTS IN SCIENCE

The science teacher should use charts in teaching pupils (Ediger, 1998, 36-38) Learners may also be actively engaged in chart construction. A chart, clearly visible to all learners in the classroom, may contain the following in a science unit on rocks and minerals:

Classification of Rocks

Igneous	*Sedimentary*	*Metamorphic*
a. basalt	a. shale	a. slate
b pumice	b. sandstone	b. marble
c. obsidian	c. conglomerate	c. anthracite coai
d. granite	d. coal	d. quartzite

The following chart on Prehistoric Life leaves space for pupils to fill in the needed subdivisions for each era:

The Precambrian Era

The Paleozoic Era

The Mesozoic Era

The Cenozoic Era

As the above named eras are studied by pupils, they may add information to each, such as the kinds of plant and animals in the Mesozoic Era included the age of dinosaurs. The chart might be quite extensive when illustrations are drawn directly related to a type of animal or plant.

In a science unit of study on The Solar System, pupils with teacher guidance may make a chart containing the names of the planets—Mercury, Venus, Earth, Mars, Jupiter, Saturn, Uranus, Neptune, and Pluto. Data on the diameter of each planet, as well as the approximate distance from the sun, may be filled in by learners as they are being studied in sequence. The chart may become quite large in size as learners write in major generalisations for each planet.

Why use charts in teaching science?

1. content shown pertains to one topic and focuses on classification of rocks only, for example, as these learnings are being taught;
2. the content is and should be large enough for all to see clearly in the classroom, or within a committee, as a related discussion pertaining to the involved subject matter is ongoing;
3. active involvement by learners is important in helping to make or in constructing a chart individually or collaboratively with teacher assistance;
4. charts vary the kind of learning activity used in the classroom to stimulate learner interest in science;
5. psychomotor skills are emphasised when pupils construct diverse kinds of charts for teaching and learning.

SCIENCE EQUIPMENT FOR EXPERIMENTS AND DEMONSTRATIONS

Classrooms need to have the latest of equipment and materials for teaching science. Up-to-date subject matter must be in the offing for each pupil, as a result of science experiments and demonstrations. Too frequently, the science teacher must furnish all the materials of instruction. Instead, it is recommendable that pupils as well as the teacher bring selected materials for science experiments and demonstrations: however, many other materials need to be at the finger tips of teacher for ease of use. The following are recommended as available materials of instruction so that the teacher does not need to spend too much time in searching and locating: hand lens, a variety of kinds of magnets, iron filings, a telescope, an aquarium, beakers,calculators, a hot plate, aluminium foil, balance and standard masses, candles, rock samples (igneous, metamorphic, and sedimentary), balloons of diverse sizes, a barometer, dry cell batteries of different volts,copper wire, small bulbs in electrical sockets, bird book guides (to check bird migration, appearance, feeding habits, and geographical environments), graduated cylinders, compasses, a mineral collection accompanied by an identification book, litmus paper,maps and globes, microscope, prisms, a hygrometer, pulleys, levers, axles, wheels, graphic paper, mirrors, stop watch, metric measurement units (liters, centimeter tape, meter stick and scales, and tables of metric measurements), thermometers, test tubes, as well as science encyclopaedias and other necessary reference books.

How might a few of the above named materials be used in unit teaching? For example the item listed first, a hand lens or magnifying glass, may be used by pupils to make observations from examining the enlarged sedimentary, igneous, and metamorphic rocks. Contrasts and comparisons may be recorded in journal form. Item second in the above listing were a variety of kinds of magnets. Here, pupils may learn that opposite poles attract and like poles repel. Iron filings may be placed on a sheetof paper directly above a magnet to notice magnetic forces. Science is a fascinating curriculum area and there are many experiments and demonstrations that capture pupil purpose and interest.

Pupils and the science teacher also may bring materials for instruction pertaining to experiments and demonstrations. Thus the following might be brought: seeds of different kinds to show rate of germinations as well as growth rates, cameras and film, cooking oil and corks, dishes and paper, feathers, flashlights, food colouring, lemon juice, measuring spoons and cups, masking tape, clay, potting soil, different kinds of soil (loam, sandy, and clay), potholders, salt, metric scales, a shell collection, sugar, sponges, a terrarium, vinegar, and dry yeast.

Pupils with teacher guidance can and do make excellent equipment in science to understand vital facts, concepts, and generalisations better than otherwise would be the case. In making magnets, for example, pupils may stroke steel needles in one direction on a magnet. The steel magnetised needle may be put on a cork and placed in a pan with water. Pupils will notice how the magnetised needle will take position according to the north/south pole orientation of like poles repel and opposite poles attract. Or, as a further example, pupils may develop a collection of and examine bird feathers with the use of a microscope. Observations made and discussed may be used to ascertain how feathers contribute to the ability of birds to engage in flight.

Pupils with teacher guidance may also make a barometer, an hygrometer, anemometer, and wind vane, among others, depending upon individual reediness factors.

Conclusion

There are a variety of kinds of learning opportunities available for teachers to use in teaching and learning situations. Science teachers always need to be on the lookout for additional and new learning activities in order to guide more and increased pupil learning. Pupils learn in diverse ways and have unique intelligences as well as different style of learning. Science teachers need to study each pupil and assist him/her to learn a optimally as possible. It is vital to stimulate and maintain learner interest in science. Pupils need to become motivated and encouraged in ongoing science achievement. Learning is a continuous process and needs to be lifelong. Most pupils are fascinated with science phenomenon and have an inward desire to learn. Individual and collaborative endeavours need to be in the offing. Heterogeneous and homogeneous experiences need to be provided to harmonise with a pupils's talents, hobbies, and interests.

Inservice experiences need to be provided to assist teachers to stay abreast of the latest knowledge, skills, and attitudinal objectives. Learning opportunities need to be noticed and applied that guide pupils in goal attainment. Accepted technology needs incorporating into science units that truly inspires and challenges learner progress in science. The focal point of instruction should always be the learner and his/her achievement and progress in science.

References

Current Science, Xerox Educational Publications, 5555 Parkcenter Circle, Suite 300, Dublin, Ohio 43017.

Environmental Protection Agency Public Information Center and Library, 401 M Street, SW, Washington, DC 20460.

Ediger, Marlow (1995), 'Designing Science Units of Study,' *School Science*, 33 (1), 14-15. Published in India by the National Council for Educational Research and Training.

Gardner, Howard (1993), *Multiple Intelligences: Theory Into Practice.* New York: Basic Books.

Ediger, Marlow (1997), *Teaching Science in the Elementary School.* Kirksville, Missouri: Simpson Publishing Company, Chapter One.

Ediger, Marlow and D. Bhaskara Rao (1996), *Science Curriculum.* New Delhi, India: Discovery Publishing House, Chapters Five and Six.

Ediger, Marlow (1995), 'Demonstration Teaching in the Schools,' *Education*, 114 (4), 371-372).

Ediger, Marlow (1995), 'Early field Experiences in Teacher Education, *College Student Journal.* 28 (3), 302-306.

Ediger, Marlow (1999), 'Issues in Curriculum Development,' *The Educational Review*, 105 (5), 90-92.

Ediger, Marlow (1998), 'Computers in the Science Curriculum', *School Science*, 36 (4), 62-71.

Ediger, Marlow (1998), 'Affective Objectives in the Science Curriculum,' *Spectrum.* 24 (2), 24-26.

Ediger, Marlow (1999), 'Objectives in the Science Curriculum,' *Exchange*, 22 (2), 24-26.

Ediger, Marlow (1995), *Philosophy in Curriculum Development.* Kirksville, Missouri: Simpson Publishing Company, Chapter Five.

Ediger, Marlow (1999), 'Attitudinal Objectives in the Chemistry Curriculum,' *NEACT Journal*, 17 (2), 15-17.

Ediger, Marlow (1998), The Pupil and Writing in Science,' *School Science*, 36 (3), 36-38.

Ediger, Marlow (1998), 'Teaching Science As Inquiry,' *Resources in Education*, ERIC, SE 06/846.

Ediger, Marlow (1998), Use of Research Results in Teaching,' *School Science*, 36 (1), 35-43.

Ediger, Marlow (1996), 'Slogans in Education and in Society, *Journal of Educational Psychology*, 24 (1), 37-41.

Ediger, Marlow and D. Bhaskara Rao (2001), *Teaching Social Studies Successfully*. New Delhi, India: Discovery Publishing House.

Ediger, Marlow and D. Bhaskara Rao (2000), *Teaching Mathematics Successfully*. New Delhi, India: Discovery Publishing House.

Mehlinger, Howard (1996), 'School Reform in the Information Age,' *Phi Delta Kappan*, 77 (6), 405-406.

Ranger Rick. National Wildlife Federation, 1412 Sixteenth Street, NW, Washington, DC 20036-2266.

9

Grouping for Instruction in Teaching Science

Much has been written pertaining to how to group for instruction. Each pupil needs to learn as much as possible to achieve optimally. Too frequently, the merits of heterogeneous grouping is favoured by educators. To be sure, pupils of unlike achievement need to be together and associate with each other. In society, individuals seek out those who have a similar ability level. Why might school not be the same? Certainly, pupils need to learn to work together with others regardless of ability and achievement levels as well as be challenged by those of a similar level of attainment. Agne (1999) raises the question, 'Are we sacrificing our children's education to satisfy a social agenda?' She wrote the following:

Parents and teachers have watched with dismay as, one by one, public schools hop on the inclusion—detracting train, seemingly in full compliance with the dictates of radical egalitarianism who, using public schools to drive their own political agendas, are bent on what they believe will save us all... .

Tracking and ability grouping are clearly not without problems... . The research is clear that all students need to be grouped with others whose learning needs are similar to their own in order to attaint their best opportunity for highest achievement in basic academic subjects. The 'one big happy family' ideal sounds lovely but stifles achievement capabilities, especially among the average and above average students, and in basic skills areas, it suppresses student achievement in all levels... .

A company recognised fact among educators is that one method, formula, style, of curriculum is never sufficient, in and of itself. Teaching is far too complex for this to be true at any level or for any area of instruction. It is no less the case for ability grouping. One prescribed grouping format is never best for everything or everyone. There are certain subject areas and differing student abilities for which certain types of grouping arrangements may be best in one case, but not necessarily in another.

Pupils differ from each other in the intelligence(s) possessed such as in the following: naturalism, verbal/linguistic, logical/mathematics, visual/spatial, musical, bodily/kinesthetic, interpersonal, and intrapersonal (Gardner, 1993). Thus, the academic area of specialty and/or preference differs from one pupil to another as well as the preferred differs from one pupil to another as well as the preferred way of learning, be it within a group or individually. The science teacher then needs to assist each pupil to learn as much as possible in science, regardless of the intelligence area of subject matter preferred. Pupils live in a world of science and technology.

GROUPING STUDENTS IN SCIENCE EXPERIMENTS/ DEMONSTRATIONS

The best plan of grouping used needs to guide each pupil to achieve as much as possible in knowledge, skills, and attitudinal objectives in ongoing science lessons and units of study. Science experiments and demonstrations, clearly visible to all in a class, might well stress using heterogeneous grouping. Gifted pupils may experience homogeneous grouping in which the experiment/demonstration is very sophisticated. The subject matter covered during these experiences needs to be explained clearly and concisely. Students should have ample opportunities to ask questions pertaining to gaps perceived in knowledge as well as knowledge that needs clarification. The science teacher needs to be very sensitive to all pupil obtaining necessary knowledge and skills as emphasised in the experiments and demonstration. Inductive learning can do much to minimise that which is not understood nor made meaningful. For example in doing experiments and demonstrations, pupils may be led to access background information so that a better job of hypothesising may be in the offing. Each hypothesis given by learners as to what will happen from the experiment/demonstration needs to be respected and printed on the chalkboard. When hypotheses are given, the teacher notices the quality of each. Thus, students reveal previous knowledge acquired and skill in hypothesising. In an atmosphere of respect, pupils fell free to participate actively in the ongoing activity. After hypothesising, the experiment/ demonstration needs to be performed and students should observe very carefully as to what truly does happen. Too many students want to jump to hasty conclusions without careful observation. Rather, students need to develop quality skills in observing carefully.

Experiments/demonstrations may be repeated to verify objectivity. Verifiable knowledge is a hallmark of principles and laws in science. If the same results are not obtained, students with teacher guidance may discuss why there are discrepancies. Students individually or collaboratively may write journal entries pertaining to what was learned. Collaboration may involve homogeneous or heterogeneous grouping. A key item here is that each pupil is respected and participates wholeheartedly. No one is minimised nor shunned. Writing observations made assist pupils to use knowledge as well as in retention. Active engagement by pupils in individual as well as in group work is commendable.

GROUPING IN USING VIDEO-TAPES, AND OTHER AUDIO-VISUAL AIDS

How should students be grouped for instruction what AV presentations are provided as learning opportunities? Generally, the class as a whole, be they heterogeneously or homogeneously grouped, may observe the AV contents. The science teacher needs to be certain that each pupil has the necessary prerequisite knowledge to benefit optimally from observing the contents as well as grasping the related ideas. If students do not have these prerequisites, they will tend to benefit only partially from the ongoing learning opportunity. To provide these prerequisites, the science teacher may ask question of students related to the AV presentation. Questioning activates the necessary background knowledge needed to comprehend the AV presentation. Having students tell about personal experiences that relate to contents in the AV activity are also appropriate. Learners do need to relate personally to the oncoming contents to be comprehended. Students then need to possess background ideas to understand the new learnings and become enthused about learning.

Vygotsky (1978) stressed the importance of the zone of proximal learning. Here, there is an initial gap between what the student knows presently and what is necessary to understand to benefit fully from the new experience. To take care of this gap, the science teacher may:

1. perform a related experiment;
2. use advance organisers by explaining what is not understood prior to the new experience. The science teacher then is filling in with knowledge needed by students to understand the new content to be presented;
3. have students take a nearby excursion;
4. read aloud a few paragraphs from the basal or library book on the understanding level of students;
5. ask questions sequentially to guide pupils in comprehending the new subject matter;
6. show prerequisite illustrations, diagrams, charts, and graphs;
7. discuss selected objects with students;
8. encourage student predictions, from viewing the pictures and topical headings, as to what the new subject matter will entail;

9. have a resource person stimulate background information which sequentially leads to the new content to be learned;
10. motivate learners to tell what they know about the new topic.

New subject matter in science can be acquired by many students if readiness is in evidence or the zone of proximal development has been narrowed greatly. If heterogeneous grouping is used in the classroom, the teacher needs to provide for a diverse set of individuals whose talents and abilities may vary greatly. If homogeneous grouping is involved, students still vary in talents and abilities in science, but the range will not be nearly as great.

Large group instruction needs to be followed with committee and individual endeavours so that all may benefit as optimally as possible. Thus, from the large group session, students may raise questions and problems to be discussed and data found within the committee setting. Each students also has subject mater that he/she wishes to learn and individualised instruction is important. An Audio-visual presentation on Fossil remains presented to the class as a whole, may be followed with committee work dealing with identified questions on these remains. In sequence, a student may wish to locate information on actual remains found of prehistoric animals, such as the woolly mammoth and the mastodon—remains found in Siberia in what is now Russia.

PROVIDING FOR INDIVIDUAL DIFFERENCES IN NEWSPAPER/NEWSMAGAZINE USE

A quality current events programme in science is vital. There are so many daily happenings in the news the involve science content. Thus, earthquakes, tornadoes, hurricanes, mud slides, avalanches, and cyclones receive much news coverage. There are several suggestions to be made in order to assist each learner to achieve more optimally in the science current events curriculum. These include the following:

1. read aloud selected science event items so that all pupils may understand salient structural ideas. Read with enthusiasm and face pupils when reading orally;

2. discuss relevant items to further assist pupils to attach meaning to content being emphasised;
3. guide each pupil to participate actively in the discussion;
4. use audio-visual aids to clarify facts, concepts, and generalisations with pupils;
5. have pupils work in small groups to elaborate on main ideas in science current events news;
6. use homogeneous groups to help pupils achieve on their individual levels of development;
7. use heterogeneous groups which involve projects whereby pupils on diverse levels of achievement may participate successfully;
8. foster respect among pupils for each other regardless of ability levels as well as foster respect for the teacher. Developing respect for each other should permeate all facets of the science curriculum;
9. have peers teach each other in small groups as well as emphasise peer teaching whereby a gifted/talented learner helps slower learners gain vital current events ideas;
10. maintain a high level of interest in current events, regardless of the type of grouping used, but the main point here is to have each pupil learn as much as possible.

FLEXIBLE GROUPING IN SCIENCE

A major generalisation to stress in the grouping of pupils for instruction in science is to assist each to learn as much as possible. Thus a variety of procedures may be used in grouping for instruction.

Interest grouping may be used. There are numerous projects that pupils may work on in ongoing science units. If pupils are studying a unit on "The Weather and How It Affects Us," a small committee may wish to develop an art project showing different kinds of cloud formations, such as cumulus, stratus, and cirrus.

Underneath each type of formation, pupils may write a description and elaborate on their effects upon the surrounding area. Pupils of similar interests may then work together on the project. Each pupil has a vital role to play in project development. All should contribute optimally. The most talented and gifted should not be expected to do all the work. Each pupil should achieve optimally here in terms of whatever he/she can contribute including as much as individual abilities permit to the project. My daughter, a computer programmer, states that in heterogeneously grouped committees, slower learners tend not to want to do any work. My challenge to teachers is to motivate each pupil do the best possible to develop an excellent science project and in any learning opportunity, regardless of grouping procedure used.

The completed project may be shared with classmates as well as be posted on a hallway bulletin board for other classes of pupils to observe. Curriculum improvement in science comes about when other teachers can see what is done in different classrooms and evaluate the end products as well as the inherent processes. Interest groups can work well in science teaching if learners.

1. perceive value in participating in a given activity;
2. attend carefully to contributing optimally;
3. desire to use individual talents in making contributions to the total committee project;
4. persevere in making a success of collaborative endeavours;
5. respect the optimal contributions of each learner on the committee.

NEEDS OF PUPILS AND COMMITTEE WORK

With flexible groups involving interest grouping for instruction, the needs of pupils may form another kind of collaborative setting. Here, the science teacher needs to be able to diagnose what a pupil needs to learn in ongoing lessons and units of study. What a group of pupils needs, provides a solid basis in grouping for instruction. Pupils may also volunteer to join a committee based on felt needs. Thus, the following needs may be experienced by pupils:

1. selected word recognition techniques to read science content in a meaningful manner;
2. comprehension skills when reading for a variety or purposes;
3. metacognition abilities to monitor one's very own success/weaknesses in reading;
4. application of what has been learned to everyday situations in life;
5. critical thinking skills.

Some of the above needs are more difficult to remedy as compared to others. For example, remedying a word recognition skill in reading science materials may be much easier to remedy than developing critical thinking abilities. Meeting needs of pupils is very important in a quality science curriculum. Pupils individually achieve more when a specific need has been mastered, such as improving in comprehension skills. With improved comprehension skills, the learner then can understand more complex subject matter when reading science content.

Even though the grouping for remediation involves homogeneous grouping of pupils for instruction, learners therein still will be heterogeneous since selected pupils are further along in achievement within the collaborative setting as compared to the others. Thus, homogeneous grouping attempts to minimise the wide range of abilities within a group to be taught. The group is taught for as long a period of time as necessary and then modified or disbanded.

GROUPS POSSESSING STRENGTHS

Groups should not be formed based on needs only, but also on strengths possessed. There are highly talented/gifted pupils in science in most classrooms. Adequate provision needs to be made to develop and maintain a challenging science curriculum for these learners. The 'sky' should be the limit for the talented/

gifted learners in science. Flexibility again is a key concept when forming collaborative settings for these pupils. Talented/gifted learners with teacher guidance may wish to engage in the following collaborative settlings:

1. planning and making scientific instruments directly related to an ongoing unit of study, such as a barometer, an hygrometer, an anemometer, a rainfall gauge, and a wind vane. These instruments may then be used in ongoing science experiments and demonstrations;

2. doing an indepth research report on causes of a specific natural disaster in the news, such as typhoons. Audio-visual aids, diagrams, and drawings may supports the research project. A variety of reference source should be used in data gathering;

3. studying and making a time line on the history of major natural disasters on the planet earth. The time line will contain the dates each occurrence with a brief write-up on the causes for each disaster, such as the Lisbon, Portugal earthquake of 1555 which destroyed fifty per cent of this city. A drawing may accompany each entry on the time line;

4. developing a video-tape on different salient space missions with accompanying drawings to show each, such as the following:

   a) the Apollo mission resulted in the first humans landing on the moon in 1969;

   b) Mariner 9 was placed in orbit around the planet Mars in 1971;

   c) Mariner 10 came within 450 miles from the planet Mercury in 1974;

   d) Pioneer Venus 1 was the first spacecraft to orbit Venus in 1978;

   e) the Hubble Space Telescope was launched from a space shuttle in 1990.

5. Identifying questions and problems which require answers from scientists whereby letter writing and/or e-mail may be used to correspond.

FLEXIBLE DISCUSSION GROUPS

Discussion groups may be either homogeneous or heterogeneous depending upon how each pupil is affected to achieve as optimally as possible. If the topic is highly complex, then homogeneous grouping should be used to guide the talented and gifted to achieve optimally. Slower learners may also have challenging subject matter to learn as much as possible on an individual basis.

Discussions assist pupil to

1. analyse content being studied;
2. ask questions pertaining to what is not understood;
3. selected problems areas for developing possible solutions;
4. probe indepth to content being discussed;
5. summarise subject matter learned;
6. develop a classroom science newspaper to correspond with parents and other interested persons;
7. brain storm possible solutions to gaps identified in knowledge being read;
8. record information presented in diary entries and journal forms;
9. use ideas given to develop dioramas, murals, and models;
10. challenge ideas presented, in a positive way.

In any discussion, pupil need to respect each other and the ideas being presented. A caring and helpful community of learners needs to be in evidence within an ongoing discussion.

GROUPING FOR A MINILESSON

There are occasions whereby a minilesson may be taught on a relevant topic. For example, supposing the temperature readings reach an all time low in a winter month during the school year, the science teacher may wish to teach a short lesson on possible causes for the low temperature readings. A deductive/inductive procedure of instruction may be used here. Generally, in whatever is taught, the teacher explains (deduction) as well as raises questions (induction). Learners too should contribute with questions raised pertaining to what is not understood as well as to identify vital questions. The grouping used here may be either homogeneous or heterogeneous. A combination of the two plans might also be used in order to assist each pupil to learn as much as possible. The minilesson needs to posses clearly stated objectives. The learning opportunities need to relate directly to the stated objectives and provide for pupils individually to learn as much as possible. Guidelines to use in teaching a minilesson are the following:

1. emphasise concrete (objects, items, experiments, demonstrations, and excursions), semi-concrete materials (audio-visual aids, illustrations, drawings, diagrams, CD ROMS, and software packages), as well as abstract learning activities (tapes, reading, writing, speaking, and listening experiences;

2. obtain the attention of all pupils so that optimal achievement may be possible;

3. use eye contact with and for each pupil in the minilesson in order that he/she may feel that a personal means of communication is in evidence;

4. stress higher order levels of cognition where feasible, such as critical and creative thinking as well as problem solving;

5. encourage and model respect for all in each lesson. Pupils as well as the teacher need utmost respect for quality learning to occur.

ACTIVITY CENTERED TEACHING AND GROUPING PUPILS FOR INSTRUCTION

Activity centered teaching involves pupils learning by doing whereby psychomotor objectives prevail, but does include cognition as well as good attitudes. There tends to be interaction among cognitive, psychomotor (use of eye-hand coordination), and attitudinal ends. It is important that pupils become skilled in use of the gross and finer muscle in being actively involved in the science curriculum. Engagement in learning is of utmost importance. Too frequently, pupils are passive recipients of knowledge, rather than being wholeheartedly involved in ongoing experiences in the science curriculum.

Which learning activities, related to a specific science unit of study, involve a learning by doing approach with active involvement by pupils in flexible grouping?

1. making dioramas of prehistoric sea life, such as plesiosaurs and mosasaurs, as well as of animal life on land, such as the ground sloth and the saber tooth tiger. Considerable research may be done on gathering information on these forms of like to present to the entire class when showing the completed dioramas;
2. drawing a sequential set of illustrations pertaining to sheet and gully erosion as well as remedies to prevent misuse of valuable topsoil;
3. dramatising important scenes from the lives of famous scientists, such as Louis Pasteur, Joseph Lister, Michael Faraday, George Westinghouse, and Anton Leuvenhook;
4. developing a classification chart of animals with backbones (vertebrates), such as fish, amphibians, reptiles, birds, and mammals. Pictures may be drawn and/or brought to class pertaining to each classification of animal;
5. a mobile may be planned and completed on animals without backbones (invertebrates), such as sponges, coelenterates, worms, mollusks, echinoderms, and arthropods.

Each of the above named five categories of activity centered approaches in learning require a considerable amount of background information which pupils may obtain from diverse reference sources. Thus, pupils with teacher guidance need to perceive a purpose for each learning opportunity, plan to achieve the purpose, carry out the planned activity, and evaluate the completed tasks. A learning by doing approach in science emphasises pupils being engaged in achieving quality objectives in science lessons and units of study.

GROUPING AND MODELLING

Frequently, pupils needs to observe good models to do well in a skill or achieve an attitude. The science teacher then may present a model for learners to observe pertaining to oral reading, writing for a variety of reasons, doing an experiment or demonstration, making a replica, doing art work, working on a construction activity, showing democratic behaviour, and being a quality member of a discussion group.

Many children and adults model themselves after the behaviour of others. Role models then are a necessity. Why? these role models give pupils an opportunity to try out and see if what is being followed from a model's behaviour is working for the well being of all. Usually, what has been observed from a role model needs to be modified, in degrees, to fit the observer's ideal. Each pupil has purposes in life and viewing diverse good role models provides more options for pupils to emulate in order to develop unique forms of desirable behaviour. Thus, for example, in writing science content, the teacher may model the following, depending on the present achievement level of pupils:

1. writing a business letter to order free and inexpensive science materials for classroom use;
2. writing a friendly letter thanking the providers for an enjoyable and productive field trip;
3. writing a set of directions for making a model object pertaining to an ongoing lesson or unit of study in science;

4. writing an outline covering vital content from the basal;
5. writing a summary of library book read;
6. writing an abstract of an article read;
7. writing a bibliography of references used in solving a problem;
8. writing an evaluation of science content read from a journal article;
9. writing a creative story on space exploration;
10. writing a synopsis of a current event science item.

From the model presented, the learner may write with the involved purpose and achieve as much as abilities and talents permit. Each pupil needs to be respected for what is being achieved in writing. The goal in writing is to move from where the pupil is presently in writing to some further ideal involving continuous progress.

GROUPING AND INDIVIDUALISED READING IN SCIENCE

With individualised reading, the issue of homogeneous versus heterogeneous grouping basically does not exist. A wide variety of titles in science content and written on different levels of pupil achievement should be in the offing at the reading corner. A pupil may then select a library book to read on his/her present level of reading achievement. The chosen library book is usually selected based on personal interests of the involved learner. The science teacher may help the pupil in book selection if the latter can not make a choice.

After a pupil has completed reading his/her selected library book, a conference may be held with the science teacher. Questions for discussion may be raised by the teacher to evaluate learner comprehension of content. This evaluation session should not destroy but encourage increased interest in reading science materials. What might be objectives, here, in the conference setting for appraisal of pupils achievement?

1. noticing pupil fluency in reading aloud a brief selection from the library book;

2. appraising word recognition skills of the learner;
3. ascertaining pupil interest in reading science subject matter;
4. determining the quality of reading comprehension;
5. progress being made by the pupil based on notes kept on a previous pupil/teacher conference;
6. improved attitudes possessed by the learner toward reading;
7. pupil's reading as many library books as possible during the allotted time;
8. selecting science materials to read during sustained silent reading (SSR);
9. wanting to improve reading skills to obtain vital facts, concepts, and generalisations, as well as to read critically and creatively to solve problems;
10. relating matter read to ongoing lessons and units of study in science.

ADDITIONAL FORMS OF GROUPING PUPILS FOR SCIENCE INSTRUCTION

There are additional ways to group pupils for instruction so that each may achieve more optimally. Thus, a departmentalised plan may be used. In secondary schools for years, departmentalisation has been in evidence, whereas in elementary schools, the self contained classroom is in vogue. In a self contained classroom, the teacher basically teaches all curriculum areas, except music, art, and physical education. Complaints here are that the elementary generalist cannot possibly specialise in teaching so many curriculum areas. Something then has to give. In departmentalisation, the teacher is specially trained to teach science. His/her undergraduate preparation indicates a major in science content and science teaching methodology. A key item in the debate has to do with how well the teacher is able to assist pupils to achieve relevant subject matter, skills, and attitudes. There are elementary schools whereby two teachers have arranged classes so that one uses talents for teaching science and the other for teaching, for example, mathematics. Modified departmentalisation has strengthened the teaching of specific curriculum areas in which each teacher uses strengths for teaching, such as in science instruction.

A second additional way to group for science instruction is to stress multiage classrooms. Here, younger and older pupils may work together on a given task, such as constructing a terrarium to observe animals in a humane environment. Pupils of different ages in a specific group may be either homogeneously or heterogeneously grouped. The argument used for multiage grouping is that in society, younger and older individuals interact with each other. Also, age levels may mean little when it comes to achievement in science. Thus, selected younger pupils achieve at a higher level as compared to older learners, as well as vice versa.

Third, cross grade grouping may also be used. Pupils from a specific grade level may be grouped with learners from another grade level. The purpose here might be to have homogeneous groups. Thus, pupils from grades one and two may work together on a project, such as making a chart on plant classification, including algae, mosses, ferns, evergreens (nondeciduous), and deciduous trees. The goal is not to have cross grade grouping for its own sake, but rather to help each pupil learn as much as possible in science. A few lower grade level pupils may have achieved at a higher level in the science curriculum as compared to those on higher grade levels.

Fourth, team teaching may be used. A teaching team may consist of two or more teachers in teaching a given set of learners in the area of science. These two or more teachers need to plan cooperatively the objectives, learning opportunities, and appraisal procedures for teaching and learning. Large and small groups need to be in the offing as well as individual study for pupils, taught and supervised by the teaching team. Plans developed and implemented need to assist pupils individually to achieve as optimally as possible in science.

Fifth, learning centers may be set up in the classroom. With learning centers, it does not matter how homogeneously or heterogeneously the pupils are within a class. If twenty-five pupils, for example, are in a classroom, eight learning centers may be set up. Each center has approximately five tasks listed on cards for pupils to select from. There are more tasks available than what any one pupil can complete. This makes for choices and decision making on the part of each learner as to what he/she would like to work on and complete in terms of learning opportunities in science. There can be individual as well as collaborative tasks to choose from. The pupil makes the decision. Time on task is vital here! The science teacher is a guide and stimulator to encourage pupil learning, not a lecturer nor a dispenser of information.

Sixth, looping has become an important concept in teaching science (Denault, 1999). With looping, a pupil stays with the same teacher for a longer period of time than one school year. The argument given for accepting looping in grouping pupils for instruction is that the teacher may provide better sequence in learning by getting to know learners well as compared to pupils changing teachers each school year. When changing teachers each school year, the new teacher starts anew with getting to know the skills and abilities possessed by a learner. This generally takes about a month. Disagreements pertaining to stressing looping in grouping pupils for instruction pertains to a pupil who may prefer another teacher who can better meet his/her personal needs.

Conclusion

There are numerous plans available for grouping pupils for instruction in science. The major goal in grouping learners for instruction is to assist each pupil to achieve as much as possible in ongoing lessons and units of study. This eliminates the need for

1. setting high standards for pupils to achieve by those outside the local classroom and school district, such as those who write standardised tests and state mandated objectives and tests. However, both standardised tests and state mandated test results

may be used for diagnostic purposes. Thus, the science teacher may notice from each pupil's results what has been missed and, if vital, needs to be stressed in ongoing lessons and units of study;

2. worrying about the homogeneous/heterogeneous grouping controversy.

Constructivism as a philosophy of instruction stresses that which is done in a classroom is what is important. Thus, the objectives, learning opportunities, and evaluation procedures developed in the classroom are of utmost importance. Within an ongoing lesson or unit of instruction, pupils with teacher guidance appraise and evaluate what needs to be improved upon. Individual and group activities need to be in evidence to provide for each learner's optimal progress. In school and in society, human beings work individually as well as collaboratively. They also interact with others homogeneously as well a heterogeneously. So both approaches may be used here in grouping pupils for science instruction with constructivism used as a philosophy of instruction.

In grouping pupils for teaching science, the following guidelines may be used, stated in question form:

1. Which procedures assist pupils best to engage in inquiry learning?
2. How can experiments and demonstrations be most successful when stressing a specific plan of grouping learners for instruction?
3. What might be done in grouping learners to minimise failure in learning in the science curriculum?
4. How might Inservice education assist teachers in grouping pupils successfully so that all may be achieve as much as possible in knowledge, skills, and attitudes in the science curriculum?
5. What is the relationship between quality grouping practices and the use of technology to help each pupil learn as much as possible in science?

References

Abruscato, Joseph (1996), *Teaching Children Science*. Fourth Edition. Boston; Allyn and Bacon, 239-241

Agne, Karen, 'Kill the Baby:' Making all Things Equal, *Educational Horizons*. 77 (3), 140-147.

Bhaskara Rao, Digumarti (2000), *Teaching of Science*. Guntur, India: Nagarjuna Publishers (in Telugu language).

Denault, Linda E. (1999), 'Restructuring? Keep It Simple...Consider Looping!' *The Delta Kappa Gamma Bulletin*. 65 (4), 19-26.

Ediger, Marlow, and D. B. Rao (1996), *Science Curriculum*. New Delhi, India: Discovery Publishing House, Chapter Five.

Ediger, Marlow (1996), 'Personalised Science Instruction, *Prism*, published by the Newfoundland and Labrador Teacher's Association, 25-27.

Ediger, Marlow (1995), Philosophy of Teaching Science, *School Science*. Published in India by the National Council for Educational Research and Training (NCERT).

Ediger, Marlow (1996), 'The Unexpected in Science,' *Investigating*, 10 (3), 24-25. Published by the Australian Science Teacher's Association.

Ediger, Marlow (1999), 'Attitudinal Objectives in the Chemistry Curriculum,' *NEACT Journal*, 17 (2), 9-14.

Ediger, Marlow (1997), 'Improving the Science Curriculum,' *The Modern Elementary School*. Kirksville, Missouri: Simpson Publishing Company, 140-160.

Ediger, Marlow (1999), *Teaching Reading Successfully in the Elementary School*. Kirksville, Missouri: Simpson Publishing Company, Chapter Two.

Ediger, Marlow and D. Bhaskara Rao (2001), *Teaching Social Studies Successfully*. New Delhi: Discovery Publishing House.

Gardner, Howard (1993), *Multiple Intelligences: The Theory in Practice*. New York: Basic Books.

Rao, D. B., and Marlow Ediger, *Scientific Attitude Vis-A-Vis Scientific Aptitude*. New Delhi, India: Discovery Publishing House. Chapter One.

Vygotsky, L. S. (1978), Mind in Society. Cambridge, Massachusetts: Harvard University Press.

10

Cooperative Learning Versus Competition in Science

Most educators appear to advocate cooperative learning in the curriculum. Pupils then are to work together harmoniously to achieve objectives in the curriculum. Heterogeneous grouping is also recommended so that mixed achievement levels of pupil work in a committee setting. These educators emphasise democratic living in the classroom when pupils are grouped heterogeneously as compared to homogeneously. Cooperative endeavours stresses democracy as a way of life, according to many educators, as compared to competition among pupils in the classroom. If full inclusion is emphasised, then a committee in cooperative learning may truly be heterogeneous with increased diversity in terms of pupil abilities. Let us examine the philosophy of cooperative learning and heterogeneous grouping more fully.

COOPERATIVE LEARNING

As we read journal articles and other teacher education materials we feel that most educators advocate cooperative learning throughout much of the school day. There is a distinctive kind of reasoning emphasised by advocates. Pupils may then learn from each other. Perhaps, more can be learned from peers as compared to the teacher. Learners are cooperative beings and like to work together with other pupils. Cooperative learning can be emphasised in all curriculum areas and throughout most or all of the school day. Pupils are serious achievers when working together with peers. Each one desires to do his/her fair share of work within a committee. Fast learners can assist the slower pupils to achieve well. They can learn from the slow learners in return. Pupils need to learn to get along with each other and to respect the abilities of others. Diversity in the curriculum is to be stressed.

We believe there are numerous loopholes in the reasoning of cooperative learning advocates. We emphasise that not all pupils by any means are cooperative. There is rivalry, hostility, and aggression among pupils. To be sure, there are many pupils who are cooperative beings in wishing to work well together with others in an harmonious manner. One has only to observe pupil behaviour to notice that pupils are both cooperative and noncooperative beings. We thoroughly agree that pupils should learn to work well with others in school and later in the work place. But to what degree in terms of the total length of the school day should pupils work on cooperative endeavours? Our thinking is that pupils should work in committees effectively since life itself consists of working well with others. However, there are many times when individuals need to work by the self. All of us find ourselves working on tasks and responsibilities by the oneself, without involvement of others. Thus there needs to be rational balance in the school curriculum between working with others as well as working individually on tasks and activities.

There is seemingly a learning style which pupils possess that prefers working with others on lessons, projects, and activities. These pupils, no doubt, might well prefer a committee or cooperative learning experience. Together, the pupil may achieve more than working individually. These pupils might be motivated more so with other learners than working by the self. Learners may motivate and challenge each other in a committee setting and yet efforts are harmonised to attain a togetherness in an educational endeavour. Pupils need to be highly accepting of each other in cooperative learning. They must respect diversity among pupils and ideas. The use of ridicule and sarcasm is to be frowned upon. Rather, the pupil needs to encourage broad participation by members of the team. Group cohesion is necessary so that the goals of cooperative learning are being attained. The committee may be evaluated together as well as individually in their team contributions. All need to participate actively and achieve maximally. Failure for one or two to achieve in cooperative learning hinders optimal attainment for these pupils. Each must be serious in persevering and working toward objectives. The individual needs to blend his/her efforts with those of others on the team. All on the team must participate optimally, no one dominate the committee endeavours. Learners should stay on the task at hand, not digress from agreed upon goals. Tasks need to become clear through interacting with each other. Achievement toward goals must be reviewed periodically in order to notice how much progress has been made and how much further the committee needs to go in order to achieve agreed upon goals.

The teacher in cooperative learning becomes a guide, a stimulator, and one who encourages, but not one who lectures nor dispenses information. He/she is a resource person who has much knowledge of keeping pupils on task. The teacher as resource person has numerous materials and necessary information from which pupils in cooperative learning may gather what is needed to achieve objectives. As a helper an facilitator the teacher is motivated to assist pupils to be creative, to engage in critical thought, and to identify and solve problems. Higher levels of cognition are necessary here. The teacher knows how to relate to learners in order that higher levels of cognition on the pupil's part in teaching and learning is in evidence.

There are selected questions that need to be raised pertaining to cooperative learning. These are the following:

1. how much time in the school day should be given to cooperative learning?
2. how should committees be formed for cooperative learning?
3. who selects members of a committee?
4. how permanent should committee membership be?
5. how flexible should committee membership be if a pupil wishes to change to a different committee?

Frequently, we have received the impression that writers/ speakers in education recommend continuous cooperative endeavours in a classroom. Certainly, learning opportunities need to be varied. Little is mentioned as to who should choose committee members. The teacher may make the choices. Pupils could also volunteer to serve on a committee. Random selection could be used to determine committee membership. Committee membership could be very short indeed for a particular group, perhaps a day or several days. Membership could be rather enduring also, such as planned tasks that last six weeks or so. There are different types of tasks such as those that are short in duration, such as planning refreshments for an end of the school year party. Cooperative learning members could also be together for an entire thematic unit of six weeks such as planning and making a model bedouin village in a unit on The Middle East. There will be pupils who do not like the project or a selected pupil on the committee. What is the answer here? This happens even if members have been chosen carefully using desired criteria.

COMPETITION IN THE SCHOOL CURRICULUM

There are a few educators, not many, who advocate a competitive curriculum. Many reasons are given for the competitive philosophy. Generally, it is based upon the free enterprise system. US pupils need to be more competitive and be first in the nation in mathematics and science as advocated by the National Governors Conference in 1989 with Education 2000. Warnings are given by newsreporters as to low achievement in mathematics and science of US pupils as compared to those of other industrialised nations. Goals have been established on the state and local levels in order that learners may measure up to these levels in terms of what is deemed necessary to be first in the world in mathematics and science. Competition here rather than cooperation is emphasised.

The voucher system has many supporters in the US. Parents receiving the voucher money may redeem it at an other school which they deem to be better than the local school. The voucher money, if it becomes law, stresses that per pupil costs of education for a school year at the local school would equal the voucher that may then be used at the receiving school. There are advocates of parents being able to use the voucher money in either public or parochial schools. Advocates believe with competition, bad schools and teachers will have no clients and therefore not be in existence. The better schools with more clients than ever will serve as models for other teachers to emulate. Competition for numbers of pupils in a school under the voucher system is strictly competitive. Poor schools will go out of business.

Merit pay has numerous advocates in the US. With merit pay teachers rated as being superior or excellent receive additional pay for their quality services. Those supporting merit pay believe that teachers individually will work harder and do a better job of teaching once they are rewarded for doing outstanding work. Differentiated pay is then desired among teachers. No longer would the single salary schedule then be in operation. The latter is based on the number of years of teaching experience and the level of attained education at colleges/universities as being sole determines of salary to be obtained by a teacher. Critics state that mediocrity is rewarded in teaching with the single salary schedule. If merit pay is implemented, competition for the higher salaries would then definitely be in evidence.

Open enrolment also emphasises the free enterprise system. Here, parents choose for their sons and daughters which kind of a school the latter are to attend. The chosen school may bypass many local schools and school systems. Parents and the child to the choosing not the local school or the locally assigned teacher. The purpose is competition in parents choosing which school and teacher is best for their offspring. Teachers and schools not selected may need statewide superintendents and newly retrained and reeducated teachers.

In a few states, e.g. Kentucky and New Jersey, schools must measure up to a definite standard in terms of standardised tests results, or the state will take over deficient schools. There is competition here in a school not being delinquent as to pupil achievement revealed by test results.

The US Secretary of Education may list state by state how well pupils are achieving in different curriculum areas. This is called the wall chart. States are compared against each other in terms of pupil achievement, money spent on education per pupil, and average daily attendance of pupils. With competition among the different states in terms of wall chart figures, personal pride of each state to improve in education might be an end result when making these comparisons, according to selected educators and many lay people.

There are schools that have arranged contracts with commercial companies to teach their children. Educational Alternatives. Incorporated (EAI) from Minneapolis, Minnesota is an example. EAI agrees with the school district how much achievement and the cost of services will be involved in a given school year. EAI then assumes responsibility for administration and instruction of the involved schools. There is competition here between the public schools and commercial companies in terms of who can provide the best education for pupils. It might well be true that school administrators and teachers remain the same with EAI as compared to earlier arrangements. EAI still does the training of teachers to use methodology as they deem to be good and profitable.

Additional means of competing with the public schools in terms of teaching pupils is to have charter schools and magnet schools.

When supervising student and cooperating teachers in the public schools, we have observed the following to encourage competition among pupils in the classroom setting:

1. a chart on the wall showing the names of each pupil in class indicating how many words were spelled correctly for each week using the basal spelling text. Gold stars were received by the top spellers, followed

by silver stars for the next best set of spellers. Other colours of stars were situated next to the name of the pupil indicating his/her spelling achievement;

2. the teacher announcing to the entire class how many problems each pupil solved correctly from one lesson from the basal text in mathematics. The announcements were made for each day of pupil practice in mathematics using the basal textbook;
3. pupil test results in social studies were posted on the bulletin board ranking learners from high to low in achievement. The teacher commented on how well or how poorly individual pupils here had achieved;
4. prizes announced prior to beginning a new unit in science. These prizes were to be awarded to pupils depending upon how many total points each received a result of participating in different projects and tasks;
5. the pupil of the day selected by the teacher being presented with and wearing 'the king's or queen's hat'. There was much competition among pupils in class in being able to wear this hat for a day.

There are many additional examples which can be given whereby competition can and is being emphasised in the classroom setting. Pupils are compared with each other as to term projects, daily assignments, oral reports, oral reading, and test results, among other items. A major purpose of standardised tests is to compare one pupil against another. A parent, after receiving information of test results from his/her offspring, may, during informal conversation, compare test results with parents of other children. I have heard parents reprimand their children for not doing better on a standardised test. Generally, the reprimand emphasises why the child did not do better than so and so. Many parents are highly competitive in wanting their offspring to be a cheer leaders, member of the first team in football or basketball, have a leading role in the school play, and/or being a class officer.

Competition can be healthy; it can also be destructive. Cooperative learning can be positive as well as negative. It all depends upon what transpires in either competitive or cooperative situations.

We will first discuss healthy competition. Here, pupils respect each other even though one or more persons in a given situation do not experience victory. Healthy competition can bring out the best within the person. Effort and perseverance is involved! There can be much interest on the part of all in competition be it between individuals or within a committee competing against another committee? We recommend the following guidelines for stressing competitive events:

1. those competing should be somewhat equivalent in talents, skills, and abilities;
2. those competing should have positive attitudes toward each other;
3. those competing should have a desire to participate and learn;
4. those competing should have definite goals to achieve in the competitive event;
5. those competing should realise that not all individuals can be winners. Best it is if all pupils can be winners! This is definitely possible.

Questions that might be raised about competitive behaviour in the classroom setting include the following:

1. does competition increase hostility among pupils toward each other?
2. does competition hinder pupils in achieving affective objectives?
3. does competition work against the learning style of selected pupils?
4. does competition compare involved pupils unfavourable due to differences in abilities, interests, and capabilities?
5. does competition increase achievement of pupils?

Teachers might wish to encourage positive competition among individuals in the classroom setting. Competition is neither good nor bad, but it depends upon how it affects individuals.

We all need to realise that as adults, we compete in numerous ways such as for jobs and occupations, promotions, marriage partners, good grades in classes taken, and for leadership responsibilities in society, among others.

Cooperative learning has its advantages and disadvantages. The advantages are the following:

1. pupils do have opportunities here in learning to work together with others;
2. selected pupils have as their favourite learning style the working together with peers, rather than working individually;
3. goals in life can be achieved in cooperating with each other, rather than through dog eat dog approaches;
4. learners can realise that school and learning may be enjoyable through cooperative learning;
5. pupils need to learn to assist each other in the school and classroom setting. We human beings are dependent upon each other for survival.

Questions which need to be raised about cooperative learning include the following:

1. might pupils become highly competitive in a negative way within a committee setting?
2. might personality clashes hinder pupil achievement in committee settings?
3. might there be learning styles whereby selected pupils do not do well in group work, but would achieve better in more competitive settings? I would like to emphasise here that pupils individually may compete against their past performance with intent of making continuous progress;
4. might there be a rational balance between individual and committee endeavours in the curriculum which could benefit most pupils?
5. might there be leaders who do their best in cooperative learning?

There are no clear cut answers to these questions. Even well designed research studies have their many weakness. Human beings write test items for the measurement device, ensuring much subjectivity in a research study. Objectivity occurs when all conditions are kept similar in giving the tests to the experimental and the control groups. Or can they be similar/ same? No, they are not. Pupils feel differently from one time to the next. Not all pupils find that revealing what has been learned occurs best through testing. There are pupils who like authentic means of revealing what has been learned better as compared to being tested.

Conclusion

Educators need to reexamine the cooperation versus competition philosophies in teaching pupils. Which approach is better of the two? It is hard to say. Neither approach in and of itself is good. There can be negative teaching in either approach. We have seen bad teaching as well as good teaching in either case. Merely having cooperative learning or saying that one has cooperative learning does not make for goodness or badness. What truly matters is how each approach affects learners in the school and classroom setting. We would recommend having rational balance among the two approaches. Pupils need to learn to work harmoniously with others as well as work well on an individual basis. Each pupil should strive to achieve optimally when working individually. After all, life in school and in society consists of both!

References

Ediger, Marlow (1997), *Teaching Science in the Elementary School.* Kirksville, Missouri: Simpson Publishing Company, 130-139.

Ediger, Marlow (1995), *Philosophy in Curriculum Development.* Kirksville, Missouri: Simpson Publishing Company 1-18.

Ediger, Marlow (1997). *Teaching Reading and the Language Arts in the Elementary School.* Kirksville, Missouri: Simpson Publishing Company, 217-236.

Ediger, Marlow (1996), *Essays in School Administration.* Kirksville, Missouri: Simpson Publishing Company, 39-48.

Ediger, Marlow (1997), *Teaching Mathematics in the Elementary School.* Kirksville, Missouri: Simpson Publishing Company, 93-118.

Ediger, Marlow (1997), 'Improving the Science Curriculum,' *Experiments in Education*, 25 (3), 55-63.

Ediger, Marlow (1997), 'Philosophy of Teaching Science,' *School Science*, 33 (3), 1-3.

Ediger, Marlow (1995), Leadership in Curriculum Development, *Education Magazine*, nr. 113, 23-28, Published by the Qatar National Commission for Education, in the Middle East.

Ediger, Marlow (1994), 'Improving the Student Teaching Programme,' *Philippine Education Quarterly*, 23 (3), 66-74.

Ediger, Marlow and D. Bhaskara Rao (2001), *Teaching Social Studies Successfully.* New Delhi, India: Discovery Publishing House.

Ediger, Marlow and D. Bhaskara Rao (2000). *Teaching Mathematics Successfully.* New Delhi: Discovery Publishing House.

11

Science and Technology in the Science Curriculum

There is strong emphasis placed upon use of modern technology in the elementary school curriculum. Technology is very strongly used in all facets of society, and elementary schools should not lag behind what is stressed in the societal arena. The elementary pupil of today will be expected to achieve in a heavily endowed work place involving technology. Many factories and farms have been strongly automated. Fewer worker are continually needed in these work places. Machines automatically do work that was formerly done with the use of human muscles and physical work.

Generally, people think of farming as stressing that very heavy manual labour is done continuously. Egg production, as one example, has eliminated most of the manual labour that was formerly done. Presently with hens in cages and the cages being placed in rows, one person can take care of 15,000 laying hens readily. Today, the eggs fall down from the cages, onto a conveyor belt. A person at the end of the long row presses a button and all the eggs come down to where this worker is located. A machine is even available to pack the eggs into a crate. The feed goes down a conveyer belt every fifty minutes so that the laying hens have plenty to eat in order to produce eggs. The feed is augurred automatically from a bin outside the laying house. Water also goes down the troughs continually for laying hens to drink. A truck comes to pick up the crates of eggs two times a week. The owner largely manages the laying house operation to see that all machines are working properly. Not all farm work, by any means is automated to this extent. In contrast, any person who has cut, baled, and hauled hay realises the heavy use of muscles that are presently involved here.

At cigarette factories everything is automated including quality control. In other words, when the cigarettes have been packaged, the machine will cull out what was not done properly. Workers are there, few in number to notice when involved machines are not working properly. They are then responsible for repair work when needed or to obtain assistance if someone else needs to do the work.

Menial work that requires human feats pays very little money, but even here the manual labour done by a human being is rather minimal, such as in fast food restaurants. At these fast food restaurants, there is a lot of movement and motion by workers in getting fast food orders fulfilled. No doubt, these workers get tired after being at the task, but the labour is not intensive.

When growing up on the farms, farmers would shovel wheat by hand, since grain augers had not yet been perfected adequately. Shoveling grain by hand with a scoop is labour intensive. They became tired after shoveling fifty bushels of wheat from a pickup into a grain bin: there were many fifty bushel loads that needed shoveling in one day during harvest time. The grain auger took most of the human efforts out of shoveling wheat since the wheat was now augurred rapidly, fifty bushels in three minutes, using an attached electric motor to the auger. What does this discussion have to do with the use of modern technology in the elementary school classroom?

PERSONAL BELIEFS ABOUT TECHNOLOGY USE

There are selected criteria from the psychology of learning that need emphasis in having pupils work with technology. We believe that technology should capture pupil interests in learning. Activities here should be fascinating to engage pupil interaction. These interests should provide for effort in pupils desiring to achieve, grow, and develop. There is little time for misbehaviour if pupils are interested in the task at hand. We have noticed, for example, first graders who had little interest in drill and practice in arithmetic using paper and pencil. And yet when a hand held calculator or computer programme was emphasised, these learners truly showed interest and fascination in learning. Interest is a powerful factor in learning since attention to the task at hand makes for increased achievement.

Second, we believe that technology may assist learners to perceive purpose in learning. If purpose is lacking, there will be little incentive for pupils to learn. Goal centered pupils achieve more than those who fail to perceive objectives in learning. We have observed many pupils who did not like to check long division problems using paper and pencil. Again, when the checking was done rapidly and accurately with the calculator or computer, there seemingly was even joy in doing the checking to see if the long division problem had been worked correctly. It appeared that pupils saw purpose, not drudgery, in checking these long division problems.

Third, we believe technology can assist pupils to attach meaning to ongoing lessons and units of study. What pupils learn then should make sense, not be nonsense tasks. There are numerous programmes in computer use which guide pupils to achieve an objective. These numerous ways stress if one procedure is not understood, there are other approaches which will guide pupils to attach meaning. It is so important that pupils understand what is being learned. Many of us have learned that to divide fractions, we need to invert the divisor and then multiply. This mechanical procedure made no sense in grade school and in high school. There should be meaning in why 'the divisor is inverted and then multiply.' With clear illustrations together with the abstract numerals on the monitor, pupils may well understand

and attach meaning as to why to 'invert the divisor and multiply.' What is learned should make sense and not merely be committed to memory.

Computer programmes should assist pupils to perceive knowledge as being related, not in isolated bits. We noticed a delightful programme on a monitor with high pupil enthusiasm working on the Egyptian system of numeration when studying a social studies unit on the Middle East. Here, pupils were fascinated to learn that individual strokes represented the numerals from one through nine. Further interests were shown in the following features of the Egyptian system of numeration:

1. each heel bone of an ox, shaped like an arch represented a value of ten. Nine heel bones represented a value of ninety;
2. each coiled rope represented a value of 100. There could be as many as nine coiled ropes to represent a value of 900;
3. each lotus flower represented 1,000. The pattern is that nine lotus flowers represent a value of 9,000;
4. each bent finger represented a value of 10,000. Nine bent fingers represent 90,000;
5. each tadpole represent 100,000; thus nine tadpoles represent 900,000.

We present this information, as an example, to show that computer programmes along with other technologies can definitely assist pupils to perceive that knowledge is related. In this case, social studies and mathematics can definitely be related so that the learner perceive the interrelationship of subject matter. Morris and Pai (1976) wrote the following pertaining to Jerome Bruner's thinking on the relationship of knowledge:

...since human beings seem to be able to store more information than they can spontaneously recall, the main problem in human memory is that of effective retrieval. Bruner is convinced that the key to effective retrieval is organisation of information. He contends there is sufficient evidence to support the assertion that, in general, any information organised around the interests and the cognitive structure of the learner can be most efficiently recalled. Hence, the only means by which we can reduce the quick rate of loss of human memory is to organise facts according the basic principles and concept for which they were inferred. Further, 'the very attitude and activities that also seem to have the effect of conserving characterise figuring out or discovering things for ourself also seem to have the effect of conserving memory.' In addition to these effects, the learning experiences resulting from self-discovery give us an increased awareness of the connections and continuities between what we learn and what we do. As a result, we are likely to see our activities in a broader context and thus gain more control of our acts in relation to an end in view. In learning by discovery, knowledge already possessed by the learner is used to gain new insights and, and in the process old knowledge becomes reconstructed.

Being very strong on learning by discovery, Jerome Bruner, stresses organising information around the interests and cognitive structure of pupils. Discovery conserves or saves what has been learned previously. Pupils need to use knowledge to obtain new insights thus connecting what we learn and what we do. There are many key ideas Bruner presents here for learners to relate knowledge and increase memory/recall. The use of technology such as video-tapes and software programmes can and do assist pupils to relate knowledge inductively and thus retain content for a longer duration of time.

Fifth, the use of technology can certainly assist to provide for individual differences among pupils in terms of achievement in diverse academic areas. When pupils work on computer programmes, they can definitely work at their optimal rate of achievement individually. Thus, in a tutorial programme for example, pupils need to possess readiness factors such as having adequate background information. The learner then may move forward on that programme at an as optimal rate as possible. Comparing this learning situation with viewing a video-tape, the contents in the latter may move forward too rapidly or too slowly.

Sixth, technology and its use might well guide pupils to develop wholesome attitudes toward learning. Pupils seem to be fascinated with interacting with technology. We have observed pupils in classrooms with little interest in achieving in mathematics, as an example, until it is time for the learner to work with the computer. Here, the pupil interacted with drawings and abstract related numerals on the monitor. Problem solving was stressed here for a fifth grade pupil emphasising finding the volume of a cone. The drawings were excellent and the hints given in finding the volume were sequential to permit the learner to determine the needed answer. Later, another pupil also came to the computer to solve additional problems cooperatively. The interest was high and the two learners worked together harmoniously. The joy that comes in working with others truly has its values for pupils.

PHILOSOPHY OF EDUCATION AND TECHNOLOGY

We are strong believers in teachers, not only stressing the psychology of learning, but also the philosophy of education in technology use. There are selected philosophies that teachers need to understand and use in teaching-learning situations.

A first philosophy and its use we would like to discuss is experimentalism. Experimentalists believe strongly in a changing environment. Changes occur in all facets of the social/natural environment. Rather rapid changes have occurred such as in technology. When I (Ediger) first started university teaching, there were no word processors on our campus. Typewriters were abundant. Electric typewriters quickly replaced the manual typewriters. Word processors rapidly replaced the electric typewriters. There is no manual or electric typewriter to be seen on our university campus today and even two decades previously! Changes can and do occur rapidly. There is hardly anything, objects as well as ideas, where changes does not occur.

With change, new problems arise. These problems need identification and delimitation so that they can be solved. An hypothesis is developed in answer to the problem. The hypothesis is tentative, never an absolute. Each hypothesis is to be tested in a lifelike situation. Problems, hypotheses, and tests of hypotheses are done in context within a practical situation. Experimentalism is utilitarian, not abstract nor theoretical. Pertaining to John Dewey and his beliefs on change, Ediger (1995) wrote the following:

John Dewey (1859-1952) lived during a period of rapid change. When he was born and even until the early 1900s, the automobile basically did not exist. When he died in 1952, manufactured automobiles, as a whole, were very dependable with hydraulic brakes, heaters, and even a few with air conditioners. Electricity had its beginning in home and factory use in the early 1890s and was highly refined with its uses in 1952, with electric ranges, dishwashers, clothes washers, and driers. Changes have occurred from zero automobiles in 1859 to more highways and interstates being built to take care of the large number of automobiles in use in the present time. In 1859 horse drawn farm equipment was utilised to plow, harrow, disk, and seed the farm land. By 1952 farm tractors had electric lights, hydraulic brakes, and could pull a plow with four to five shears in plowing the land. Tremendous changes then occurred from 1859 (year of birth) to 1952 (year of death of Dr. Dewey).

With these and many other changes, problems arise. Problems need identification and careful delineation in the school curriculum, as well as in society. Each problem is vital. Information acquired in school needs to be utilised to solve problems. Knowledge is not attained for its own sake, but is instrumental to the solving of identified problems. In society also, information is secured from a variety of reference sources, useful to solve each chosen problem.

From the data gathered, directly related to the problem, a hypothesis is developed. A hypothesis results for each identified problem. The hypothesis is tentative and subject to change through testing. Testing is done in a life-like situation. The results of the test may confirm or refute the hypothesis. Minor revisions of the hypothesis may also be needed. Generally, change will occur rather continuously.

Experimentalists believe that one can only know experience. One cannot know the real world in whole or in part as realists advocate nor does one know ideas only, of what exists out there in society, as idealists stress. With the world of experience as experimentalists believe, one identifies and solves necessary problems. Eichelberger (1989) wrote the following pertaining to pragmatism, also called experimentalism:

The relationship between knowledge and reality (truth) that is used by researchers today is that of the pragmatist, which states that all knowledge is produced by human beings and that we can never distinguish between knowledge and truth. In empirical research, this means that if something works in practice then it is true, or we can assume that it is true. A truth (knowledge) that is not supported by further empirical study will be modified or discarded.

How does any philosophy of education relate directly to the use of technology? We have noticed numerous computerised programmes that are excellent for pupils to use in problem solving. Thus pupils in context have identified a problem for which they wish to have or find a solution. A software programme carefully selected might well provide data to test a hypothesis. Generally, additional technological sources will be used to evaluate an identified hypothesis in answer to a problem. However, there are numerous programmes which may provide information in the problem solving arena. Then too, there are simulated programmes which tend to be lifelike and real. These entire software programmes go through flexible steps of problem solving. A delightful computerised simulation is Choice or Chance (1984) which contains the following sequential content on the Age of Exploration:

Little is known of Hudson's life before his travels as an explorer began in 1687. During his sailing career, he sailed for both the Dutch and the English.

Hudson's voyages in 1687-1688 were founded by an English trading company, the Muscovy Company. His goal was never reached. In 1689 Hudson was hired by the Dutch East India Company, also a trading company, to lead another expedition. He again headed northeast hoping to avoid the ice floes. After the crew and supplies were in place, the ships set sail from Amsterdam, Holland on April 6, 1689. Their goal: find a northern route to Asia. Follow their journey (a relevant map is shown on the screen):

* Sail north and east to Novaya, Zemla, and an Island in Russia.

* Crew threatens mutiny, but Hudson convinces them to sail southwest.
* Arrive at the coast of Maine and cut a mast for the ship on July18, 1689. Some trading was done at that time. Sail south, along the coast to what is called the Chesapeake Bay. Arrived on August 3. 1689.
* Sail north along the coast to what is now called the Delaware Bay.
* Continue to sail north along the coast until a large inlet is spotted.

Imagine that you are Hudson. Use the map, called Dutch Exploration, to help you make decisions, consider the geographic factors presented and how they affect your decisions on the map page. You are now ready to sail upstream and explore. Good Luck! As you continue further into the inlet, a large island is seen. The island is covered with oaks.

Strong saltwater tides occur. A suitable harbour with a depth of 4-5 fathoms is seen. The inlet is continually windy. Do you wish to

a. settle in this area?

b. explore further upstream?

c. return to Amsterdam?

Feedback is then given on the screen pertaining to choice(s) made. Additional content is presented so that new sequential decisions need to be made by students. The Choice or Chance simulation.

1. relates history and geography;
2. brings reality into the programme;
3. emphasises active involvement on the part of learners;
4. presents background information to pupils before decisions are considered and made;
5. involves a logical sequence in that the programmers present sequential problems for pupils to consider;

6. stresses low risk on the pupils's part in interacting since the materials are not first hand, but are reality based.

Changes in technology abound. Rose and Fernland wrote: During the 1980s, computer assisted instruction (CAI) was an important part of classroom use. Teachers, department chairs, and district technology coordinators purchased commercial and public domain programmes in the subject areas, stored on one or more floppy disks, including drill and practice programmes, tutorials, simulations, and games. During the next decade there were four major changes that improved CAI: (1) the decline of the use of floppy disks, replaced by the enhanced storage capability of CD-ROM and videodisc, (2) enhanced interactivity in software in which students play a more active role, (3) sophisticated graphics, video clips, colour and sound, creating a multimedia presentation no longer dominated by screens of text; and (4) the growing marriage of CAI and telecommunications, allowing a seamless transition from single computer use to collaborative work with distant partners and access to internet-based sources.

The use of CAI in the social studies classroom continues to be strong, although such use is being eclipsed by the tool uses of computers; word processing; communications, research, and multimedia production. CAI is available on the internet, a helpful tool for teachers who want to review the product and consult other teachers who have used the programme with their students. CAI has greatly improved in creativity and quality; many programmes offer motivating experiences for students in analysis, problem solving, and decision making.

IDEALISM AS A PHILOSOPHY OF EDUCATION

Previously, it was mentioned that experimentalist believe we can know experiences only from the physical and social world. Idealists state that we receive ideas only, not experiences; nor can we know what the real world is like in whole or in part as realists indicate. Idealism is an idea centered philosophy of education. Mind is real and needs to receive nourishment through quality ideas in different academic disciplines. There are numerous tutorial programmes with computer use that stress learners achieving important concepts and generalisations. Knowledge objectives predominate, according to idealism as a philosophy of teaching and learning. Ediger (1997) wrote the following:

> Idealism is a more traditional approach in making decisions as compared to experimentalism and existentialism. According to idealists, individualists cannot know the world as it truly is in terms of a objective reality. Each person, however, obtains ideas pertaining to objects and items in the environment. The mind brings order to what is observed and seen. Thus, of all facets of human development that is significant to develop, the mind or intellectual achievement must come first. Rich learning experiences will need to be in evidence to guide pupils to achieve maximum development mentally. Thus experiences may well be selected in terms of leading pupils to attain universal ideas and knowledge of the Absolute (God). These universal ideas need seeking and finding. Any person may not achieve perfect understanding of these universal ideas and of God. However, each person may continually move closer in achieving ideals of universal ideas and of the absolute.

From the thinking of idealists, the following implications apply for teaching and learning:

1. broad generalisations need emphasising that have much use to the learner in terms of mental and moral development;
2. quality ideals for pupils to emulate need adequate emphasis in the school curriculum;
3. intellectual objectives should receive primary stress in the curriculum;
4. quality course work in literature and history, in particular, should guide pupils to achieve worthy generalisations;
5. abstract ideas are more important to emphasise as compared to the concrete and the semi-concrete.

Key ideas in understanding idealism in teaching and learning are written by Bigge (1982) in the following statements:

The heart of idealism is the belief that basic reality consists of ideas, thoughts, minds or substantive selves, not physical matter. Since priority is given to minds, minds have bodies, but bodies do not have minds. Idealism usually carries with its view the ideas of the subsistence (the superexistence) of God, who also is basically mind or self. The universe is an expression of intelligence and will; its order is due to an external, spiritual reality. For idealists, people are just good-active substantive minds; they are absolutely real selves endowed with free will or genuine moral choice. This philosophy has ancient roots; It dates back to Socrates (469-399 BC) and Plato (427-347).

Idealism is really idea-ism. The source of this title is based on Platonic thought. For Plato, ideas alone were genuinely real; they consisted of immaterial essences. That which people perceive is a shadow of reality; each thing that they perceive gets its existence from its Thingness; an idea. A book is a book because of its being more or less an imperfect replica of Bookness. A woman is a woman because she is a replica of Womanness. Plato's assumed world of 'eternal' verities' consisted of the True, the Good, and the Beautiful.

We can trace the development of idealism by listing some of the leading philosophers who contributed to this position and stated a leading idea that each has contributed to the philosophy. Socrates believed that children are born with knowledge already in their minds, but they need help to recall this innate knowledge. Plato contributed the idea of ideas, which are the universal forms of all existing things and are the essence of reality. St. Augustine (350-430) held a dualistic (mind-body) theory of humanity within which the mind or soul is the set of the force of goodness.

What then are the implications of the idealism for teaching and learning in the classroom involving computer use? I have seen selected excellent software packages which stress an idea centered curriculum. It seems as if for each academic area, there are tutorials which might well assist any pupil to achieve subject matter knowledge.

These software packages should assist pupils to

1. achieve abstract content which is challenging and yet attainable;

2. learn content in depth with emphasis placed upon mental development of pupils;
3. acquire subject matter which makes sense and has meaning;
4. relate relevant content from an academic centered curriculum;
5. attain vital facts, concepts, and generalisations in each academic discipline.

An idea centered curriculum might also guide pupils to use what has been learned in problem solving. This belief assists in relating idealism with experimentalism.

EXISTENTIALISM AND THE CURRICULUM

Existentialists are very much concerned about the every day life and its anxieties of individuals. Individuals are concerned with choices that need to be made regardless if the desire is there to make these decisions. There is dread, fear, anxiety, and uncertainty in making choices. Many existentialists believe life to be absurd and ridiculous. There is dread in choosing when so many alternatives are available in the making of these choices. People do not live in a subject centered world, nor in a world of science. Rather they live in an open-ended world where there are no standards in and of themselves. These standards, rules and regulations, need to be developed. Human beings make their own world; there are no absolutes nor are there given rules to live by. People, past and present, have developed standards to go by in life, but these are human made in an open environment where people, individually and collectively, develop the kind of society they wish to have. Pertaining to existentialism, Ozman and Craver (1990) wrote:

> Because the individual human is so important as the creator of ideas, existentialists maintain that education should focus upon individual human reality. It should deal with the individual as a unique being in the world, not only as a creator of ideas, but as a living, feeling being. Most philosophies,...existentialists charge, tend to focus upon only as a cognitive being. The individual is this, but he is also a feeling. Aware person, and existentialists think that this side deserves attention.

Which implications in the curriculum might follow some of the tenets of existentialism?

1. pupils individually need to choose freely, from among alternatives, those learning activities which are purposeful and meaningful;
2. content in the curriculum should reflect human feelings of loneliness, alienation, anxiety, and tension;
3. personal feelings of the pupil should be reflected in ongoing lessons and units of study. These feelings might well be expressed in art and construction projects, as well as of personal writings of learners.

The pupil needs to realise that choices to need to be made. If others make decisions for the personal self, choices are still being made, but the individual has abdicated responsibility in the decision making arena. Choices made do involve dilemma decisions, but authentic decisions must be made. Coercion is definitely not a part of the decision making philosophy of existentialists. Quality decisions made do not always make for good human relations. Alienation may also be an end result. The individual always needs to consider the consequences of choices made. Moral decisions made in a free environment is the goal of existentialists. Individuals should remember they are responsible for choices made; no one else can assume this responsibility. Choices are Subjective, not objective by any means.

With technology in the curriculum, existentialism advocates

1. individuals selecting from among others computer programmes to complete. The individual should also choose which tasks to engage in when additional forms of technology are used;
2. the human condition with all of its uncertainties and anxieties should be stressed in the technology curriculum;
3. the pupil needs to have ample opportunities to study situations in which dilemmas are present. Decision making is not clear cut nor an absolute. Content in technology can emphasise these ideas;

4. the learner needs to express his/her feelings in diverse projects and activities. Thus a variety of writing experiences, fine arts and practical arts activities, speaking and reading learning opportunities, as well as listening may be stressed as evaluation techniques as well as enrichment activities in the technology curriculum;
5. heavy pupil involvement and choice in the technology curriculum should always be in evidence with existentialism as a driving philosophy in education.

REALISM AND THE TECHNOLOGY CURRICULUM

Realists are strong advocates of individuals knowing in whole or in part what the real world is like. Their model comes from the world of science and mathematics. Precision and extreme accuracy are major tenets of realism as a philosophy of education. Thus the realist is strongly interested in having pupils achieve precise, measurably stated objectives in each curriculum area. With these kinds of objectives, carefully chosen by teachers and other educators, pupils do or do not attain each objectives as a result of instruction. Learning activities selected by the teacher harmonises with what pupils are to learn as contained in the stated objective(s). Evaluation techniques need to be aligned with the stated objectives. Validity is then in evidence in testing and measurement. Reliability needs to stress test-retest, split half, and/or alternative forms of appraisal. Results from pupil tests should indicate numerical data such as percentile ranks, per cent of items correct, standard deviations, quartile deviations, and standardised scores. Subjectivity in testing is definitely not wanted. Rather objectivity in testing is advocated to determine what any one pupil has learned as a result of teaching.

Pertaining to realism, Wild (1955) wrote the following:

The child, of course, should be interested in what he is learning. But it does not follow that whatever the child is interested in is, therefore, valuable. This is absurd. The skill of the elementary teacher lies in eliciting the interest of the child in the right things, especially in grasping the truth for its own sake. At the early stages no psychological or rhetorical technique should be neglected which is capable of strengthening this urge. When a mathematical principle has been understood, the child's attention should be drawn at once to the problem this enables him to solve. No opportunity should be lost to point out the principles of pure science which underlie modern technology. Language and grammar should be taught at essential phases of that mysterious process of apprehension by which the actual structure of things is mentally reflected and expressed, and by which such knowledge is achieved.

Realists do place very strong emphasis upon the following in teaching and learning situations:

1. carefully selected ends for pupils to achieve need to be written in precise, measurable terms;
2. learning opportunities chosen by the teacher align with the ends or objectives mentioned in number 1 above;
3. pupil achievement in having attained the precise objectives are measurable and presented in numerical terms;
4. the models of mathematics and science with its accuracy and specificity should be incorporated into the curriculum;
5. research studies can provide much data on what learners should study such as, for example, which words pupils should master in spelling. Many excellent studies have been made which indicate the words pupils use most frequently in functional writing. Words that are misspelled in these writings provide a scientific basis for determining practical words to be chosen by the teacher for pupil mastery.

Technology needs to be matched with the chosen objectives of instruction in lesson plans and units of study. After the use of technology in teaching and learning situations, the teacher may measure what pupils have learned. The results are given in numerical terms, not vague subjective data. The objective results may be reported to parents to indicate learner achievement in the school curriculum.

LEADERSHIP IN TECHNOLOGY USE

Teachers need to be and are leaders in curriculum development. They select objectives, learning activities, and appraisal procedures. Teachers organise the classroom for instruction. Organisational work includes grouping pupils for instruction, disciplining pupils, as well as devising a schedule for teaching. Technology is definitely involved in making curricular decisions. For example, there should be an ample number of software programmes in the learning activities section to guide pupils to achieve objectives. Definite leadership skills are necessary here. In addition to the classroom teacher, the principal plays a vital role in curriculum development.

Ritchie (1996) wrote the following pertaining to reasons why the use of technology is minimal in schools:

* A lack of administrative support
* Inadequate staff development and technological support
* Low quantity, quality, and access of technologies in the classroom.
* Nonexistent or cursory plans for adopting and implementing technology into a school
* The failure to allocate a technology coordinator to help train teachers and coordinate the technologies
* A lack of funds and personnel to maintain equipment
* Continual assessment of content acquisition through traditional methods.
* Establishment of a broad participatory clientele to establish a technology culture (Hoffman, 1996).

From the above statements, it is quite clear that school administrators need to understand and value technological use in the classroom. School administrators should perceive the necessity of implementing technology use in the classroom so that pupils may achieve more optimally. No doubt, there are school administrators who lack quality experiences with technology and therefore do not see the need for pupils experiencing learning activities involving technology. Each principal and supervisor should avail themselves in learning more about technology and how to integrate its use into the school curriculum. Talking to and learning from classroom teachers should assist the school administrator in realising the importance of technology in a modern elementary curriculum. Staff development programmes in using technology in the curriculum should be in the offing. Teachers and administrators need to realise the importance of an updated curriculum. The school of today and the work place of tomorrow should not be in isolation from each other, but rather become integrated entities. Definite goals in inservice education using technology are musts! These goals and experiences for participants need to be chosen carefully. Relevance and importance are two concepts that need careful consideration when inservice education programmes are developed and implemented. The goals of the workshop need to be clearly stated and should be cooperatively developed by workshop participants. There should be a large group session to hear a speaker or two who introduce vital inservice education goals. In the large group session, participants need to identify problem areas pertaining to the use of technology. Cooperative endeavours and committee work should follow to solve identified problems from the large group session. Consultants need to be available to assist in clarifying ideas and raising important questions to consider. A hands on approach should be in the offing. Individual endeavours need to also be pursued in the inservice education programme. Participants individually have concerns that need addressing with consultant assistance. There should be opportunities to try out what has been studied in the inservice education programme to the level of application in the regular public school classroom. Feedback from the classroom to participants in the inservice education programme is a must!

There need to be definite plans to integrate technology into the school curriculum. This should not be left chance, but rather quality goals and plans have been developed to use technology to its fullest in teaching and learning situations. Teachers need to have easy access to technology in lesson plan and teaching unit construction. A trained and educated coordinator of technology use can assist teachers to educate children for more optimal achievement. The coordinator of technology needs to develop good human relations with teachers with the later having access readily to technology.

Adequate money needs to be budgeted and used to develop a curriculum with technology as a guiding principle. The lay public needs to be informed continuously about the merits of using technology in the classroom to assist each pupil to achieve as optimally as possible. The school culture reflects the importance of technology use with pupils, teachers, and administrators indicating its importance to child growth and development in the school setting.

Maskin (1996) wrote the following:

Promoters of computers in the classroom claim that exposing pupils to Web sites, e-mail, and newsgroups promises more than the means of securing a job in the next century. Technology boosters also predict that the use and mastery of the internet and the World Wide Web will produce affective changes that can be measured to produce increased student self-esteem and confidence. Whether working at home or in school, as an individual or in a cooperative learning or team setting, students will become 'infotectives', i.e. independent thinkers, researchers, inventors, inquirers, capable of solving problems that often required the active direction of a teacher or supervisor...

In expanding the learning environment to include data bases, computer networks, and other library resources throughout the world, the internet makes it possible for students to shape their own education. Once the easy accessing protocols are learned, the student can dive into these resources in the comfort of his or her home and/or library without the constant supervision and intervention of the teacher. Lao Tzui's' dictum, 'He who teaches least teaches best,' describes a student centered teaching, learning, and assessment environment in which the student can access information from multiple perspectives and learn to use this information to solve complex problems.

Freedom, however, also opens up the possibility of choice. The emerging information technologies can just as easily be used to access sports trivia as they can explore issues being debated in Congress or at the World Bank. Many students, if left to their devices, might choose to spend hours surfing the 'Net for their own enjoyment rather than using it to complete a school assignment. The job of the teacher, therefore, is to involve students, individually or in teams, in internet projects that are fun to do and skill enhancing. Students exposed early on to such educational endeavours are more likely to feel comfortable and confident in Drucker's knowledge based society...

I am convinced that internet connectivity empowers students, gives them a research advantage, and generally gets them excited about learning.

We are truly in an information age in which there are so many outstanding sources of content for pupils acquisition. Pupils need to have ample opportunities to secure a variety of subject matter on a topic. It does cost money to have the latest of technology in our schools. But can we afford to be without it? Pupils today, in a few years, will be in the work place where the information age will even more be clearly defined as compared to today. Pupils of every race, creed, and religion must have the chances in an equitable manner to be able to use the latest in data securing sources. The upper income level pupils will have these opportunities of obtaining information through World Wide Web and Internet in the home setting. Other pupils also should have equality of opportunity to use state of the art sources to obtain information.

Pertaining to the future of technology, Mehlinger (1996) wrote the following:

Without going into detail regarding specific pieces of hardware, we can say with confidence that schools should expect more *integration, interaction, and intelligence* from future technology. In their early days in school, computers and video were regarded as separate entities, and it was assumed they would stay that way. In fact, we can expect a continuing integration of these technologies. Voice, data, and images will be brought together into one package. One current example of this process is desktop video. In a single, relatively inexpensive unit, one has telephone (voice), computer (data storage and manipulation), and video (sending and receiving moving images) capabilities. Those who use the machine can talk to people at a distance, exchange documents, work collaboratively, and even see collaborators on the screen.

Technology will also become more interactive. In the field of distance learning, rather than strictly rely on one-way video and two way communication, teachers and students will see another simultaneously, thereby making distance learning more like face-to-face classroom interaction. Computer based instruction will also be designed to respond to learners' interests and abilities, giving them greater control over what they need to learn and the pace at which they will learn it. And computer searches, which can be bewildering to the casual observer, will become easier and more responsive to what a user needs. Greater interactivity will make instructional programmes even more powerful than they are today.

Finally, technology will have greater intelligence. This intelligence will be displayed in several ways. First, the technology will have more features and greater capacity. Second, it will have the capability to learn from the user, so that it can customise its services to fit the user's learning style and interest. Future technology will provide not only data bases but knowledge bases. And technology will be able to stay abreast of that information most valued to the user and alert him or her to its availability.

Integration, interaction, and intelligence. These are three features we can expect of technology in the future. And they will change the way technology is employed in schools.

Conclusion

From the psychology of learning, there are numerous criteria recommended for teaching pupils. These are that interest needs to be developed within pupils for learning, purpose should be there on the learner's part to achieve, meaning should be inherent in ongoing lessons and units of study, relationship of knowledge is salient in the instructional arena, individual differences among pupils need to be provided for, and good attitudes need adequate emphasis.

Four philosophies of education were discussed and need to be appraised so that the best one(s) are used to meet individual pupil learning styles. These philosophies are experimentalism with its stress upon pupil problem solving; idealism with its emphasis upon an idea centered curriculum advocating learner's achieving abstract subject matter; existentialism with values placed upon the individual pupil selecting, from among alternatives, learning opportunities to pursue; and realism with its stress upon pupils achieving measurable stated objectives.

The future seemingly looks bright for use of technology in the classroom. The use of World Wide Web and Internet, e-mail, faxing, and the electronic bulletin board, among others, will guide pupils to attain vital objectives of instruction. Desktop videos, as a truly modern device in technology, integrate voice, sound, and the pictorial.

References

Bhaskara Rao, Digumarti, ed. (2000), *International Encyclopaedia of Science and Technology Education*, 11 Vol. New Delhi, India: Discovery Publishing House.

Bigge, Morris L. (1982), *Educational Philosophies for Teachers.* Columbus, Ohio: Charles E. Merill Publishing Company, pp. 25 and 26.

Choice or Chance (1984), Chicago, Illinois: Rand McNally and Company.

Ediger, Marlow and D. Bhaskara Rao (1996), *Science Curriculum.* New Delhi, India: Discovery Publishing House, Chapter Three.

Ediger, Marlow and D. Bhaskara Rao (2000), *Teaching Mathematics Successfully.* New Delhi: Discovery Publishing House.

Ediger, Marlow (1995). *Philosophy in Curriculum Development.* Kirksville, Missouri: Simpson Publishing Company, pp. 86-87.

Ediger, Marlow (1997), *Social Studies Curriculum in the Elementary School.* Fourth Edition, Kirksville, Missouri, p. 241.

Ediger, Marlow (1994), 'Teaching Science,' *Investigating*, 10 (3), 24-25, published by the Australian Science Teachers Association.

Ediger, Marlow (1996), 'Personalised Science Instruction, *Prism*, 5 (1), 25-27, printed by the Newfoundland and Labrador Teachers Association.

Eichelberger, Tony R. (1989). *Disciplined Inquiry: Understanding and Doing Educational Research.* White Plains, New York: Longman, Inc., p. 11.

Hoffman, Bob (1996). 'School Technology Integration: An Automated Needs Assessment and Planning Tool..' in *Technology and Teacher Education Annual.* Edited by Robin, Price, Willis, and Willis. Charlottesville, Virginia: Association for the Advancement of Computing in Education.

Maskin, Melvin (1996). 'Infotectives on the Infobahn: Designing Internet-Aided Projects for the Social Studies Classroom, *National Association of Secondary School Principal's Bulletin*, Vol. 80, No, 582, pp. 59-69.

Mehlinger, Howard D. (1996), 'School Reform in the Information Age', *Phi Delta Kappan*, Vol. 77, No. 6, p. 405-406.

Morris, Van Cleve and Young Pai (1976), *Philosophy and the American School.*: Houghteon Mifflin Company, p. 378.

Ozman, Howard, and Samuel Craver (1990). *Philosophical Foundations and Education.* Fourth Edition. Columbus, Ohio: Merrill Publishing Company, p. 249.

Ritchie, Donn (1996), 'The Administrative Role in Integration of Technology,' *Bulletin of the National Association of Secondary School Principals*, Vol. 80, No. 582, p. 43.

Rose, Stephen A., and Phyllis Maxey Fernlund (1997, 'Using Technology for Powerful Social Studies Learning, *Social Education*, Vol. 61, No. 3, pp. 161-162.

Wild, John (1955), *Modern Philosophies of Education.* Chicago, Illinois: The National Society for the Study of Education, p. 31.

12

Improving Leadership in the Science Curriculum

Leadership is needed in schools to overcome problems in the school setting. Richardson and others (1989) emphasised that principals be proactive and not reactive persons. Thus problems tend to be identified before they happen rather than reacting to crises situations only. Ediger (1993) stressed the importance of administrators and supervisors being highly knowledgeable about the curriculum in providing for optimal learner achievement. Much parental dissatisfaction might well be avoided if leadership capabilities were used to guide each pupil to attain as much as possible.

KNOWLEDGE OF THE CURRICULUM

To assist pupils to achieve as well as possible in the school setting, attempts need to be made to identify effective schools. This is indeed difficult. Wallberg (1979) identified more than 2,700 research studies that emphasised effective schools. Squires, Huitt, and Segar (1985) in summarising research pertaining to effective schools raised the following questions:

1. Does the school leader have purpose in mind when administering and supervising in the school setting?
2. Are high academic standards being stressed?
3. Is the principal supportive of efforts in school improvement?
4. Are adequate staff development programmes in evidence to improve the curriculum?
5. Do faculty and staff work together to harmonise endeavours in instructional improvement and discipline of learners?
6. Is the principal visible to observe teaching and learning as well as to confer with teachers on curriculum and instruction matters?

Questions arise here as to what is meant by school and curriculum improvement, having purpose in mind in making changes in the educational setting, as well as which inservice education programmes to stress for faculty development. A need exists to make decisions based on theory and research. Something must provide direction and guidance in whatever is done in education, teaching, and learning. Writers frequently write about the necessity of theory guiding instruction. These writers tend not to state which theories should be emphasised in the curriculum. There are numerous recommendable psychologies and theories of instruction that can be emphasised in the school curriculum. We recommend strongly that all administrators, supervisors, and teachers become thoroughly familiar with each theory. Depth learning of each theory should be in the offing for educational leaders which includes classroom teachers. These theories have stood the test of time and tend to be classical in nature. We will discuss what we believe to be selected relevant theories of instruction which educational leaders must be able to implement in ongoing lessons and units of study.

THEORIES OF TEACHING

Dewey (1916) emphasised problem solving approaches in teaching-learning situations. The problems need to be real and lifelike to pupils. Committee work to identify and solve contextual problems in a creative atmosphere was stressed. The teacher is a guide and resource person, not a dispenser of information.

In a science unit on 'Animals Without Backbones,' pupils individually or in a committee setting might identify problems such as the following based on ongoing learning opportunities:

1. How to sponges obtain food since they do not move around?
2. How do coelenterates, such as jelly fish and the Portuguese man-of-war, paralyse their prey?
3. How do parasites such as flatworms (Platyhelminthes) obtain energy for living?

For each problem area identified, pupils may volunteer to serve on a committee to obtain solutions. A variety of reference sources need to be used to gather information in answer to the problem. The answer(s), which are stated as hypotheses, are tentative and subject to testing.

Piaget (1950) stressed a development psychology by identifying four stages that most pupils go through as they progress from birth through the elementary school years. These developmental stages are sensorimotor (birth to two years of age), preoperational (ages two to seven), concrete operations (ages seven to eleven), and the stage of formal operations (age eleven and beyond). The ages given are approximate in Piaget's research findings.

For the sensorimotor stage of development, which is prior to the public school years, parents may provide models of animals without backbones. These young children may touch, feel, smell, see, and hear sounds of these models when they are being shaken.

At the preoperational stage of development, pupils may raise questions about the invertebrates being observed. Piaget, like

Dewey, was strong on using problem solving methods of learning. At this stage of development, Piaget believed that pupils see one variable only or largely such as the length of the object only, or the width only. Comparisons may be too difficult for these preoperational pupils to make such as comparing annelids with Platyhelminthes (flatworms) and nematodes (roundworms).

In viewing a videotape, preoperational pupils on the first grade level may notice and reflect upon annelids, such as the earthworm, having a segmented body, and a well developed nervous system. It then might not work for preoperational pupils to make comparisons among invertebrates. The pupils at the stage of concrete operations understand several variables at one time and yet the teacher needs to refer pupils to the concrete situation which are directly related to the abstract. Thus if pupils are studying mollusks, they need to relate abstract learnings (words, phrases, sentences, paragraphs, and diagrams) to the model or real mollusks, including snails, slugs, oysters, and squids. From the concrete to the abstract would be a good model to follow here. Much use needs to be made of real objects and items in teaching pupils on the concrete stage of operations.

At the stage of formal operations, pupils with teacher guidance may discuss arthropods, for example, without referring to realia or concrete situations, according to Piaget. We would recommend, however, that learning activities should stress the concrete facets adequately. Content can become too abstract whereby learners individually do not understand what has been taught.

Marlow (1954) emphasised a theory of motivation with its hierarchy of needs that individuals should have fulfilled such as physiological (adequate nutritious food, clothing, and shelter); safety and security (a safe home and neighborhood, freedom from abuse), love and belonging (acceptance in the home and school setting), esteem (being recognised for talent and/or skill), and self actualisation (becoming the kind of person desired). Personal needs of pupils must be met if they are to do well in school. Pupil-teacher planning of the curriculum is salient.

The objectives, learning opportunities, and appraisal procedures must meet needs of pupils in the science curriculum.

Bruner (1968) emphasised a structure of knowledge be identified for each curriculum areas. These structural ideas represent key ideas or major generalisations as perceived by academicians in science in their respective areas of expertise. Leaders in science education and teachers might well identify their own structure of knowledge to emphasise in teaching each curriculum area. Bruner's theory of instruction is practical since its implementation might well provide objectives, learning opportunities to attain the objectives, as well as evaluation procedures to ascertain learner progress. Methods of learning, according to Bruner, emphasise what the scientist would stress in a laboratory setting.

Behaviourism, as a psychology of learning, has a long history of importance (Bobbitt 1916, W. W. Charters 1923, B. F. Skinner 1979). Behaviourism stresses the importance of precise, measurably stated objectives for pupil attainment, written prior to instruction. Mastery learning, instructional management systems, and criterion referenced testing are present day examples of behaviourism. Reinforcement theory is also directly relate to behaviourism. The following are examples of behaviourally stated objectives for pupils to achieve:

1. The pupil will list in writing three regions of an insect and explain the purpose of each region;
2. The pupil will write a fifty word paragraph on differences between monerans and bacteria;
3. The pupil will state orally three differences and three likenesses of amphibians versus reptiles.

The science teacher may announce prior to instruction what pupils are to learn from a teaching/learning situation. This provides security to pupils when they know what is to be learned from an ongoing lesson or unit of study. Tests given are aligned with the precisely stated objectives. To provide reinforcement, based on test results, the science teacher may offer sincere praise to pupils for doing well. Ideally, the success rate for pupil learning is high since the teacher teaches directly for pupils achieving the stated objectives. The learning activities aligned with the objectives of instruction make for high validity.

With objectives being stated so that pupils either do or do not attain success as a result of interacting with learning opportunities, little leeway is left for interpretation as to what any one objective means.

The basics (Bagley 1905, Bestor 1953, Smith 1959) in the curriculum also had a relatively long history in education. It has never been determined at any age in time what is basic for pupils to learn. Former President of the United States Ronald Reagan and his Secretary of Education William Bennett continually emphasised that teachers should teach the basics and not waste time on the frivolous. They too did not define what the basics were that pupils should acquire. If we only could know what these are, much time would be saved in teaching learners. To be sure, effort must always be put forth to determine what is basic and essential for pupils to achieve.

More is expected of administrators and supervisors than ever before. Knowledge of the curriculum is no exception. Missouri since 1985 with the Excellence in Education Act, among other states in the United States, mandates that principals evaluate each nontenured teacher at least once a year and tenured teachers at least once every three years. This means that principals need to have knowledge of the curriculum when appraising teaching performance. Teachers will grasp how knowledgeable the principal is during an observation to the classroom followed with a conference. The purpose of observational visits and fillip conferences should be to improve the teaching of knowledge, skills, and attitudes of the classroom teacher.

Theories of learning to provide direction in teaching-learning situations differ from each other. What then can be done to assist teaches and administrators/supervisors in providing for optimal pupil attainment in the classroom? Determine which theory or theories benefit individual learners in teaching and learning. Pupils differ much from each other and need guidance to learn as much as possible. Since pupils are human beings and are different one form the other, it behooves educational leaders to determine which theory in use will assist the pupil to attain as optimally as possible.

FUNCTIONS OF THE EDUCATIONAL LEADER

Leaders in education must emphasise the importance of good human and public relations (shoemaker and Fraser 1981). Principals and supervisors need to assist teachers to have pupils achieve goals. Assisting teachers can largely be done if there is mutual respect and acceptance between the leaders and the teachers. Hindrance in quality communication among participants results in a lack of sharing ideas, results, and work completion in the school setting. Oliva (1984) stresses careful attention be given to methods of nonverbal, written, and verbal communication skills.

Gestures, facial expressions, and body movements do convey something to the receiver of nonverbal communication. A friendly countenance emphasising a willingness to work together and collaborate on salient tasks to improve the science curriculum are musts. People realise rather quickly in most cases in which selected individuals indicate non-verbally that they do not wish to serve on a committee, nor give the time to do so, nor indicate feelings of cooperation in moving toward an ideal or have a vision of what should be accomplished in the school setting. The educational leader must present a role model here. The principal/supervisor sets examples for teachers to follow. His/her enthusiasm, knowledge, empathy, and understanding of teachers as human beings having much worth should be an inherent facet of the non-verbal role model. Written communication skills are further needed by the educational leader to convey, clarify, and confirm meaningful information to teachers be it in a bulletin, E-mail, or Fax pertaining notices of staff development, in trends in teaching for teachers to think about, as well as issues in the curriculum. Modern technology has made it so that word processors make the act of written communication easier, neater in the final copy, and more flexible in making revisions and modifications. Mechanical errors must be omitted in all written messages used to communicate to receivers of the message.

Verbal communication must be comprehendible with appropriate stress, pitch, and juncture used to convey information to others. Quality eye contact is a must in verbal communication. Ellis (1986) wrote that, in terms of research results from the studies of William Rutherford and associates, the most successful principals, clearly communicated expectations, provided technical assistance, and monitored the results.

Being able to communicate well comes up again and again in research results pertaining to educational leaders. Hallinger and Murphy (1986) in emphasising effective school research summaries list the following as being salient:

1. determining and communicating the goals of the school;
2. supervising and evaluating teaching and learning;
3. coordinating curriculum efforts;
4. developing high standards in the academics as well as high expectations;
5. monitoring and evaluating student achievement;
6. encouraging professional development of teachers;
7. maintaining time on task for instruction;
8. developing incentives for teachers and students.

Stocklinski and Miller—Colbert (1991) emphasise the Comer Process, a research based model for school improvement that has as its basis collaboration, consensus, and communication for the solving of problems in academic, social, and staff development areas. This process permits teachers, supervisors/ principals, and parents to harmonise efforts in working together for the good of the pupil. Among other items of importance here is the emphasis placed upon quality communication to achieve goals of the school and of education.

TRAITS AND CHARACTERISTICS OF PRINCIPALS

More is expected in a complex society than ever before of school supervisors and administrators

Duttweiler and Hord (1989) state that educational leaders who are effective desire a participatory style of supervision. These principals and supervisors want input from others, particularly teachers. Thus there needs to be collaboration skills in working together for the good of the student. Skills in being able to foster cooperation among participants in selecting objectives of instruction, learning opportunities to attain the objectives, and evaluation procedures to assess progress are desired from school leaders. These leaders need to be able to motivate, encourage, and stimulate others in the school setting to participate in school improvement endeavours. Thus principals and supervisors should be skillful in working effectively with others to achieve the goals of the school. An open school environment assists participants to become actively involved to improve the total school curriculum.

Society is continually changing. It does not stay stable. With the many societal changes, the school curriculum also needs modification and revisions. The world of work and the personal needs of individuals require that student competencies need developing in the areas of creative thing, problem solving, critical thinking, as well as reasoning skills (Dede 1989). Educational leaders should think of change as being relevant in society. These changes have tremendous implications for objectives and goals in the curriculum, learning opportunities to attain the stated ends, and assessment procedures to determine how much pupils have learned and what is left to be done to guide more optimal learner attainment.

The new leader in the school setting must be

1. highly knowledgeable of workable procedures of teaching;
2. an effective leader possessing skills to work with others;
3. able to motivate teachers and others in the school setting;
4. proficient in curriculum development;
5. knowledgeable of child development characteristics;
6. proficient in a variety of communication skills;
7. skillful in interpersonal relations;
8. able to plan and implement decisions made through collaboration;

9. knowledgeable of societal trends and quality school practices;
10. able to apply technology to instruction and management;
11. skillful in the use of political processes to attain objectives of instruction;
12. knowledgeable about school site management and its implementation;
13. secure parental cooperation and input;
14. obtain information to use in making relevant decisions;
15. empower individuals, especially teachers, in a rich school cultural climate.

School leaders need to provide opportunities for science teachers to try out new ideas in ongoing lessons and units of study. Thus, science teachers with supervisor leadership may wish to assist pupils in new ways to develop rich science vocabularies. Condrey (1996) wrote the following:

> Every science teacher knows that showing students how concepts apply to everyday events is quite a challenge. We describe real world applications in class, conduct demonstrations to illustrate concepts in action, and give students applications they can replicate in the lab. Yet they still have difficulty connecting classroom activities to their own lives.
>
> We could spend hours previewing videos in search of the perfect visual to illustrate concepts germane to teenager's lives. A better idea is to provide them the opportunity to produce a video that illustrates concept applications from their own experiences.
>
> Student teams can design and produce three to five minute instructional videos that define a concept and apply it to their personal experiences. For example, physics students might film applications of inertia in skating or stock car racing: biology or anatomy students might show how a gymnast's muscles work together to perform a manpeuvre on the parallel bars; or chemistry students might produce a video illustrating the effects of chemical reactions in food preparation. Making these videos

helps students to see the connections between science and 'real life' by taking the experience out of the classroom and putting it into their personal areas of knowledge and relevance.

Producing a short video involves much more than haphazard filming. The purpose is to define and illustrate the application of a specific concept, so that video should be instructive and follow a logical sequence. It must be able to stand alone without further explanations from the presenters. Students should be encouraged to use creatively and humour in their productions.

Conclusion

Foresight of educational leaders is vital so that a vision of the ideal is possible. Efforts need to be made to achieve the vision. It is an ongoing process. Much knowledge of the curriculum is necessary to attain and grow. Purposes need to be involved in moving from what is to what should be. The educational leader needs to provide support to those working toward positive changes in curriculum improvement. Staff development is needed in making these changes. Collaboration among participants is necessary to work toward a desired curriculum.

Diverse theories of instruction that have stood the test of time may be used by teachers to guide pupils to achieve as much as possible. The theory used must harmonise with what assists the learner(s) to attain and achieve. Each theory provides the teacher guidance and direction in making educational decisions.

Quality supervisors/principals are able to communicate well with others. Diverse forms of communication must be used to achieve purposes in the school setting. The goals and objectives of the school need communicating to parents and the lay public. Learning opportunities being emphasised in the school setting should harmonise with quality goals and objectives. Monitoring of learner progress in goal attainment is a must. There need to be high standards for pupil achievement with time on task involved. Incentives for learning and for teaching should be in the offing.

Society changes rather continuously making it necessary for the school curriculum to change. Higher levels of cognition must be stressed in teaching-learning situations. Knowledgeable, skillful leaders should possess abilities to work effectively with others, especially teachers. These leaders must be proficient in curriculum development procedures. Child growth and development characteristics should be used in improving teaching and learning. Good interpersonal relations are needed to guide staff development efforts as well as involve parents in matters pertaining to curriculum improvement.

There are principles of learning from educational psychology which teachers and educational leaders tend to agree with. These principles of learning provide guidance in choosing objectives of instruction, learning opportunities for pupils to achieve the objectives, as well as appraisal procedures to ascertain what pupils have learned. Ediger (1994) lists these principles of learning as follows:

1. pupils need to attach meaning and understanding to ongoing lessons and units of study;
2. pupils need to experience interest in learning;
3. pupils need to perceive purpose in learning;
4. pupils need to experience sequence in learning opportunities;
5. pupils need to experience rational balance among objectives in the curriculum, such as knowledge, skills, and attitudinal goals.

The long range goal of educational leaders is to assist teachers in guiding pupils to achieve more optimally. Supervisors/ principals need to challenge teachers to provide the best curriculum possible for pupils in the school setting. Ward, et. al. (1996) wrote the following:

As student continue to explore the observations and relationships found in the above activities, the teacher guides students to "construct" the concept that air expands when heated and contracts when cooled. The teacher then provides opportunities for pupils to apply that concept to new situations in which differences in air pressure are caused by the temperature changes.

Providing a classroom environment that encourages collaborations among students is an important component of a constructivist classroom environment. When teachers use questions that probe, clarify, and explore the relationships between student's prior experiences, students develop more accurate science concepts.

Students within this classroom environment change from passive receptors to active learners responsible for their own construction of meaning. The challenge for teachers is how to help students effectively construct meaning. Teacher continued to be responsible for selecting which science concepts to study and how their students learn these concepts. Within a constructivist environment, however, these decisions are based to a much larger degree on the abilities of teacher to know what their students bring to the classroom. When teachers are attuned to students' prior knowledge, they enable students to accommodate their previously held ' understandings' by providing experiences that develop increased understanding of science concepts.

The leader in science curriculum improvement needs to be very knowledgeable about study groups that have done much work in curriculum development. One such group, among others, is The American Association for the Advancement of Science (AAAS). The AAAs (1989) developed Project 61 which has four broad categories:

1. The scientific endeavour;
2. The scientific study of the world;
3. Perspectives on science;
4. Scientific habits of the mind.

The AAAS four broad objectives, listed above, provide guidance and direction for further consideration of listed high quality objectives, useful to teachers and leaders in providing leadership to improve the science curriculum.

References

American Association for the Advancement of Science (1989), *Project 2061*. Washington, DC: AAAS.

Bhaskara Rao, Digumarti (2000), *Educational Psychology*. Guntur, India: Nagarjuna Publishers (in Telugu language).

Bhaskara Rao, Digumarti, ed. (1999). *Education for the 21st Century*. New Delhi, India: Discovery Publishing House.

Bruner, Jerome, *Toward a Theory of Instruction*. Cambridge, Massachusetts: Harvard University Press, 1968.

Bobbitt, Franklin, The Curriculum. Boston: Houghton Mifflin Company, 1918.

Bagley, William, *The Educative Process*. New York: The Macmillan Company, 1905.

Bestor, Arthur, *Educational Wastelands*. Urbana: University of Illinois Press, 1953.

Condrey, Jean Friend (1996), Focus on Science Concepts, *The Science Teacher* 63 (4), 17.66.

Charters, W.W. Charters, Curriculum Construction. New York: The Macmillan Company, 1923.

Dewey, John, *Democracy and Education*. New York: The Macmillan Company, 1916.

Duttweiler, F.C., and S. Hord. *Dimensions of Effective School Leadership*. Austin, Texas: BEDL, 1989.

Dede, C. (1989), 'The Evolution of Information Technology: Implications for Curriculum,' *Educational Leadership*, Volume 47 (1), 23-26.

Ediger, Marlow, 'Goals of School Administrators,' *Michigan Principal*, Fall, 1993, pp. 12-14.

Ediger, Marlow (1997), *Teaching Science in the Elementary School*. Kirksville, Missouri: Simpson Publishing Company, Chapter One.

Ediger, Marlow (1996), *Essays in School Administration*. Kirksville, Missouri: Simpson Publishing Company, 6-12.

Ediger, Marlow (1995), *Philosophy in Curriculum Development* Kirksville, Missouri: Simpson Publishing Company, 19-36.

Ediger, Marlow (1995), 'The Psychology of Learning and the Teacher,' *Philippine Educational Quarterly*, 23 (4), 1-11.

Ediger, Marlow (1994), 'Shared Leadership in the Curriculum,' *Education Magazine*, nr. 110, 11-15.

Ediger, Marlow (1997), 'Computer Literacy in the Public Schools' ERIC # ED 412919.

Ediger, Marlow (1999), 'Attitudinal Objectives in the Chemistry Curriculum,' New England Association of Chemistry Teachers Journal, 17 (2), 15-17.

Ellis, T.I., 'The Principal as Instructional Leader'. ERIC Document Reproduction Service # ED 274 031, 1986.

Ediger, Marlow, 'Early Field Experiences in Teacher Education,' *College Student Journal*, September, 1994, pp 302-307.

Hallinger, P., and J. Murphy. 'Instructional Leadership in Effective Schools.' ERIC Document Reproduction Service # Ed 309 535, 1986.

National Association of Elementary School Principals, *Principals for the Twenty First Century Schools.* Alexandria, Virginia: NAESP, 1990.

Oliva, P.F., *Supervision for Today's Schools.* Now York: Longman, 1984.

Piaget, Jean, *The Psychology of Intelligence.* New York: Harcourt Brace Jovanovich, 1950.

Richardson, M.D., and others, 'A Descriptive Analysis of Kentucky Elementary School Principals.' ERIC Document Reproduction Service # ED 311557.

Squires, David, and others, *Effective Schools and Classrooms: A Research Based Perspective*, Alexandria, Virginia: Association for Supervision and Curriculum Development, 1985.

Skinner, B.F., *Beyond Freedom and Dignity.* New York: Alfred Knopf, Inc, 1979.

Smith, Mortimer, *Diminished Mind.* Chicago: Regency Press, 1959.

Shoemaker, J., and Fraser, H. W 'What Principals Can Do: Some Implications from Studies of Effective Schooling,' *Phi Delta Kappan*, November, 1981, pp. 178-182.

Stocklinski, J., and J. Miller-Colbert, 'The Comer Process Moving from I to We.' ERIC Document Reproductive Service # EJ 419 920, 1986.

Ward, Kathleen, et.at. (1996), Constructing Scientific Knowledge, *The Science Teacher*, 63 (9), 23.

Wallberg, H., and others, 'The Quiet Revolution in Education Research,' *Phi Delta Kappan.* November, 1979, pp. 179-183.

13

Staff Development Programmes in Science

Much is written in educational literature pertaining to staff development. It appears that writers stress staff development for each innovation presented. For example, if the interdisciplinary curriculum needs emphasis, then staff development is needed. Or, if full inclusion is wanted, then staff development should be in evidence. We believe the first issue in staff development is how many sessions should be devoted to staff development when writers bring in new ideas in teaching and at the same time advocate staff development for implementing that idea. Is it necessary to have staff development for each new or innovative idea adopted in teaching and learning? Might teachers be trusted with implementing the new concept(s) on their own?

FURTHER ISSUES IN STAFF DEVELOPMENT

Who should determine what should be emphasised in staff

development? A common vision is being emphasised as to what our schools should be like as a result of this vision. How is the vision to be achieved? A staff development programme, in part, may help. Ediger (1988) recommends that staff development programmes have three integrated parts such as a general session, small group or committee endeavours, and individual study. Teachers here should determine what is to be emphasised in the general session to identify problem areas, they should volunteer as to which committee to work on to solve problems, and then work individually on a problem of their very own choosing. The teacher and teaching here are at the center of the stage in staff development. Principals and supervisors are there to assist teachers in working toward solutions of problem areas.

Toward the other end of the continuum, supervisors and principals, after consultation with teachers, may desire to bring in a certain programme whereby staff development is necessary. The teachers are trained and educated to use a certain model in teaching after a quality programme of training. This approach at staff development has unique features that the first did not possess. The latter procedure in staff development is more principal/supervisor oriented, even though there was consultation with teachers about the new approach. Second, a commercial approach or one proposed by a team of educators was emphasised. The ideas for problem areas to be solved basically did not come from local teachers. Third, teachers must develop into having completely new teaching styles. The teaching model selected for staff development and implementation might not intrinsically be wanted by teachers. There may be a different procedure in teaching desired by teachers. Fourth, an external training team may be involved in the training of teachers. Trainers then come from outside the local school system or district. Fifth, trainers sequence experiences for teachers in staff training sessions. A logical approach is then involved in sequencing experiences for trainees.

WHAT SHOULD TRAINING SESSIONS STRESS?

The objectives of instruction may be changed or modified. Generally cognitive objectives have received major emphasis in the curriculum. There are different levels of pupil achievement in the cognitive domain. Changes may be made from stressing the lower level cognitive objectives to those emphasising higher levels of thinking. Bloom's (1956) is still popular in discussing objectives form the lower to higher levels of cognition. His sequence is the following: recall of factual information by learners, comprehension of what has been recalled, application or using what has been learned, analysis involving critical thought, synthesis stressing unique ways of putting the information together after analysis, and evaluation of what has been learned in terms of standards or criteria. Staff development programmes may stress teachers having children move for lower to higher cognitive objectives using Bloom's taxonomy. Learning opportunities need to be designed to guide pupils in thinking at a more complex level in ongoing learning opportunities. Feedback from teachers to members of the staff development programme should be in the offing after the teacher has used higher cognitive objectives in the classroom.

There is much discussion in education about having pupils apply what has been learned. Perhaps, a staff development programme will stress the level of application in ongoing training sessions. Teachers then put to use ideas developed and acquired in the staff development programme to the regular classroom. These teachers report back to the training session how the ideas worked out in the classroom.

Modification of objectives stressed in teaching and learning may also emphasise minimising cognitive and advocating affective ends in teaching. Affective objectives put more emphasis upon attitudes that pupils need to develop. Hopefully, quality attitudes will assist pupils to achieve cognitive objectives more effectively. Krathwohl stressed five levels of affective objectives in moving from the lowest to the higher levels. These are the following: paying attention to relevant content presented, responding to content with feeling or emotion, responding to content in a value oriented way, organising values and feelings into a structure, and characterising the attitudes in terms of being consistent and following a pattern. A quality affective curriculum emphasises pupils developing positive feelings and values.

A learning stations philosophy might well stress an affective curriculum. Here, the teacher together with pupils develop an adequate number of stations as well as tasks for each station. Pupils might then choose which tasks to complete and which to omit. Decision-making by learners is important. Ideally, pupils choose tasks which possess interest and perceived purpose. Motivation for learning should be higher if the pupil has had input into what he/she has planned and wishes to learn. The learner also is involved in planing and selecting—two concepts which no doubt are at the heart of democratic thinking. The learner chooses form among alternatives and he/she is affected by choices made, from among alternatives. Involvement by pupils in selecting objectives, learning activities, and appraisal procedures emphasises increasingly democratic living. Also the attitudes of the pupil determine, in part, what will be learned. A psychological curriculum stresses pupils sequencing their very own learning opportunities; opposite of a psychological curriculum is a logical curriculum whereby a teacher arranges the order of learning for pupils.

In noticing that an almost complete absence of statements advocating democracy and democratic ideals from policy makers, Fenstermacher (1995) write the following:

...We hear a great deal about readying the next generation of workers for global competition, about being first in the world in such high status subjects as maths and science, and about having world class standards for what is learned in school. We hear almost nothing about civic participation or building and maintaining democratic communities, whether these be neighbourhoods or governments at the local, state, or federal levels. The advancement of democratic ideals and institutions goes largely unmentioned, taken for granted or insufficiently important to rank up there with such world-shaking events as our playing Avis to Japan's Hertz.

Workshops and staff development programmes might then be arranged for the teacher to stress democracy as a way of life with the inclusion of affective objectives.

A third change in the curriculum may reflect the use of psychomotor objectives. Here, the school curriculum stresses the use of the gross and finer muscles of the learner. Harrow (1972) listed six levels of psychomotor objectives. These are the following:

1. reflex movement;
2. basic fundamental movements, including locomotor, non-locomotor manipulative movements;
3. perceptual abilities containing several subcategories:
   a. Kinesthetic discrimination that refers to body awareness, body image, body relationship of surrounding objects in space;
   b. visual discrimination including visual awareness, visual tracking, visual memory, figure ground differentiation, and perceptual constancy;
   c. auditory discrimination including auditory activity, tracking, and memory;
   d. tactile discrimination;
   e. coordination.
4. physical abilities including endurance, strength, flexibility, and agility;
5. skilled movement including simple adaptive skill, compound and complex adaptive skill;
6. non-discursive communication including expressive movements and interpretive movements.

In emphasising psychomotor objectives, the teacher assists pupils to become actively involved in making, constructing, artistic endeavours, doing, and other forms of using physical movement and motion. Psychomotor objectives may be used in any curriculum area and receive more emphasis in teaching and learning as compared to cognitive and affective ends of instruction (Earnest, 1995).

Staff development programmes may be needed to change from a cognitive or affective objectives emphasis to one stressing the psychomotor domain. Psychomotor objectives truly emphasise an activity centered curriculum for pupils. In teaching a unit on 'Weather and How It Affects Us,' pupils with teaching team guidance discussed and constructed a barometer, a wind vane, a hygrometer, and an anemometer. Each object was goal centered, planned, constructed, and appraised in terms of criteria.

LEARNING OPPORTUNITIES TO ACHIEVE OBJECTIVES

In changing from previously used activities and experiences to a new approach takes effort, knowledge, skill, and, motivation. If pupils are to use modern technology in the curriculum, it may truly revolutionise the curriculum depending upon the amount of change being empathised. In using the word processor, world wide web and internet, graphing techniques, CD ROM's, video disks, among other items, teachers may need to experience two to three years of quality staff development programmes. Objectives need to be determined for pupils to achieve sequentially in using modern technology. Progress by pupils may well be slow, but sure with good teaching, in using technology to achieve objectives.

Second, staff development programmes might well be extensive if an interdisciplinary curriculum is to be in evidence. An allied arts programme of instruction may well emphasise a team teaching approach. Allied arts attempts to integrate art, music, dance, drama, poetry, and architecture, among other possibilities. Thus a teaching team consisting of the following teachers, each qualified in his/her area of expertise—an art, a music, a physical education, and a literature of English teacher—must be in the offing. If possible, an architecture from the community might be hired part time. If the school system has an architect, it becomes easier for this person to work on the team to plan the objectives, learning opportunities, and evaluation procedures than would otherwise be the case. Staff development programmes might then include members learning to plan together, developing means of curricular integration of content, and evaluating to ascertain the effectiveness of the teaching team. Team teaching has built in inservice education opportunities since members may learn from each other during planning sessions.

Third, cooperative learning, as activities and experiences for pupils to achieve objectives, may need staff development programmes. The goals of the staff development programme might stress how to form groups for coorperative learning, how to work effectively as a teacher with diverse groups in the classroom, and how to appraise pupil performance within a group. The classroom teacher needs to believe in cooperative learning for it to become effective in the classroom setting. There needs to be a caring attitudes toward each other in cooperative learning endeavours. Pupils who feel neutral to each other or possess feelings of hostility might well fail to become good members of a committee in cooperative learning endeavours. Noddings (1995) wrote the following:

> The greatest structural obstacle, however, may be simply legitimising the inclusion of themes of care in the curriculum. Teachers in the early grades have long included such themes as a regular part of their work, and middle school educators are becoming more sensitive to developmental needs involving care. But, secondary schools—where violence, apathy, and alienation are most evident—do little to develop the capacity to care. Today, even elementary teachers complain that the pressure to produce high test scores inhibit the work they believe is central to their mission: the development of competent and caring people. Therefore it would seem that the most fundamental change required is one of attitude. Teachers can be very special people in the lives of children, and it should be legitimate for them to spend time developing relations of trust, talking with students about problems that are central to their lives, and guiding them toward greater sensitivity and competence across all the domains of care.

Fourth, peer coaching may be used to assist teachers to hone and perfect teaching skills in any curriculum area. Two teachers working together may observe each other's teaching and discuss the quality of objectives to be stressed, the aligning of learning opportunities with the objectives, and evaluation to ascertain if the objectives have been achieved by pupils. Showers and Joyce (1996), strong advocates of peer coaching, wrote the following:

When staff development becomes the major vehicle for school improvement, schools should take into account both the structures and content of training, as well as changes needed in the workplace to make possible the collaborative planning, decision making, and data collection that are essential to organisational change efforts. As we ponder ways to ensure that training/coaching fuels the school renewal process, we are also examining how the culture of the school can increasingly provide a benign environment for collective activity.

A cohesive school culture makes possible the collective decisions that generate school wide improvement efforts. The formation of peer coaching teams produces greater faculty cohesion and focus and, in turn, facilitates more skillful shared decision making. A skillful staff development programme results in a self-perpetuating process for change as well as new knowledge and skills for teachers and increased learning for pupils.

Peer coaching might then be used to improve the quality of learning opportunities for pupils as well as select objectives and evaluation procedures for learners. Learning opportunities (Ediger, 1994) should emphasise that pupils experience:

1. meaningful lessons and units of study. With meaning, pupils understand and comprehend that which was contained in ongoing learning opportunities;
2. interesting content and skills in the curriculum. With interest, the pupil and the curriculum become one, not separate entities. Pupils attend and achieve from ongoing lessons and units of study;
3. purpose in learning. With purpose in learning, pupils accept reasons for attaining relevant facts, concepts, and generalisations presented...
4. sequence in learning. With quality sequence, pupils relate newly acquired content with that previously achieved. Previous knowledge attained provides readiness for the new objectives to be achieved...
5. balance among objectives stressed. Thus, knowledge,

> skills, and attitudes—three kinds of objectives need to be achieved by students. These objectives interact and are not in isolation from each other. For example, if pupils possess positive attitudes, they should achieve needed knowledge and skills more readily.

Traditional organisation of learning opportunities stress using textbooks heavily, workbooks, work sheets, and recitation methods of instruction. A separate subjects curriculum tends to be in evidence with traditional approaches in teaching. Moving away from the separate subjects curriculum is correlation, then fusion, and finally the interdisciplinary curriculum. Skill in planning is needed to move away from the usual ways of teaching to that which harmonises more so with learner growth and development characteristics. Each pupil is to realise optimal development in knowledge, skills, and attitudes or the affective dimension. A multimedia approach is recommended in teaching to provide for individual differences.

EVALUATION OF PUPIL PROGRESS

Traditional procedures of evaluating pupil achievement has been to use standardised and norm referenced testing. Teacher written test items have also been used much in the past to ascertain pupil progress. These procedures are still recommended to determine pupil achievement. However, addition procedures must be used. Teacher observation needs to be used to notice learner progress in contextual situations. Thus within a given activity, the teacher notices how well each pupil is progressing. Assistance is given to pupils as is necessary. Pupils might then continue to work in context on the project or activity being pursued.

A relatively recent development is for pupils with teacher guidance to develop a portfolio of achievement and progress. In the portfolio, the pupil places samples of activities completed. These include written work, art projects, snapshots of construction experiences, videotapes of dramatic endeavours and cassette recordings of speech activates, among others. The portfolio may also contain test results, journal entries, rating scales, rubrics, and checklists to indicate learner progress and achievement.

Materials for the portfolio must be carefully chosen; otherwise it may become too voluminous. Contents in the portfolio are to show interested persons accomplishments of the involved pupil. A variety of learning opportunities experiences by a learner must show its related accomplishments to others who are interested in seeing the individual pupil's achievements.

Kane and Khattri (1995) wrote:

Some questions related to performance assessment remain to be answered b future research... . They have to do with basic and secondary issues in educational reform. What knowledge and skills are students expected to demonstrate after a certain period of schooling? What other systematic reforms must be undertaken in order for assessment reforms to be effective? Which assessment formats are most useful for which specific purposes? The greatest challenge ahead lies in designing systems of school reform that synergistically support the core educational functions of teaching and learning for which teachers are the most powerful 'engine'.

References

Bloom, Benjamin S. (1956), *Taxonomy of educational objectives, Handbook one—Cognitive Domain.* London, England: Longmans Publishing House.

Earnest Vimala (1995), *The relative effectiveness of teaching volumetric experiments in chemistry using Simpson's taxonomy of educational objectives for the psychomotor domain—an experimental study*, Ph. D. Thesis, University of Madras, India, pp. 4-21.

Ediger, Marlow (1999), 'Evaluation, the Language Arts and the Student,' *Focus*, 25 (2), 12-16.

Ediger, Marlow (1988), *The elementary curriculum*, 2nd Edition. Kirksville, Missouri: Simpson Publishing Company, pp. 117-126.

Ediger, Marlow (1994), 'Early field experiences in teacher education,' *College Student Journal*, 28: 302.

Ediger, Marlow (1998), 'Staff Development and Reading,' ERIC # ED 416458.

Ediger, Marlow (1998), 'Objectives in the Science Curriculum,' *The Progress of Education*. 22 (3), 23-29, published in India.

Ediger, Marlow (1998), 'the Unexpected in Science,' *Exchange*, published by the Pennsylvania Science Teachers Association, 23-25.

Ediger, Marlow (1995), 'Philosophy of Teaching Science,' *School Science*, 32 (3), 1-2.

Fenstermacher, Gary D. (1995), 'The absence of democratic and educational ideals from contemporary educational reforms initiatives,' *Educational Horizons*, 73:70.

Kane, Michael B., and Nidh Khattri (1995), 'Assessment reform,' the *Phi Delta Kappan*, 77: 32.

Krathwohl, David, et. al. (1956), *The taxonomy of educational objectives. Handbook two, affective domain.* London, England: Longmans Publishing House.

Noddings, Neil (1955). 'Teaching themes of care,' *Phi Delta Kappan*, 76 : 679.

Rao, D. Bhaskara and Mariow Ediger, (1996), *Scientific Attitude Vis-A-Vis Scientific Aptitude.* Chapter Two.

Rao, Digumarti Bhaskara (1996), *Teacher Education in India.* New Delhi, India: Discovery Publishing House.

Showers, Beverly, and Bruce Joyce (1996), 'The evolution of peer coaching,' Educational leadership, 53 : 16.

14

Writing and the Pupil in the Science Curriculum

Pupils need to become quality communicators of content in writing. Why? Scientists in laboratory setting must be able to write their findings in an accurate, objective approach so that effective communication among experts, as well as others, is in evidence. Not being able to communicate effectively in writing would greatly hinders scientific achievement in sequence on a continuing basis. Thus, in poorly developed written communication, scientists could not benefit from each other's research and findings. It behooves the teacher to encourage, assist, and motivate each pupil to do as well as possible in writing in ongoing science units of study.

Pupils may engage in writing on an individual or committee basis. Pertaining to committee or cooperative learning endeavours, Ediger (1997) wrote:

Cooperative learning is receiving considerable emphasis in

curriculum development. It is difficult to say how operative learning is different from the earlier term 'committee endeavours' stressed in curriculum development. Presently, it appears that most writers and speakers in education recommend using cooperative learning rather heavily in the classroom. Thus, pupils a class work cooperatively in projects. Activities, and experiences. The teacher becomes a guide or assistant to help learners achieve as much as possible. It is important here to emphasise that pupils work as a unit, not separately. Quality group dynamics becomes salient in cooperative learning. Learners then need to achieve goals and be goal centered. Competition among individuals is deemphasised and cooperation is salient. Individuals may work on different tasks in a team setting; however, these endeavours should represent cooperation in goal attainment.

Why is cooperative learning important? Presently, as well as in the future work place, individuals will be asked to work harmoniously with others. The individual who cannot work well with others will be handicapped. The are people from diverse cultures and abilities in any work place. Thus a pupil presently should be able to work with children of different values and talents. Being able to accept others is of utmost importance. Pupils individually need to be responsible to contribute optimally in cooperative endeavours. They need to think of themselves as a part of a group, not as competitive individuals. At issue here is how much time should be placed upon cooperative learning as compared to individual achievement. To think about individual endeavours in the curriculum, one must admit this is also important. Each person interacts with others and yet also needs to be able to use spare time wisely on an individual basis. A person is not a member of a group always but is also a person who has unique interests, needs, and purposes.

WRITING AND THE PUPIL

The science teacher needs to determine where each pupil is presently in achievement in writing. At this starting point, the teacher must guide learners on an individual basis to attain optimally and in a sequential manner.

A. Writing Experience Chart in Science

Early primary grade pupils tend to enjoy writing experience charts. A cooperative teacher who supervised a student teacher of mine taught a unit on *Animals in Our Lives.* She had three goldfish in an aquarium, tadpoles in a jar, a frog in a terrarium, a small garter snake in a different terrarium, and a pet canary in a bird cage. Pupils observed the goldfish carefully as they swam in the aquarium. Pupils were then asked to present ideas on what they saw to the teacher who in return recorded in writing observations presented. The following sentences, among others, were given in which first grade learners could see talk written down and experience writing:

1. The gold fish swam rapidly;
2. The bright colours mixed with the sunlight;
3. Water in the aquarium has bubbles inside of it;
4. Fish come up to breathe air;
5. It is fun to watch the fish being fed.

The numerals were then removed from the above experience chart and pupils read the content with teacher guidance. The teacher pointed to the words as the young learners orally read the content together with the teacher. There were numerous pupils who could not read the subject matter initially, but developed confidence to do so as the teacher patiently pronounced the words sequentially in the group exercise using the experience chart. The experience chart was saved and pasted on the wall. Pupils could then view the chart as the need arose. A week later, the teacher again read the contents of the chart with the children involved. Several asked to read it individually to the entire class. This developed considerable enthusiasm. The teacher announced to the class that anyone wishing to read the contents off the chart to her (the teacher) should do so at any time. At this point and stage of achievement, most of these first grade pupils read the subject matter on the chart, making very few errors. This chart and later ones developed were saved for learners to reread at their own convenience.

With the use of the experience chart approach in teaching writing, pupils can see talk written down. Thus what is said orally can be printed with the use of abstract symbols in grapheme-phoneme relationships. The experience chart concept of teaching reading is based upon learners having a personal experience. In this situation, the experience was to look at goldfish. Later experience charts would be based upon pupils seeing tadpoles, frogs, a snake, and a canary. This brought to the attention of pupils, fish, amphibians, reptiles, and birds as sequential classification of animals with backbones. Still later, the teacher brought her pet cat to class to show a mammal.

With concrete experiences of viewing lifelike, real animals, pupils began to use language to describe what was viewed. The use of oral communication was then inherent. Pupils listened to the ideas presented by others. The content that resulted was printed in neat, manuscript letters by the teacher. Learners then read the content orally with teacher guidance as the latter pointed to the words and phrases within each sentence. Thus oral communication, listening writing, and reading were experienced by each learner. The four language arts areas then become an inherent part of the science unit currently being studied.

When pupils are ready, they should write their own experience charts. This activity can be appropriate on any grade level.

Art work may well be related to writing experiences for pupils. Ediger and Rao (1996) wrote:

Learning activities involving art work can do much to enrich the elementary school science curriculum. Thus, the science teacher must provide a variety of learning experiences involving art in the science programme.

1. Developing murals. Pupils in a committee may plan and develop a mural pertaining to an ongoing unit of study in science. Thus, if pupils, for example, are studying a unit on 'Animals with Backbones,' they may decide upon scenes involving:

    a. diverse kinds of fish;

    b. amphibians. e.g. toads and frogs;

c. reptiles, e.g. snakes and turtles;

d. various kinds of birds;

e. mammals, e.g. human beings, monkeys, chimpanzees, gorillas.

2. Developing friezes. A series of pictures developed by a committee of pupils is inherent in cooperative planning and implementing the frieze concept in art work. A variety of media should be available to pupils when working on a frieze. Thus, crayons, coloured chalk, water colours, coloured pencils and finger paints should be readily accessible at the frieze center. If pupils, for example, are studying a unit on 'Animals Without Backbones,' they may develop a series of illustrations (a frieze) on:

a. protozoans, e.g., the amoeba, the paramecium, and the euglena;

b. porifera (sponges);

c. coelenterates, e.g. hydras, jellyfish, coral, and sea anemones;

d. platyhelminthes (flatworms) e.g. planarian, flukes, and tapeworms;

e. aschelminthes (roundworms), e.g. hookworms, ascaris, and the trichineilla;

f. annelida (segmented worms) e.g. earthworm and sandworm;

g. echinodermata (spiny animals) e.g. star fish, the sea urchin, the sea cucumber, and the sand dollar;

h. molusca (shellfish) e.g. clams, scallops, oysters, snails, and slugs;

i. arthropods, e.g. shrimp, lobsters, crayfish, and crabs. Insects are also members of this phylum—praying mantis, grasshopper, walking stick, dragonflies, ladybugs, and potato beetles.

B. Outlining Content in Science

Outlining content read from the basal or other reference source might well assist pupils to be able to organise information better in terms of sequence. A quality outline should possess the following parts:

1. The title;
2. Roman numerals to show the main ideas or divisions;
3. Capital letters under each main idea to show the relationship of these subdivisions with the main idea;
4. Details with ordered numerals under each subdivision to show relationships between the subdivision and the related details.

In outlining content, such as from the basal textbook in science, pupils may perceive the relationship of subordinate ideas to the main idea, the details to the subordinate idea, and the general sequence of subject matter. A pupil that focuses too much upon isolated facts tends to forget content sooner as compared to those who perceive that broader ideas exist such a subordinate and main ideas. Then too, broader ideas tend to become a part of the general repertoire of the learner sooner as compared to the acquisition of isolated facts. Thus, there is a structure of knowledge in science for the learner when he/she perceives that key ideas can be selected and subordinate content and details can be related rather readily to the main ideas. We recommend that when pupils are ready, not before, they experience practice in outlining subject matter, not for the sake of doing so, but to perceive knowledge as being related.

A quality outline on a purposeful topic provides the learner with an excellent tool to present an oral report to others in the classroom setting. The pupil should never read ideas from an outline, but use the ideas therein to present well organised subject matter to listeners. Thus, if the learner forgets sequential content in the report, he/she may then refer to the outline. Quality organisation of content assists the listener to acquire what is being presented. If an oral report contains randomly presented ideas, the chances are that comprehension by listeners will be difficult.

Pupils may receive practice in reading content in science that is poorly organised and rearrange the sentences so that coherence is in evidence. Noticing the differences between the two is important.

C. Writing Results From Science Experiments

A very useful writing experience for pupils is to write up science experiments that have been or will be performed in ongoing units of study. We believe that a plan developed by the teacher with pupil involvement will aid in writing that which is clear and distinct. First of all, the experiment needs to have a title which is meaningful to readers. If pupils are studying a unit or partial unit on water erosion of soil, a science experiment that is salient might well be entitled 'Water and Soil Erosion.' A problem then needs to be stated. The problem should be written clearly so that related information may be located as solutions. Hazy problem areas do not lend themselves to finding needed answers. A clearly worded problem might be the following: How does rainfall affect the soil in our schoolyard? Learners might then brainstorm answers to this question. No value judgement should be made of contributions of individual pupils. Respect for the thinking of others is necessary to generate ideas. The answers proposed in brainstorming should be recorded on the chalkboard to avoid unnecessary duplications. Higher levels of cognition are involved when pupils continue to offer answers. Initially, it probably is relatively easy to offer answers to the identified problem or question. After brainstorming, pupils need to ascertain which answers are acceptable and which are not. Science experiments should be performed in the classroom to determine the affects of water upon soil as well as observing in the out-of-doors what happens to soil with different levels of intensity of falling rain. As many variables as possible must be observed too, such as the slope of the land, the covering (grass) of the soil, and the kind of soil (clay, sandy, loam, among others). Inside the classroom, two boxes of equivalent soil with equal slope may be used initially. A similar amount of water should be poured over each box containing the soil. The only variable tested here is that one box has a grass covering over the soil whereas the other box does not. The amount of runoff of the soil for each box may be determined with a small container as broad as each box at the base to catch the eroded soil. Other variables to test for include different cover crops, different kinds of soil, as well as different amounts of water with variable intensity poured over each box.

These activities can also be used in testing the different answers given in brainstorming:

1. reading from diverse sources which shed light on water erosion of soil;
2. viewing audio-visual aids on causes and prevention of erosion of soil;
3. listening to qualified resource persons;
4. doing additional experiments and observing demonstrations;
5. making models of soil preservation including terracing, strip cropping, and trees/vegetative coverings to prevent erosion in its diverse forms.

Answers to questions should be viewed as tentative with chances of making necessary modifications as the need arises. Each step discussed above should be written with clarity and precision. Thus the problem or question, the brainstromed ideas, the data gathering, and needed modifications sections should be written with meaning and comprehension. Quality writing assists in communicating ideas more effectively.

A long standing debate has been in evidence in the teaching of science as to should it stress processes or products. A very popular approach in teaching science is Science—A Process Approach SAPA) developed by the American Association for the Advancement of Science (no date given): their advocated objectives are the following processes:

1. observing;
2. recognising and using number relations;
3. measuring;
4. recognising and using space time relations;

5. classifying;
6. communicating;
7. inferring;
8. predicting;
9. defining operationally;
10. formulating hypotheses;
11. interpreting data;
12. controlling variables;
13. experimenting.

The science teacher may stress the above named SAPA with or without using their materials of instruction. For example, objective number one above which is observing is very important in all science units of study. Here, the teacher may emphasise pupils observing a science experiment and all the sequential steps therein. The teacher may then appraise if pupils are observing carefully. This may be determined by teachers viewing attentiveness of learners during an experiment. Pupils might reveal their observational skills by writing up what happened sequentially in the ongoing experiment.

D. Writing Book Reports

Summarising what has been read from a library book directly related to an ongoing science unit can be highly educational for pupils. The learner should have had the opportunity to choose his/her own book to read, from among others, at a reading center. There are several kinds of writing activities that can be implemented here. The pupil needs to select which procedure to use when writing about subject matter read from a library book. Thus, the pupils may choose from among the following:

1. writing a certain number of main ideas covered in the chosen book;
2. writing what was perceived to be the most interesting content contained in the reading material;

3. writing one or more paragraphs pertaining to the central idea contained in the library book;
4. writing questions that remain unanswered pertaining to the content;
5. writing a different beginning or ending if the contents of the library book are highly creative, such as the book Miss Pickerel on Mars.

Writing summaries pertaining to content read from library books should encourage, not destroy interest, in reading and writing content in science. The teacher should evaluate achievement here and in all writing experiences based on the following criteria:

1. use standards that assist the learner to notice that which needs to be improved upon;
2. have reasonable standards for each pupil, not excessively difficult nor at too low a level of achievement;
3. do not emphasise too many corrections for any one pupil to make, lest the involved child is overwhelmed with corrections that need to be made;
4. focus upon ideas in the written product, into exclusively upon the mechanics of writing such as spelling, punctuation, and grammar;
5. emphasise clarity of ideas expressed, not quantity in content written.

It is important for teachers to have conferences with pupils, one on one, too assist learners to improve over previous attempts at written work. The conference should stress caring for the pupil in becoming a better writer. Negative criticism must be avoided in the conference setting. A positive attitude toward the learner and his/her ability to improve in writing in all school endeavours is a must.

Relevant principles of psychology in teaching and learning must be followed when pupils engage in ongoing units of study... in the science curriculum. Thus, experiences for pupils should follow these standards or criteria:

1. learning activities should be interesting and meaningful;
2. pupils must have needed background information and possess adequate readiness for new units of study;
3. learners should perceive purpose in learning in ongoing units of study;
4. each pupil should be guided to achieve optimal development in understandings, skills, an attitudinal objectives;
5. learner progress must be continuously evaluated to determine progress in achieving stated objectives.

E. Journal Writing in Science

Pupils need to be given time to engage in journal writing. This provides opportunities for learners to reflect upon what has been learned in ongoing science units and lessons. Journal entries may be dated. What is written in the journal is up to the pupil. A pupil may then write what transpired in a science experiment or demonstration. The learner may wish to focus upon salient ideas discussed in a committee setting. With reflection, the involved learner will remember better what has been learned due to thinking upon key ideas or concepts stressed in science. The pupil might desire to write about attitudes and interests developed in science as a result of teaching and learning experiences.

Should the teacher appraise the quality of these journal entries? If not, how does a teacher know if the time devoted to journal writing is worthwhile and assists the learner to attain relevant objectives? If the teacher appraises the quality of journal writing, should the contents be graded? These and other vital questions need careful consideration.

We would suggest that teachers encourage pupils to share their writings. This can be done by sharing content written with the teacher on a voluntary basis. Pupils might also meeting committees to share what has been written. It is best if pupils are not coerced to show what was written in the journal. However, a pupils may waste time and pretend he/she is writing, but is day dreaming or writing irrelevant content. We believe the teacher can and must observe pupils to notice that achievement is taking place in all learning opportunities. A general overview in observing learner achievement may suffice in appraising pupil progress in writing journal entries. The teacher needs to be a good observer and use quality criteria to appraise pupil progress. A listing of criteria may assist the teacher to make justifiable decisions pertaining to pupil journal writing. Among others, these include the following:

1. time on task is vital;
2. conscientious and judicious statements are a must;
3. proper order of written subject matter is salient;
4. clarity of content is necessary;
5. accurate mechanics in writing are needed to the degree it makes the written content more meaningful.

There should be a variety of kinds of learning opportunities in writing so that pupils feel that written work is utilitarian and purposeful.

F. Writing Diary Entries

Pupils individually or in committees need to have ample opportunities to write on a day to day basis what was learned in a science lesson. Each entry should be dated. By writing what was learned on a daily basis in science, writers review previously acquired information. With review, subject matter learned will be retained for a longer period of time than would otherwise be the case. Pupils should participate on a rotating basis in writing these diary entries. The following are examples of diary entries written by a committee of learners:

October One. The teacher explained to us the differences between sheet and gulley erosion. Emphasis was also placed upon the amount of top soil lost each year due to erosion. Farm crop yields decrease when rich top soil is not available for the growing of wheat, soybeans, and corn, among other grains. Marginal and tilled hilly land, in particular, are subject to increased erosion.

October Two. We went outdoors to notice gulley erosion beginnings on our playground. We leveled the soil and seeded grass to avoid erosion. We then came into the classroom to watch a video-tape on 'Preventing soil Erosion.' Before observing the video, we hypothesised on ways to prevent soil erosion. During the video, we were asked to list and describe different ways to prevent or minimise soil erosion as presented in the video. These ways include using terraces, seeding grass and planting trees, as well as emphasising strip cropping, among others.

The teacher may discuss with the entire class what might be added to each diary entry. These entries should be kept so that pupils might use these for review. Individual or committee members' names may appear on each page of diary entries and bound for future reference. Hopefully, the learning opportunity will increase learner interest, purpose, and meaning for writing in science.

G. Writing Log Entries

Pupils may review and combine the diary entries so that a log may be written. A log covers a longer period of time in terms of lesson content as compared to diary entries. Thus a log may pertain to recording what was learned within a week. The diary entries then become a part of the log. Individuals and committees who record the log entries must read carefully each diary entry so that broader generalisations may be written such as in a log. Log entries should be bound together with the diary entries so that pupils might review and rehearse what had been learned previously. Log entries provide a good basis in reviewing for a oncoming test.

Standards to follow in writing log entries include the following:

1. ideas should be specific enough so that misinterpretation is not possible;
2. quality human relations need to be stressed in any committee endeavours;
3. appropriate order of content is necessary so that sequence is in evidence;

4. correct spelling of words, punctuation, indentation of paragraphs, and grammar should be in evidence in order to communicate effectively. However, the focal point is on ideas in the logs, not the mechanics of writing;

5. log writing must encourage an increased desire to write rather than writing being perceived as a chore.

If pupils are to become good writers, writing should be emphasised across the curriculum. The curriculum area of science provides its many opportunities for pupils to become good writers. The are numerous purposes in writing in science. The author here recommends that pupils participate actively and fully in written work in ongoing lessons and units of study in science.

USING WORD PROCESSORS

One of the greatest boon to writing has been the use of the word processor. The word processor indeed eliminates much drudgery attached to writing. The mistakes made in typing can quickly be corrected on the monitor before a final copy is sent through the printer. Once can secure the desired copy, reading it on the monitor, before printing occurs. A perfect copy may then results even if a person's typing is not the best. A spell check programme eliminates spelling errors in a hurry without retyping any part of the document. There are limitations here in that the computer does not catch errors in homonyms nor in selected other kinds of errors such as in punctuation or capitalisation. The user of the word processor still needs to be able to proof read typed content carefully and oh so carefully. However, spelling errors can all be taken care of in a very short time indeed with a spell check programme. Typing errors can be taken care of quickly by looking to see what is on the monitor and making needed revisions when proofing. We find it enjoyable to use a word processor in typing manuscript content each day. One can make much headway in typing with a persona computer that is very user friendly. A person who can type using the old typewriter can learn very quickly to use a word processor and be amased at its capabilities!

Pupils who use word processors, when ready, feel ownership of the tasks involved thereon. The pupil with teacher assistance determines the content to be put into the computer. He/she sequences the content to be typed. Revisions are made in terms of the writer's goals. When changes need to be made such as rearrangement of ideas in the typing, this can be done quickly. No longer does a writer need to start all over in typing a page if a single error has been made. Whiteout does not need to be used in making corrections as was true of typewriter use. The writing curriculum must be updated so that each learner can benefit from modern technology and its applications. With word processors, the following conclusions may well be emphasised:

1. writing tends to be more enjoyable since errors made can quickly and conveniently be corrected with user friendly technology;
2. the rearrangement of ideas for quality sequence can be rapidly implemented, making it unnecessary to start over again in the typing process;
3. pupils may feel that what is done using the word processor is completely in their hands. The pupil gives the commands to the computer and completely controls what will follow in terms of content and the mechanics of writing;
4. content types can involve diverse purposes such as formal and creative writing. Each of the purposes discussed throughout this manuscript pertaining to writing may be emphasised using the word processor;
5. pupils individually or in dyads may writer using the word processor depending upon goals stressed in writing in science. Goals may stress individual as well as group or committee endeavours in the curriculum.

Conclusion

The science teacher needs to provide a variety of writing activities for pupils. This is necessary to provide for individual differences. Pupils should be guided to become increasingly proficient in writing. One cannot expect a pupil. to blossom immediately into becoming a good writer. Rather, sequentially, each pupil can build repertoire of writing skills. By comparing a pupil's past written product with his present written work, the teacher can notice the degree to which a learner is achieving more fully. Writing is a basic in the curriculum. The science teacher should incorporate writing experiences when it assists pupils to acquire more subject matter content. Acquisition of facts, concepts, generalisations, principles, and laws of science are vital. So too must skills objectives be emphasised in teaching-learning situations. Thus writing for a variety of purposes in science is salient. The science teacher needs to notice if quality attitudes are a by-product of subject matter and skills stressed in the science curriculum. Each pupil is unique in achievement and needs adequate provision so that continuous progress is possible in science. Pertaining to stressing a variety of writing activities in science, Ediger and Rao (1996) summarised the following:

1. develop an outline. Each pupil with teacher guidance may develop an outline pertaining to content that has been read relating to an ongoing unit of study...
2. develop a written report. The content of the outline may be used to develop report. Written reports may deal with:
    a. summaries of experiments conducted in ongoing units of study in science;
    b. diary entries kept by pupils on a daily basis pertaining to understandings, skills, and attitudes acquired. Members on a committee may be rotated in writing these diary entries...
3. write poetry such as haiku, free verse, couplets, triplets, and quatrains...
4. other forms of written work such as writing plays announcements, and notices, as well as writing biographies of famous scientists.

A variety of kinds of written work should be emphasised so that pupils learn to communicate clearly and accurately in science.

References

American Association for the Advancement of Science (no date given). *Science A Process Approach*. Washington, DC: Ginn and Company.

Ediger, Marlow (1997). *The Modern Elementary School*. Kirksville, Missouri: Simpson Publishing Company, page 63.

Ediger, Marlow (1996), 'The Pupil, Geology, and the Science Curriculum, *School Science*, Vol. 34, No. 34, page 26.

Ediger, Marlow and D. Bhaskara Rao (1996), *Science Curriculum*. New Delhi, India: Discovery Publishing House, pages 90-91, 91-92.

Ediger, Marlow, and D. Bhaskara Rao (2000), *Teaching Mathematics Successfully*. New Delhi, India: Discovery Publishing House

15

Reading in the Science Curriculum

Science teachers need to be teachers of reading since the act of being able to read and comprehend is necessary in problem solving activities. There should be a variety of learning opportunities in ongoing lessons and units of study, and reading subject matter is one important facet of achieving. It certainly is true that some classrooms stress reading of content to the point that other kinds of experiences are almost non-existent. Reading is one approach in learning in science.

What might the teacher do to assists pupils to comprehend science subject matter more thoroughly in reading? There is always the problem of new words that pupils cannot identify in reading science content. How should these situations be handled? We will offer several suggestions that our student teachers and cooperating teachers whom we supervised in the public schools used.

1. A good reader pronounces words that are unknown to pupils as they read silently. As a first grader during

the 1934-35 school year, and later elementary school years also, one of the authors was asked by the classroom teacher to pronounce unknown words to pupils when they raised their hands during silent reading. This approach can be overdone if the same pupil is asked sequentially to pronounce unknown words to others. Pupils individually would also like to pursue their own reading interests. Sometimes, a pupil pronounces an unknown word too quickly to a learner, not permitting adequate time for the latter to ascertain what the unknown word is. If a pupil does not know what the unknown is, he/she should have enough time to determine what the correct word is. The opposite situation occurs also whereby a pupil has to wait too long to obtain help with identification of unknown words when reading science content.

2. The teacher should write new words on the chalkboard in neat manuscript letters prior to pupils reading a selection in science. He/she needs to go over each printed word several times with pupils in class. The teacher needs to be certain that pupils are looking at each word as it is being pronounced by the teacher or individual pupils. Using this approach assists pupils to see the new words on the chalkboard in print before seeing them while reading. Hopefully learners will recognise each word as it is being read in science.

The printed words may be written individually or within a sentence on the chalkboard. We prefer the latter approach since it is more contextual. Pupils may learn to use context clues more thoroughly when seeing new words printed within sentences. Learners need to attach meaning to these new words. Context clues many times provide the needed information for pupils to understand needed meanings. Sometimes, a word needs to be defined so that pupils know intended meanings and can read content more proficiently.

3. cassette recordings may be made of science content pupils are to read, be it from the basal or from a library book. The teacher need not always make these

recordings, if his/her schedule is very busy. We have observed good readers make excellent cassette recordings of science subject matter. The same content may be listened to by a reader as he/she reads sequential ideas from a book. If the reader does not identify selected words in context, the recorded voice will provide the necessary information. This approach can be used very successfully when pupils read in science. Carlo (1996) wrote:

For many young children and poor readers, there's a substantial time lag between when they see and hear a word. That lag produces slow, laborious reading that makes comprehension all but impossible. It's terribly difficult for students to recall what a passage is about when they have to spend so much time figuring out each new word.

A recorded book can, in effect, do what the child is not yet able to do naturally. It verbalises the printed words with the correct pace, phrasing, and expression. As a result students make fewer reading errors, and the possibility of forming incorrect reading patterns is diminished.

Best of all, it's not necessary to recall dull, simple reading materials to develop a student's sight vocabulary.

4. instead of reading from the basal text, pupils may read subject matter from library books related to the ongoing lesson or unit or study. There needs to be an adequate number of library books so that a learner may choose a book that is on his/her reading level. We observed several lessons in public schools where this procedure worked very successfully. Pupils would then share with the entire class that which had been read. Ediger (1996) wrote:

One approach in emphasising sequence is to have students choose the order of experience within a flexible environment. Thus, for example, in individualised reading, a learner selects which library books to read sequentially. After reading a book, the pupil has a conference with the teacher to appraise progress. After the completion of the conference with the teacher, the learner is ready to select the next library book to read. The teacher intervenes in library book selection if the student is unable to choose and complete reading a book.

In situations involving individualised reading in science, the pupil orders his/her own experiences. Sequence, it is felt, resides within the involved learner. Others, the teacher included, cannot select the order of goals for a learner to attain. The student in individualised reading must do the processing of content. A teacher determined science reading curriculum does not work, according to advocates of individualised reading. Humanism, a psychology of learning, strongly advocates concepts such as the following:

1. student-teacher planning of the science curriculum;
2. learners choosing from diverse objectives which to achieve and which to omit;
3. learning centers from which pupils may select their learning opportunities;
4. students being involved in determining objectives within a contract system. In contract form, the pupil with teacher guidance plans which experiences to complete along with the date of completion. Both pupil and teacher sign the contractual agreement in science;
5. a good reader might read the selection for the day from the basal science text orally to slower learners in reading. The latter may follow along in their own textbooks as the words are read orally. These participants may be seated close together in an atmosphere of respect so that optimal listening is involved. The good reader should explain difficult concepts to pupils as they are being met in print. After hearing the science content read orally, we have noticed slow readers who desire to read the entire selection to themselves;
6. peer teaching can be quite effective in reading science content. With peer teaching, two or three pupils read the contents orally from the basal text; each follows along in his/her book as the other reads. If a slow

reader does into wish to read orally, the other two pupils my do the oral reading. These learners may also discuss salient ideas from the science content read. The goal in all of these reading endeavours is to assist pupils to comprehend and understand science content, not to ridicule or minimise. Respect for others is always salient in each science lesson and unit of study;

7. we have observed where no basal texts are used in science and pupils read content from library books directly related to the unit being taught in the science curriculum. Pupils then have done an outstanding job of telling what was read as it relates to the ongoing discussion in thematic unit teaching. Pupils individually tend to select library books that are on their reading level to comprehend well. We believe many pupils feel more at ease reading from library books as compared to the basal. Canney and Neuenfeldt (1993) wrote:

Most elementary teachers still use a basal for reading instruction. However, it appears that teachers combine children's books and basals, which is a change from previous reports. Teachers perceive themselves to be in line with school district policy to support their preference for a basal/tradebooks combination. Most teachers also say that they have access to an adequate supply of tradebooks and 85 per cent believe that children should read independently for 15 to 30 minutes daily. Finally, regardless of teaching experience, formal training in reading, or grade level taught, most teachers prefer a combination of basal and tradebooks in their reading programmes.

8. one of us have also successfully observed whereby two volunteers from the community assisted selected learners who had difficulty identifying words in reading from the science textbook. The volunteers listened carefully to pupils read orally in a designated area. They helped pupils with recognising unknown words and pronouncing selected words to these learners as was needed. Seemingly, these same pupils were then ready to read the same science selection on their own. They were also able to enter the discussions effectively in the classroom pertaining to what had been read;

9. there are teachers who have simplified content contained in the text. By using less complex words and shorter sentences, select pupils might now read and understand the revised subject matter. Generally, teachers have confided in me that the approach is good but the work involved in rewriting takes up an excessive amount of time;

10. sometimes, slow readers have read well from the basal after having listened to the class discussion covering the related subject matter. By listening carefully to the discussion, slow readers may be able to read the same content from the basal science textbook due to possessing readiness information for reading. We are not entirely in agreement with this procedure; however, the teacher needs to assist pupils with a variety of procedures in word recognition and comprehension so that each pupil may attain more optimally in the science curriculum. McNinch and Gruber (1996) wrote:

What children ultimately learn about literacy is heavily influenced by the expectations, skills, and concerns that parents, teachers, and principals share. All players in literacy development should possibly share common perceptions, especially in the basic philosophical and pedagogical beliefs. If children are to receive coordinated instruction. Do parents, teachers, and principals agree on the basic reading issue of whole language versus traditional skill development?… .

Parents, teachers, and principals each perceived that the development of literacy in young children is developed broadly both through traditional practices and whole language, emerging literacy routines. The research groups find favour with traditional readiness activities… . Also, they perceive that children learn literacy as an emerging activity through such activities as repetitive listening, shared story telling, invented spelling, and creative writing.

Emerging literacy is a mutual product of the home and school environment acting together with common interests. It does appear that the literacy providers, parents and teachers, are supporting each other in an eclectic approach to learning.

How much assistance should be given in Word Recognition Techniques? There is no easy answer to this questions. So often, it is felt and believed that the teacher of reading alone should assist pupils in word recognition and identification. A problem then results with pupils who need much guidance to identify unknown words in reading in the content fields, such as in science. Certainly, pupil achievement, in part, will be due to how well a learner reads and comprehends subject matter to solve problems. Thus, it behooves the teacher to assist pupils in reading science materials. The more that reading is stressed as a means of learning the more likely it will be that pupils need assistance in word recognition.

There are six word recognition skills that pupils need to develop skill in. The use of picture clues to unlock unknown words will be used more so on the early primary grade levels as compared to later times. Why? There are more pictures in a basal science text on the early primary grade levels as compared to later times. If a first grader, for example, does not know a word, he/she may look at a picture on the same page and the unknown word will usually become known. There are exceptions here so the primary grade pupil, as well as at later sequential stages of learning, will need to learn additional procedures, other than using picture clues, to unlock unknown words.

Phonics is taught more than any other techniques to unlock unknown words. There are degrees of regularity in using phonics to recognise words. Thus there are many sound/symbol relationships that are consistent in the English language. The words—ban, can, dan, fan, man, nan, pan, ran, tan—follow a consistent spelling between each grapheme and phoneme. Sometimes, only a few letters in a word will have consistent spelling between symbol and sound, such as the following words—globe, scale, miles, and agriculture. Selected words are spelled very irrationally, such as through, bough cough, bought, and dough. Thus, there are words or word parts that need to be learned through the sight method, not phonics. Learning words through the sight method makes it so that the learner has no approach to use to unlock unknown words in science.

The use of context clues is a very valuable procedure to

use to unlock an unknown word in science. Thus if a pupil does not know how to pronounce a word, he/she looks careful at the surrounding words and may be able to identify a word that fits in and makes sense. Sometimes, there are not enough clues in the surrounding words to assist in determining what the unknown word is, such as 'I see a... . There are too many words that make sense contextually. But if the reader uses phonics also, perhaps the unknown can be identified, such as 'I see a l... .' Here, the 'l' letter is very consistent in sound and the pupil may now be able to determine what fits in.

There use of syllabication skills may prove very helpful to the reader to unlock unknown words in science. A word that appears to be new and unknown may not be so if the pupil divides the 'unknown' into syllables. For example, the word 'unimportant' looks long until the pupil notices the prefix 'un'. If the pupil knows the prefix 'un' means 'not', then it should be very possible to identify and attach meaning to an unknown word. Many prefixes and suffixes appear again and again in reading and the pupil soon becomes skillful in dividing a science word into syllables to identify and pronounce it correctly.

We recommend that teachers of science be teachers of reading and assist pupils to learn approaches in word recognition which make for independent readers. Science lessons and units do emphasise reading as a means of acquiring information; therefore, pupils need to comprehend subject matter through reading.

DIVERSE PURPOSES IN READING

There are many purposes for reading in science and not one purpose or reason only. Comprehension of science content is an overall goal. Certainly, pupils should read for meaning and not for the sake of going through the motions only. The concept of 'comprehension' need to be broken down to more specific aims in the reading of science content. We believe that reading to solve problems in science should be the major goal. Most science educators put high priority in having pupils read to solve problems. Certainly, life in society demands that we identify and solve vital problem areas. There is much confusion as to what can be termed as a problem. Should these come from pupils only with teacher assistance? Might teachers select problems which pupils accept once readiness for learning has been developed? We have observed in classrooms where pupils do accept problems identified by teachers if there are stimulating ways of doing this. With stimulating audio-visual aids presented meaningfully to capture learner interest, pupils might well accept teacher identified problems in science for solving.

In addition to reading to solve science problems, pupils should read critically. Here pupils analyse subject matter read. When analysing, learners separate component parts so that each facet may be assessed thoroughly or at the developmental level of the learner. We have observed pupils debate the accuracy of selected statements after analysing. Reference books and other sources are looked at to check accuracy. There are many slogans that abound in society and these may be found in content being viewed carefully by pupils. Are slogans, for example, like the following true?

1. That government is best which governs least. Is there a chance that so little government makes for anarchy?
2. It's not guns that kill, but people kill;
3. Let's get government off our backs and our of our pockets;
4. Lets's not throw money at problems;
5. Long prison sentences deter crime.

Each slogan should be evaluated in terms of being based on evidence or are they myths? Sometimes, the bandwagon approach is in evidence in society in that everyone joins the majority in whatever is being stressed. We believe we are very guilty of this in education. For example, in the early 1970s, performance contracting came in big into American education. Thus the business world entered the educational arena by contracting for providing educational services to public schools. They promised larger gains in pupil achievement than what traditional approaches could produce. For every pupil that achieved, according to what was in the business contract, the company would receive that amount as specified in the agreement. There were many schools wanting to join in on performance contracting since "pupils would achieve at a higher level." This plan soon fizzled out in that pupils did poorer as compared to using traditional approaches in teaching. Second, many teachers taught directly to the test in performance contracting which other schools could not do. Teaching directly to the test items should make for higher achievement if test results are used to determine pupil progress. Performance contracting has reappeared but under much less publicity and fanfare, such as in Educational Alternatives, based in Minneapolis, Minnesota. The band wagon approach needs to be analysed in critical thinking situations. 'The everybody is doing it' philosophy can be very harmful to individuals and groups in society, as well as in the science curriculum.

Pertaining to critical reading, Harris and Sipay (1985) wrote:

An important kind of critical reading involves comparison of two or more sources of information. Children are usually amazed when they first find two authorities contradicting each other. An experience like that can serve as a preliminary to discussion of such questions as the reputation and prestige of each author, his impartiality, or bias, the comparative recency of the two sources, and so on. Reading experiences of this sort develop naturally when children do wide reading to find data on a problem. The teacher should be alert and should make use of such occasions as stepping stones toward a more mature attitude on the credibility of reading matter. In the study of current events, comparison of treatment of an event by two newspapers or magazines of opposing points of view can form an effective point of departure.

A second kind of critical reading involves considering new ideas or information in the light of one's previous knowledge and beliefs. The thoughtful reader asks... Is it reasonable. Is it possible? He does not, of course, automatically reject the unfamiliar idea or challenging conclusion. But... becomes doubly alert when he finds disagreements with what he has previously accepted as true.

Creative thinking is another relevant goal for pupils to.

achieve in reading science content. Learners need to be able to brainstorm and come up with unique, novel ideas in ongoing lessons and units of study. In the area of reading science content, pupils, for example, might have heard the following:

1. the planet Saturn has a solid core or ring around itself;
2. there is no relationship between dinosaurs and birds on the evolutionary scale;
3. amphibians are not becoming fewer in number on the planet earth;
4. all dinosaurs were cold blooded animals.

The teacher needs to stimulate pupils to raise innovative questions as well as come up with unique responses to statements made by others or read from older reference sources. Thus pupils may come up with updated information pertaining to the above four statements. There are numerous ways that pupils can come up with creative answers to problem areas:

1. Have a committee read from a variety of recent reference sources and give a report to the class on ringlets that encircle the planet Saturn. Illustrations may be shown as the oral report is given. A model solar system might also assist pupils to understand contents in the report;
2. assist a committee to discuss and summarise contents on recent discoveries in Patagonia, Argentina pertaining to a possible linkage between dinosaurs and birds in prehistoric times. A map should be used/drawn showing the region of these findings.

In addition to giving science reports, pupils may also show what has been learned through

1. the making of dioramas, models, movie sets, and flannel boards with cutouts;
2. dramatic activities including formal, creative, pantomime, and role playing;
3. outlining, summarising, concluding, and paraphrasing;

4. developing parts for and presenting a reader's theater presentation;
5. doing a collage, a bulletin board display, and an outside the classroom series of displays, placed on corridor walls;
6. engaging in discussions, debates, committee work, individual study plans, use of learning centers for enrichment, reading library books, and pupil/teacher planning of learning opportunities;
7. performing science experiments and demonstrations. This is the heart of the science curriculum.

In addition to problem solving, as well as creative and critical thinking in reading science content, pupils should also practice reading for causes and effects such as in the causes for natural disasters. Events read should be evaluated in terms of causes for happenings. This is a precise aim of reading instruction in the science curriculum. Pupils then should use methods of acquiring and appraising information in the same way as does the professional scientist.

An additional skill in reading science content is reading for factual information. Sometimes, it seems, according to many educators, that factual acquisition is not necessary. But, this should not be the case. Facts provide the building blocks for pupils to use in developing concepts and generalisations. A relationship of facts, perceived accurately by the learner, should make for quality generalisations. Within a concept, there also are many facts. Look at the following generalisation that might well be important for pupils to achieve in a unit on Rocks and Minerals:

1. there are igneous, sedimentary and metamorphic rocks. There are four concepts here—igneous, sedimentary, metamorphic, and rocks.

Inside of each concept, there are numerous facts. Thus the concept—igneous—refers to molten materials such as lava or magma that come from the interior of the planet earth.

Reading for facts then is important to develop concepts and generalisations. Should facts be read for their own sake? We do much reading of subject matter and find factual reading for its own sake can be quite interesting and enjoyable. For example, we have found very little practical use for knowing facts pertaining the thinking of Aristotle in ancient Athens whereby he believed the brain to be the place of cooling of the human blood. We have noticed that many others do not find Aristotle interesting to read pertaining to his beliefs on physiology and the natural environment. Thus our students, in most cases, cannot recall these events and yet all admit having studied Aristotle's philosophy on the human body and nature. Maybe, this says to us that much of what is learned in science is personal and purposeful to the individual. Thus the science teacher needs to have an ample number of reading activities selected/or designed for the individual. Cooperative learning in reading is important, but so are individual endeavours. The teacher needs to stress group endeavours as well as individual projects and experiences in reading.

Also, adequate emphasis should be placed on how to do something in reading. We have noticed and observed pupils making models by following directions. Thus model cars, planes, trucks, among others, are assembled through reading. Here, pupils tend to perceive much purpose or reasons for reading. Teachers need to locate materials for pupils which the latter finds interesting and purposeful. These ingredients assist pupils to become better readers. Exercises in workbooks, textbooks, and project construction contain directions which need to be followed accurately. Wrong responses from pupils can come about if directions are not followed accurately and thoroughly. Pupils need much practice in reading to follow directions. They should be able to state directions read into their very own words so that meaning and understanding are there.

Pupils should develop skills early in the public school years of becoming research orientated. We believe that scanning information is very important. The skill of scanning can be learned by pupils at a young age. Many of our pupils will be going on to higher education where this skill becomes important in locating information for term projects and papers developed. In the workplace, workers may also need to scan pages to see where relevant information is located, such as an automobile mechanic scanning pages in a manual to notice how to repair an air-conditioner in an older car.

Closely related to scanning is the reading skill of skimming content. Skimming also is a rather rapid type of reading since not every word is read when a person skims for a few ideas such as names, dates, and places. If a pupil reads to determine the birth and death of Louis Pasteur he/she will look for numerals in skimming an entire page or more. Or, if a learner is looking for Edward Jenner and his inoculation procedures for small pox the name of that person will have capital letters for each name. The capital letters set the name off from other subject matter on the page, except for the beginning of a sentence or the names of cities. Generally, there are very few items that start with capital letters on a page of content. Knowing this assists the individual in doing a better job of skimming. Pertaining to skimming, Ruben (1983) wrote:

Setting purposes for reading is a crucial factor in reading. Students need to learn that they read for different purposes. If they are reading for pleasure, they may either read quickly or slowly based on the way they feel. If they are studying or reading information that is new to them, they will probably read very slowly. If, however, they are looking up a telephone number, a name, a date or looking over a paragraph for its topic, they will read much more rapidly. Reading rapidly to find or locate information is called skimming. All skimming involves fast reading: however, there are different kinds of skimming. Skimming for a number, a date, or name can be done much more rapidly than skimming for the topic of a paragraph or to answer specific questions. (Some persons call the most rapid reading scanning and the less rapid reading skimming.) Teachers should help pupils recognise that they read rapidly to locate some specific information, but that once they have located what they want, they may read the surrounding information more slowly.

It is quite obvious that there are numerous purposes for reading in science. The purpose involved determines how rapidly one will read or how slowly. The amount of background information possessed as well as the complexity of the materials will also determine the rate at which something is read.

Teachers need to assess reading comprehension of pupils. Barr and Sadow (1985) wrote:

An assessment of reading comprehension serves a twofold purpose. It enables the teacher to make an informed decision regarding the level of materials that would be appropriate for instruction, and it alerts the teacher to a student's specific instructional needs. Such an assessment is generally undertaken when there is some question concerning a student's present placement in instructional materials or the type of instructional emphasis that would enable the student to make better progress. For the most part these questions arise when a student is not performing well during daily lessons. But they should arise also when a student is performing extremely well. For instructional materials should be neither so difficult that the student can have little success with them nor so easy as to require little thought or intentional effort. Thus the student who is always able to answer the teacher's questions may need more challenging materials, while the student who can seldom answer questions correctly may need less demanding ones. Teachers must make every effort to see the instructional materials are optimal from this point of view.

HOW SHOULD A READING ASSIGNMENT BE INTRODUCED?

The science teacher should have several strategies available to guide pupils in reading a new selection. We would recommend first that the teacher try to ascertain which words in the lesson to be read, pupils may have difficulty with. Certainty is not involved here. The teacher, however, should know his/her pupils well enough to do a good job of hypothesising which words pupils may have trouble identifying unless there is assistance prior to reading. We recommend that these words be printed on the chalkboard so that all can see them clearly, written in sentences. Have pupils trade off reading an entire sentence with the new word therein. It is best if pupils get as much practice as possible in pronouncing what are perceived, by the teacher, to be new words. Go over the new words within sentences as often as is necessary so that pupils may master these words and identify them when reading science content silently. We would make certain that there is meaning and understanding of these new words as a part of learning to identify each word. Then too we believe learners need to identify one or more reasons for reading in science. These reasons may be stated in question form and printed on the chalkboard. Thus pupils have a better idea as to what to read for and that being to obtain answers to questions.

After pupils have had a change to read the selection silently or orally, the teacher may lead a discussion of science content read which may answer each question. The discussion should be relaxed and not hurried. Pupils need to have opportunities to think of possible answers to science questions. Questions raised by pupils other than what was read from the text may also be discussed.

We believe there should be enrichment activities for pupils following the discussion of the story read from the basal. The following are possibilities:

1. learners individually may read library books on the same topic or by the same author. The teacher needs to introduce selected library books to pupils to what appetites for reading;
2. performing science experiments, dramatising, pantomiming, model making, and constructing items that relate directly to content read can be good ways to make use of knowledge acquired;
3. rewriting the contents from the library book involving science fiction;
4. explaining the content orally or through reader's theater might well be challenging for a few pupils;
5. writing test items in science to cover the contents in the reading selection can be interesting for selected learners. The test items may be exchanged among pupils in order to take the test. Pupils should receive feedback on the quality of their writing of each test item.

SELECTING SCIENCE TEXTBOOKS

Teachers are generally involved in a committee to choose basal science textbook series for the oncoming school year. Certainly, each team member needs to have quality standards in mind when making textbook decisions. We have had numerous science teachers say to us that they believe the following criteria assist in making the best choice possible:

1. The text needs to bring in a reasonable number of new concepts on each page or chapter. If too many new words are mentioned per page, the reading task could be overwhelmingly difficult. Should there be too few new words per page, the book may lack challenge for pupils;
2. Pupil should have a chance to read from each series being considered for adoption to assist in determining which text would best meet the needs of learners;
3. The textbook being considered needs to be written in a style and manner which optimalise comprehension of contents;
4. There needs to be a helpful related manual for teacher use in choosing objectives, learning activities, and appraisal procedures. Generally, there are marginal notes which may assist teachers in the task of teaching science;
5. An ample number of illustrations and diagrams should be in evidence in each chapter to guide pupils to understand content more optimally;
6. The size of the type should be appropriate for the pupils who will be reading from the text;
7. There should be an adequate number of headings and subheadings in each selection of reading to orientate the learner to what the ensuing content will be about;
8. An adequate number of study aids for pupils should be in the textbook. Experimentation should be at the heart of teaching science;
9. The textbook should contain an adequate number of summaries and previews for pupils;
10. There should be a table of contents, index, and glossary for pupil use. An index and glossary may not be in a text for young learners.

Participants on the committee to select the science text should invite comments from other teachers who will also be using the adopted textbook. Members of the selection team need to have available for all teachers an adequate number of science series so that decisions can be made on which text should be adopted. Comments made in the selection process should be courteous and clear. Respect for the thinking of others is important. Due consideration should be given each book. Slighting a series is not in the best interests of selecting a truly quality book in teaching science.

PERSONALISED READING IN THE SCIENCE CURRICULUM

There are times when pupils should select their very own library books to read that directly relate to the ongoing science unit. Generally, when pupils individually choose what is to be read, they select that which is interesting and on their very own reading level. The text may be too difficult for a few children to read even with quality methods of obtaining pupil readiness for reading a given selection. Thus an answer may be to have pupils individually choose a library book that has similar information as does the basal textbook.

After choosing a book, from among many others, the learner settles down to read the content. The teacher does not intervene unless a pupil cannot decide upon which book to read or gets bogged down on what is being pursued presently. If a pupil cannot decide upon which book to read, the teacher needs to provide assistance. If a pupil gets bogged down on what is read, the teacher needs to determine reasons for doing so. The following could be inherent reasons:

1. the book is too difficult for the pupil to read and understand;
2. The pupil needs to be encouraged to pursue what is difficult to read;
3. a peer approach may be used whereby two pupils change off reading the contents to each other and assist where there are problems;
4. the contents may be cassette recorded by a good

reader and the involved pupil may listen to the contents, following along in his book, as the tape is being played. The learner then may be able to read the book on his/her own;

5. rewards may be given to honour those pupils who read a designated number of library books within an interval of time. Following the completion of the reading of the library book, the learner may share the contents with others during discussion time in the ongoing science unit of study. The learner may also have a conference with the teacher to appraise comprehension and understanding of what had been read. The teacher may also check fluency of oral reading, word attack attack skills, and attitudes toward reading content in science. Ideally, the pupil should share during class discussions what was learned from reading library books. Each library book read relates directly to the ongoing lesson or unit of study in science being pursued.

EXPERIENCE CHARTS IN SCIENCE

Primary grade pupils, in particular, like to develop experience charts with teacher guidance. Although when pupils can do their very own writing, they should do so. As the name indicates, an experience chart relates directly to what pupils have experienced in science. For example, a first grade teacher may have the following objects on an interest center to initiate a unit:

1. a model self-propelled combine and a tractor. Here, pupils may study simple machines, involved in physics, inherent in the combine and tractor;
2. model farm implements for the tractor to pull. A further study of simple machines involved in performing work may be stressed;
3. a model farm truck to haul grain. An overview of how gasoline powered engines operate may be emphasised;
4. samples of corn, wheat, and oats. Tests on germination may be made;

5. a model set of farm animals. Here, learners may study automation in feeding farm animals.

Pupils may study the models on the learning center and ask questions of each other and of the teacher. Perhaps, questions such as the following are raised by pupils after viewing the models:

1. how does a self propelled combine work to cut grain?
2. how is soil prepared for drilling and seeding grain?
3. what determines which grain to seed in a given field?
4. how is automation used to feed farm animals?
5. how is grain stored on the farm?

The above questions, as an example, provide a basis for pupils with teacher guidance to develop an experience chart. Ideas come from pupils pertaining to what was experienced from the learning center. The teacher assist and guides pupils to present content for the experience chart. The teacher prints the ideas from pupils in neat manuscript letters on the chalkboard or on a transparency for overhead use. We have observed numerous teachers type the ideas presented by pupils using a word processor and a large screen to project the resulting ideas. Learners may then see their talk written down. From the concrete experiences of objects at the learning center, pupils may see the abstract words on the large screen.

After the content has been printed/typed, pupils with teacher help may read the content together orally. The teacher needs to point to the words and phrases as they are being read. This guides pupils into becoming better readers. For some, these are beginning experiences in reading on the early primary grade levels. With the types/printed subject matter in a transparency in the computer, pupils may enjoy reading the same content at a later time. Rereading content is good for pupils and provides increased opportunities to develop a good stock of sight words in science. If the ideas from pupils have been printed on the chalkboard, they may be transferred to a flip chart so the content is saved and can be read later in a loosely bound volume. Sometimes pupil's ideas are printed immediately onto the flip chart. This saves the time of the teacher if this is done; however, many teachers feel they cannot immediately print the ideas correctly from pupils as they are given.

There are numerous questions that arise pertaining to the use of experience charts. Should the teacher write the ideas down directly as given orally by learners. The content may lack completeness, correct grammar, and usage. We would say that the teacher can ask for other ways to state a sentence if the one given has its many weaknesses. A short period of time for brainstorming might well provide the quality of sentences desired by the teacher of science. The experience chart may be written individually, within a cooperative learning endeavour, or the class as a whole. There are times when individual pupils have content they desire the teacher write for them. At other times the teacher may wish committee work on an experience chart so there are more chances for learner interaction within a small group. If the class size in large, the teacher may wish to have a smaller group work on an experience chart. The ideas presented by each pupil should be respected by all involved in developing the experience chart.

Closely related to experience charts approaches in science reading is the whole language programme of reading instruction. Instead of segmenting reading instruction in terms of phonics instruction and other word recognition procedures whole language advocates advocate the wholeness of content read. It is the entire story or event that is salient. Ediger (1997) wrote the following pertaining to whole language philosophies of teaching and learning in reading:

Teachers, whom we supervise, advocating a strong whole language approach in teaching reading stress the following:

1. reading involves wholeness in that ideas are read sequentially by learners;
2. the wholeness involved in reading should not be interrupted with phonics or other word recognition techniques. Obtaining ideas, not phonics, is salient;
3. interest in reading generates motivation to learn: interest overcomes problems in word recognition. Much

reading then assists pupils to identify an increased number of words;

4. providing assistance to pupils, as needed, is sufficient for learners to recognise unknown words. This, as needed approach, also prevents pupils from fragmenting content read in reading;

5. learner enjoyment in reading needs to be whole, not segmented into parts.

Toward the other end of the continuum, student teachers and regular teachers whom we supervised believed that whole language approaches are more suited toward pupils who can read well, such as in recreational reading. These readers can sequence their very own reading materials at a personal, optimal rate of speed. Little assistance is then needed in identifying unknown words. Teachers, here, agree that selected pupils do use context clues heavily to identify unknown words. Science pupils are different one from another, it stands to reason that some pupils will be orientated toward the whole language approach... .

HELPING THE MAINSTREAMED PUPIL

The Education for All Handicapped Pupils law (PL 94-142) emphasises that handicapped pupils be placed in the test restricted environment. Too frequently, all handicapped pupils had been placed in a special education classroom. Presently, many of these handicapped pupils are placed into the regular classroom. Here, the regular teacher teaches the handicapped together with normal children in a mainstreamed class. An IEP (individualised educational plan) is written for each pupils who is mainstreamed. The plan spells out with measurable stated objectives what a pupil is to achieve within a given interval of time. Learning activities are indicated for teachers so that they may assist pupils to achieve the IEP objectives. Auditing is possible to determine if objectives have been achieved by the mainstreamed pupil. I have served as an auditor to audit if a pupil has/has not achieved selected objectives. The auditor needs to notice if there is evidence to show that a pupil was successful in goal attainment.

IDEA (Individuals with Disabilities Education Act) was

passed by the United States congress and signed by the president in 1990. This law further protects the rights of handicapped pupils with a free and appropriate education. Appropriate means that the pupil needs proper placement and assistance for those who are impaired in speech, hearing, and sight. Orthopaedically handicapped pupils also need adequate provisions made for them as to pupils with learning disabilities. Parental involvement, including placement of the disabled was also emphasised in IDEA.

In research on mainstreaming or inclusion of the handicapped into the regular classroom, Gottlieb and Leyser (1996) wrote:

The present findings revealed two primary findings. First, that parents who indicated that they had a family member with disabilities were more positive of mainstreaming in 1991 than in 1981, and second that the more positive shift in attitude was not evident for the numerically larger group of parents indicated they did not a have a family member with disabilities.

From the perspective of families that had a member with disabilities, the data suggest that the relative commonplace fact of mainstreaming, and inclusion, has reduced concerns and fears of the unknown regarding what might happen in integrated classrooms serving students with disabilities alongside their nondisabled peers. For this community of families, mainstreaming seems now a more acceptable, programmatic option for all children. The magnitude of the change may be indicated as follows: for parents indicating that they have a family member with disabilities, the power of the differences in means attitude scores between 1981 and 1991 was 1:00, with an effect size of 3:00. This represents a powerful difference in attitude scores.

Parents who did not report the presence of a family member with disabilities did not express a shift in attitudes, either in the positive or negative direction. Evidently, mainstreaming did not arouse parental concerns that their non-disabled children would be negatively affected by the presence of classmates with disabilities... .

The IEP protects handicapped pupils so they are not ignored

in teaching and learning. There are goals that need to be achieved by these learners. The IEP's also spell out what kinds of services are to be received by each handicapped child such as speech correction for the impaired child in speaking. Teachers, the principal, and parents need to be involved in developing the IEP as well identifying the necessary services to be provided.

The teacher of science then needs to provide for the handicapped pupil who is mainstreamed into the regular classroom. The IEP objectives need to be met in teaching. Hopefully an aide will assist the regular teacher to provide for the mainstreamed handicapped pupil. There are no easy ways of teaching any pupil, be it mainstreamed or normal pupils. We, however, recommend the following in teaching the handicapped:

1. Determine where each pupil is achieving presently and then, based on these findings, develop an IEP. Involve teachers, the principal, parents, and the guidance counsellor in developing an appropriate IEP;
2. Provide all needed services for the handicapped, such as speech correction and ways to remedy learning disorders such as dyslexia;
3. Use learning opportunities that stimulate and encourage pupils to achieve objectives;
4. Evaluate to notice learner progress in achieving objectives;
5. Use evaluation information to improve the quality of teaching the handicapped;
6. Make certain aides have been properly instructed as to their roles in teaching handicapped pupils;
7. Discuss with parents which is better for their child, mainstreaming or being taught in a special education class.

Slow learners, in general, may be guided through a variety of learning opportunities in achieving more optimally. A good reader or the teacher may read orally to these pupils as they follow along in their own science textbooks. The content read orally might then be discussed with the slow learner. These same pupils should receive practice reading the same content that was read orally. The background information as well as seeing and hearing the words pronounced accurately provides the kinds of knowledge and skills needed to read on their own.

If there is teacher time, simplified content will assist the slow learner to do a better job of reading. Subject matter can always be simplified by using easier terms in context as well as sentences that are more readily understood. We have found that pupils who lack reading skills appropriate for what others are reading may select and read related library book content in science. There should be an atmosphere of respect when provisions are made for individual differences. There are so many people not able to work and achieve, is it not a blessing to be able to do more than others who are unable to do so, for various reasons? We believe most children in school want to learn much and achieve at a high level, as much as abilities permit. We believe there is an inward feeling of satisfaction with high achievement. An inadequate self concept says, 'I can't do this.' Or, 'It is impossible for me to learn as much as others do.' The self concept needs to be nurtured and supported of each pupil. Learners need to achieve success through hard work and feel they can be successful. We have found, numerous times, that there are pupils who do not learn as much as they are capable of. This hurts the self concept of the pupil. The learner is not achieving and can do better, regardless of ability levels. There is joy in achieving and learning, be it utilitarian to be used in a practical situation or in having worth for its own sake. Learning activities should be there to assist pupils to learn as much as possible on an individual basis.

In addition to reading orally as well as simplifying content for pupils in reading, the teacher also may use the experience chart idea whereby, from an experience, pupils may present the subject matter orally for the teacher to record on a chart. Pupils then see talk written down and may then read it back to the teacher orally. This procedure is very sound. Pupils are reading their very own ideas; they have the necessary background information from personal experiences such as an excursion on the school grounds to notice sheet or gully erosion. These learners also know and can identify words in reading since the words came from involved pupils. By saving the experience charts, pupils may read again and again, if they wish, the printed content.

The Reading Recovery Programme, brought to the United States from New Zealand, is a one on one programme of instruction. One teacher for one child can make much difference on achievement in science. Here we recommend securing volunteers from the community to guide slow learners in reading science content. One teacher for one child should ensure for success in reading. The aide may then assist pupils in word recognition as well as read science content to the child orally. There are ways of teaching whereby all pupils may be successful in learning. With the many audio-visual materials of instruction available, where no reading is required, pupils can learn many salient concepts and generalisations in science in ongoing lessons and units of study.

ASSISTING THE GIFTED

The gifted and talented, too frequently, are left out of the spectrum in providing for individual differences. These learners also need their fair share of time with the classroom teacher. They need quality, challenging objectives, learning opportunities which truly emphasise reaching for the stars, as well as valid and reliable evaluation techniques. What might the science teacher do to assist each pupil to learn as much as possible? We would recommend individual and cooperative projects that stimulate and encourage the gifted/talented to lofty, attainable goals. A research project might then be stressed that relates to, but goes beyond regular classroom work. The research project should have a clearly stated problem. The problem is important and relevant. A variety of reference sources and activities should be used to gather information directly related to the identified problem. Pupils are clear on the reference sources to be used. The teacher needs to provide direction on available references and the use of each. The internet, along with other sources, may provide necessary information in answer to the problem. A tentative answer may then be developed. The answer here is tentative since it needs to be.tested in a utilitarian way. Additional resources may be used in the testing of the answer. This may mean revising the answer, if evidence warrants. Integration of content is a key concept in using problem solving as a means of teaching and learning. Pertaining to an integrated curriculum, Harp and Brewer (1991) wrote:

A scope and sequence decision that will profoundly alter the way you teach is whether you will integrate the curriculum, by which we mean combining instructional objectives from two or more curriculum areas into one lesson or unit. We believe that teachers face an impossible task when they view each piece of the curriculum as a single building block and teaching as stacking those blocks one on to the other. There are too many curriculum blocks to build a tower successfully. In making scope and sequence decisions you need to search for ways to integrate the curriculum. Obviously, we believe that reading and writing should be taught together. Other possible combinations are music and reading, reading and art, social studies and writing and reading, and science and physical education.

We concur that reading and writing in a research project are one, not separate entities. Certainly there is much reading that gifted/talented pupils need to do as well as considerable writing in conducting research in the science curriculum.

Newsmagazines and daily newspapers from the centralised library may provide further information sources for the gifted/ talented. Pupils may read and discuss current events items in science within a cooperative learning endeavour. The teacher needs to be on the lookout for learning activities to optimalise learning for the gifted/talented.

A quality teacher is a proficient evaluator of learner progress. A variety of appraisal procedures need to be utilised. Among other evaluation techniques, the following may be utilised:

1. Teacher observation;
2. Anecdotal records;
3. Sociometric devices;
4. Teacher written tests;

5. Checklists and rating scales;
6. Standardised achievement tests;
7. Personality tests;
8. Interest inventories;
9. Criterion referenced tests;
10. Self-evaluation by the learner.

Conclusion

There are numerous means available to guide pupils to achieve more optimally in reading in science. The teacher should assist pupils in word recognition in context. This is a powerful way to have learners recognise unknown words. At the same time, recognising words in context does not hinder in securing sequential ideas while reading. Reading science content then needs to be as holistic as possible. However, teachers must be available at teachable moments whereby analysing words may be highly beneficial to pupils. Thus a small amount of time, as needed, may be given by the teacher to guide learners in phonics or syllabication. By giving time in analysing unknown words, the teacher is helping pupils to develop a wider array of sight words. Reading fluently and in a manner stressing diverse approaches in comprehension is an ultimate goal in reading in science. Basal texts may be wisely used as a part of the science curriculum, but this does not, by any means, stress the entire unit of study. It is one learning activity among many others. Learners need to use content from science textbooks to identify and solve problems. The basal textbooks might also be used to check hypotheses and in their revision. If textbooks have a quality manual section, this aids the teacher in selecting objectives, learning opportunities, and evaluation techniques. Suggestions for improving teaching should always be welcome by the teacher.

Basal science textbooks may be used to guide pupils in securing needed facts, concepts, and generalisations within the framework of problem solving. Higher levels of cognition should be stressed in the science curriculum. Certainly, a good teacher is not satisfied with pupils achieving facts only or largely, but has pupils move in the direction of thinking critically and creatively about content being pursued. Individual differences need to be provided for in reading content in science. Ediger (1997) wrote the following for a quality programme of reading instruction in the science curriculum:

1. Each pupil begins at a point where he/she is ready to achieve as optimally as possible;
2. The learner experiences continual progress successfully in reading;
3. The four vocabularies—listening, speaking, reading and writing—are integrated into a quality reading programme;
4. Word recognition skills, such as phonics, syllabication, context clues, and structural analysis, are taught within a framework of interesting content to be read;
5. Major emphasis placed upon reading literature, not analysing words into component parts;
6. Multimedia approaches are used to motivate pupils so that an inward desire in learning to read is inherent;
7. Problem solving, critical and creative thinking, as well as application of salient concepts stressed in teaching reading;
8. The best sequence is used to guide each pupil toward optimum achievement in reading;
9. Learning to read as a lifetime endeavour is stressed;
10. The use of relevant research results is important in the teaching of reading.

References

Barr, Rebecca, and Marilyn Sadow (1985), *Reading Diagnosis for Teachers.* White Plains, New York: Longman Inc., page 143.

Cagney, George, and Christine Neuenfeld (1993), 'Teacher's Preference for Reading Materials,' *Reading Improvement.* Vol. 30, No. 4, page 244.

Carlo, Marie (1996), 'Recorded Books Raise Reading Scores,' The *Education Digest*. Vol. 61, page 56.

Ediger, Marlow (1984), 'Goals in the Reading Curriculum,' *Reading Improvement*, Vol. 21, No. 3, page 243.

Ediger, Marlow (1996), *Elementary Education*. Kirksville, Missouri: Simpson Publishing Company, page 39.

Ediger, Marlow and D. Bhaskara Rao (2000), *Teaching Reading Successfully*. New Delhi: Discovery Publishing House.

Ediger, Marlow (1997), *Teaching Reading and the Language Arts in the Elementary School*. Kirksville, Missouri: Simspon Publishing Company, page 24, page 37.

Ediger, Marlow (1998), *Teaching Reading Successfully in the Elementary School*. Kirksville, Missouri: Simpson Publishing Company, 14-17.

Ediger, Marlow (1997), *Teaching Science in the Elementary School*. Kirksville, Missouri: Simpson Publishing Company, 162-190.

Harp, Bill, and Jo Ann Brewer (1991), *Reading and Writing: Teaching for the Connections*. New York: Harcourt Brace and Jovanovich, Publishers, page 98.

Harris, Albert J., and Edward Sipay (1985), *How to Increase Reading Ability*. White Plains, New York: Longman Inc. page 504.

Gottlieb, Jay, and Yona Leyser (1996), 'Attitudes of Public School Parents Toward Mainstreaming Changes Over a Decade,' *Journal of Instructional Psychology*, Vol. 23, No. 4, page 263.

McNinch, George W., and Ellen Gruber (1996), 'Perceptions of Literacy Acquisition (Traditional Vs. Whole Language): Teachers, Principals, and Parents,' *Reading Improvement*, Vol. 33, No. 3, pages 130-136.

Ruben, Dorothy (1983), *Teaching Reading and Study Skills in Content Areas*. New York: Rinehart and Winston, pages 109-110.

16

Evaluation of Pupil Achievement in Science

There needs to be a variety to approaches used to evaluate pupil achievement in science. Since no approaches perfect, it behooves teachers and supervisors to use diverse methods to determine learner progress in science. Then too, there are numerous facets of a learner's achievement that need to be evaluated making it necessary to use different procedures. These facets include knowledge, skills, and attitudes, among others. We would like to start with discussing teacher observation to appraise pupil achievement.

TEACHER OBSERVATION OF PUPIL PROGRESS IN SCIENCE

Observation by the teacher of each pupil in the classroom during time devoted to teaching science can be rather continuous and ongoing. Perhaps, it is the most common way to evaluate achievement in science teaching and learning. The teacher needs to use quality criteria in appraising pupils in ongoing lessons and units in science. These criteria should include the following:

1. pupils being a on task and not digressing from paying attention to ongoing learning activities;
2. pupils being actively involved in identifying and solving problems;
3. pupils developing and testing vital hypotheses in problem solving situations;
4. pupils working harmoniously with others in committee settings and with the class as a whole;
5. pupils making application of what has been learned previously;
6. pupils putting forth optimal effort in individual endeavours;
7. pupils reading science materials with comprehension;
8. pupils writing content clearly and meaningfully in science;
9. pupils evaluating their own achievement in science in a conscientious manner;
10. pupils observing carefully during time devoted to science experiments and demonstrations;
11. pupils speaking accurately and precisely so that quality communication in science takes place.

What has been observed by the teacher may be recorded periodically so that retention of learner achievement is an optimal as possible. One approach in recording pupil achievement is to use anecdotal records. Shepherd and Ragan (1982) wrote the following:

Teachers have many opportunities to observe pupils in the classroom, on the playground, in the cafeteria, and in the auditorium. Observations over a period of time in these situations may provide information not revealed in an artificial test situation. For example, pupils may answer yes to a test item, 'Do you prefer to work with others rather than by yourself? When careful observation of their behaviour may reveal that they seldom participate in the activities of a group. Observation also provides an opportunity to report actual behaviour. The pupils who are asked to report on their own behaviours in a formal test situation are likely to give what they perceive to be the expected answer. The report of direct observations is likely, in this instance, to be more reliable than test results. The teacher may also learn a great deal about the personal-social development of children by observing their creative activities. Do the pupils enjoy the activity for its own sake, or do they primarily work for good marks? Do they express their own feelings in their drawings and paintings, or do they prefer to copy the ideas of others?

ANECDOTAL RECORDS

With anecdotal records, the teacher records learn progress individually at selected intervals. Photocopies may be made to make it convenient in using anecdotal records to record each pupil's achievement. The following form has been used very successfully by teachers whom we have supervised to record information about a pupil through teacher observation:

Name of Pupil *Date* *Observations Made*

What might be written, for example, pertaining to pupil's achievement in the classroom, according to teacher observation? The following is provided as an example:

Alex Smyth September 10—Alex worked well with others in the committee to develop a mural on volcanic eruptions. He needed to do more reading and looking at a video so that the opening to the volcano looked more real. Alex seems to enjoy working on the mural with others. He read additional materials on lava and magma, beyond what was discussed in class. Alex enjoys discussing current events items pertaining to volcanic eruptions.

From the above anecdotal record, it appears that Alex tends to do well in science at this point. If a pupil is deficient in an area, the science teacher may then assist the learner in overcoming a difficulty. By looking at the anecdotal record, the teacher may quickly notice what a pupil needs more help in. The teacher may write anecdotal statements on two or three pupils per day so it does not become an overwhelming activity. There must be a purpose in writing anecdotal records and that purpose being to assist pupils to achieve more optimally.

There are other procedures whereby a teacher may observe learner progress and file the results also, in addition to anecdotal records. Journal writing is another procedure for the teacher to use in recording observations made of pupil progress.

WRITING JOURNAL ENTRIES

As is true of anecdotal records, journal writing stresses contextual situations of evaluating pupil progress. 'Contextual' means pupils are being evaluated within specific learning activities in terms of observations made by the science teacher to notice what the strengths and weaknesses are of a pupil's progress. Journal entries are written in narrative form, not as precise statements as was true of anecdotal records. The science teacher may focus upon one or two pupils per school day when writing journal entries. It is good to have records of pupil achievement in science. The date for writing in the journal is important. Comparisons might then be made of later with earlier journal entries. A good science teacher is a good evaluator in that he/she knows where each pupil is in achievement and can guide pupils to make continuous progress.

When field studies are being made, pupils need to record comprehensively what was achieved and accomplished. Pertaining to pupils doing field studies in connection with Prince George's Community College, in Largo, Maryland on ospreys and whooping cranes, Cunniff and Mcmillen (1996) wrote the following:

At the end of the research week, students rank the four research areas in order of preference so that project directors can establish teams to do the data analysis, research presentation, and poster for each area. As expected, working with each species, the ospreys and cranes, is the first choice of many students. However, the project directors are able to place students work in their first or second ranked research area. Letting students work in their area of interest promotes a sense of ownership and motivation.

For each research area, the student teams make numerous null and alternative hypotheses. Statistical analysis, done both by hand and computer, is then used to test these hypotheses.

This final week is intense. Each of the four groups analyse the field data along with data from existing databases. Students are graphing software packages to analyse and graph data, test hypotheses, and help reach conclusions. Students develop posters to summarise the research methodology, data analysis, and conclusions. Each team develops a 12 minute presentation, and every student is required to speak. Research presentations are given the Thursday evening of the fourth week to more than 100 persons—parents, teachers, and friends. This activity gives students an opportunity to strengthen communication skills, learn how to give a scientific presentation, use overheads and slides, and work together as a team to deliver a final project, all under a very tight deadline.

There are numerous skills being acquired by pupils in the above named science project; these include doing research, using statistics, reporting orally, and writing observations made.

USING PORTFOLIOS TO APPRAISE PUPIL PERFORMANCE

Pupils individually or in committees with teacher guidance need to develop a portfolio to indicate the quality of school work that has been accomplished. Isele (1995) raises questions and provides answers pertaining to portfolio development:

What are student portfolios? A purposeful collection of work that illustrates the student's efforts, progress, and achievement in given areas.

What is the purpose of a student's portfolio? Portfolios provide an ongoing and authentic record of student performance that enable:

students to reflect upon and articulate their progress;

teachers to tailor their instruction to the student's.

strengths and needs and to use the student's work as a basis for instructional planning;

parents to gain greater insight into their child's learning;

administrators/policy makers to base decisions about student achievement on authentic and meaningful information.

What are benefits of portfolios? Portfolios

* portray students's processes as well as products;
* involve students in reflecting upon their learning, and thereby, provide individual responsibility, self-sufficiency, and active involvement;
* increase time spent on learning an the quality of teaching;
* provide a tangible and meaningful basis for discussions among students, teachers, and parents;
* link curriculum, instruction, and assessment;
* inform instruction.

Portfolios have a rather recent history in their use to appraise pupil achievement. What should go into a portfolio containing products to pupil achievement in science?

1. snapshots and videos of pupils working on science experiments;
2. cassette recordings of pupils working on committees in collaborative endeavours;
3. art products and written work of the pupil in ongoing lessons and units of study in science;
4. diary entries kept by the learner on a daily basis and dated pertaining to what was learned in science. Written products may come from word processor use;
5. log entries which summarise the diary entries;
6. pupil summaries of major concepts and generalisations acquired in science units of study;

7. descriptions of pupil/teacher conferences covering a science unit of study;
8. self evaluation by the pupil on strengths acquired during the entire unit of study. The pupil may wish to list what areas he/she needs more assistance in;
9. results from teacher written, standardised tests, as well as norm referenced tests;
10. a listing of computer packages completed. Internet may well be used to obtain information in problem solving experiences. A table of contents should be developed for the portfolio.

Collins and Dana (1993) suggest that four kinds of data or evidence be in a portfolio: these are the following:

1. artifacts are documents normally created or used in schools such as tests, book reports, work sheets, projects, etc.;
2. reproductions are items that typify events of activities in which students normally engage but often are not captured. For example, audio/visual taped discussions, presentations or photographs of projects or other work;
3. attestations often take the form of a letter prepared by someone other than the student verifying his/her work or contributions;
4. productions take two forms, both of which are especially created for the portfolio. The first is a reflective entry which articulates what was learned from the project or activity. The second is a caption affixed to each portfolio entry describing what it is and why it is included.

Pupils with teacher guidance need to have definite categories in mind when having the former develop a portfolio. These identified categories assist the learner in thinking about how to organise the portfolio and its contents. A wide variety of processes and products should be in evidence in a portfolio. Interested, responsible persons, especially parents, may then see what the learner has accomplished and what needs to be worked on to further the progress of the pupil.

After appraising diverse procedures used to evaluate pupil achievement, Ediger (19950 wrote:

Approaches used to appraise pupil progress depend upon the philosophy of education involved. Each specific philosophy has uniqueness attached in determining that which learners have acquired.

The testing and measurement movement stresses the utilisation of predetermined objectives written in measurable terms. The objectives are written prior to instruction of learners. With appropriate learning opportunities, either a pupil does or does not achieve one or more precise objectives. Measuring pupil progress against the stated objectives emphasises the concept of criterion referenced testing (CRT).

The testing and measurement movement also advocates using norm referenced tests (NRT). Pupils are spread out on a continuum from highest to lower based on test scores. Predetermined objectives tend not to exist when utilising norm referenced tests to measure pupil achievement. Norm referenced tests spread pupils' results in terms of test scores much more so than criterion referenced testing. Pupils attempt to attain predetermined objectives with CRT's. The measurably stated objectives represent absolute standards. A high number of pupils might well achieve the measurably stated objectives, as the teacher usually intends.

Self evaluation by the pupil is an opposite approach to appraisal of learner progress as contrasted with the testing and measurement movement. With self evaluation, the responsibility rests upon the learner himself/herself to acknowledge strengths, weaknesses, and modifications to attain at a higher level. Learners when evaluating the self need to perceive the processes and products completed from the frame of reference of personal improvement. Truth, in results from the evaluation, may well reside within the pupil. Subjectivity in results is to be expected, since open-ended criteria are utilised to appraise progress. With self evaluation, the pupil might well perceive increased purpose in assessing the self. The teacher is a stimulator and initiator when guiding the self evaluating process.

TESTING TO DETERMINE PUPILS ACHIEVEMENT

Using tests as a sole determiner to ascertain pupil achievement has lost its popularity and luster than what it once had. However, test results can still provide the teacher with feedback pertaining to a pupil's achievement. Testing occurs in a non-contextual situation and thus does not have the utilitarian features that a contextual situation has. For example, if a pupil writes a 'thank you notice' to a person or place where the classroom took an excursion, the situation is practical and the letter will be mailed to the proper destination. The involved letter of appreciation was written in context in a lifelike situation. Tests taken by pupils are outside the framework of a utilitarian situation. People in society then do not take tests to show how well they are doing their work. Rather they are appraised in terms of how well they perform at the work place. An automobile mechanic might then be appraised in terms of how few complaints are received from customers as to faulty work having been done on their cars and trucks. The carpenter on the job does not take a paper/pencil test to show how well he/she did in building a home or other structure. Instead, the carpenter reveals proficiency by his/her skills and abilities to build a cabinet in the house, shingle the roof of the dwelling, and lay tiles for the basement floor, among other needed tasks.

To use the same analogy, the pupil in school has purposes for writing such as writing a 'get well notice' to a friend who is ill, inviting friends to a birthday party, sending a thank you notice for a gift or favour received, and/or corresponding with pen pals. Here, the pupil is not evaluated in letter writing through a paper pencil test using multiple choice test items. In context, the pupil should be appraised in how well he/she writes, not how well a test can be taken. The term 'constructivism' is also given to appraising pupil achievement in writing within a contextual situation. The contextual situation stresses practical and utilitarian situations. Knowledge and skills are put to use. Application is then made of knowledge and skills possessed by the learner.

Now getting back to testing of pupils in the curriculum,

should testing be avoided? We think not. Why? Testing is one method of appraising pupil achievement. The teacher when writing these test items needs to use quality standards. Subject matter contained should be valid for the test. In other words, the teacher in teaching and learning situations has covered the content written as test items, generally multiple choice in nature. The teacher needs to be certain that the test items are clearly written; ambiguity has been omitted. The stem of the multiple choice item is grammatically correct with each of the four distracters. The following is given as an example:

Reptiles have all but one of the following characteristics:

a. temperature readings are comparable to that of the environment;

b. their live are born from eggs that have hatched;

c. babies are very dependent upon adults for at least a month;

d. in their phylum are animals such as turtles, snakes, and alligators.

The responses should be quite similar in length when writing multiple choice items so that clues are not available to the pupil as to which the correct answer would be. It is much easier to write multiple choice items measuring factual responses as compared to higher levels of cognition.

Many teachers write true-false items to measure pupil achievement. If a test item here is false, pupils should correct wnat is incorrect so that a minimal amount of guessing is involved. In the following true-false item, the pupil needs to correct what is false:

Fish start their lives breathing through the use of gills and later develop lungs.

There are teachers who write matching test items to measure pupil achievement in science. What is matched is usually factual in nature. There are important facts for pupils to understand in science. To match column A with column B, there needs to be more items in one column as compared to the next so that the process of elimination may not be used excessively. There should not be more than ten items in one column for intermediate grade levels. One column in the matching test should have single words of phrases; it is difficult to match column A with column B if both have lengthy sentences.

Teacher written test items should possess reliability. Thus if a test is taken a second time by the same set of learners, the results would be similar from one testing time to the next for individual learners. Should these test results vary much for one child from one testing to the next using the same items, the test would lack reliability. It would not be too useful to notice where a pupil is, on the same test, if on the first testing, John has 90 per cent right and for the second testing 30 per cent correct. The question would then arise as to where is John in achievement since the scores vary much on the same text from one testing to the next. There are basically three kinds of reliability statistically. These are test-retest, split half, and alternate forms.

Teacher written tests are one kind to be taken by pupils. Generally teachers align their tests with what has been taught. Thus, there are degrees of validity there.

There appear to be weaknesses no matter which procedure is used in testing. Thus, in standardised testing, teachers have no objectives to go by to know which subject matter will be covered in the test. The manual section will say how the items were selected to be on the standardised test. But, it leaves the science teacher in a precarious situation in terms of having some guidance as to what pupils should learn in ongoing science units of study in order to do well on the standardised instrument. Quality standardised tests will contain in the manual section the validity and reliability figures from schools having used these tests. Reliability figures given are high since it is relatively easy to develop quality reliability figures when spending a considerable amount of money to secure needed test-retest, alternative forms, and/or split-half reliability It is much more difficult to obtain quality 'validity' for the standardised test. The science teacher should have statements of clearly stated objectives so that he/she may teach in a manner which will assist pupils to achieve objectives. The learning activities in science would then be valid for the stated objectives. Otherwise, the teacher would be uncertain in knowing what to teach so that pupils do well on the test.

A publishing company of standardised tests has specific rules to follow, indicted in the manual, as to how to administer the test. Each pupil taking the test follows the same rules and has the same time limits. Thus there are standard procedure in test taking. To score the tests, the same key is used for all pupils and with machine scoring, no errors should be made in checking each pupil's paper. Test results, if checked again, should be the same for each pupil no matter who or what scores the tests.

From pupil results, there should be quite a range from high to low in pupil's test scores in any one grade level. The standardised tests are constructed in ways which make it possible to have this wide spread of scores.

Criterion referenced tests have taken some of the weaknesses out of standardised testing. Here, teachers have statements of objectives to use in teaching science. The teacher needs to choose learning opportunities in order that learner may attain the objectives. Thus the learning opportunities harmonise with the stated objectives and provide for validity. The testing device also aligns with the stated objectives, thus making for validity in testing. Ideally, there should be a small range in pupils' test scores from a criterion referenced test. Why? The science teacher teaches so that as many pupils as possible achieve the stated objectives. Thus, it can be expected that the range of scores from high to low on criterion referenced tests will be much more marginal as compared to standardised tests.

There are numerous states that mandate criterion referenced tests for pupils to take on selected grade levels. Accountability of teachers may be tied in with criterion referenced testing. Thus, teachers are held accountable for pupils achieving the precise objectives whose subject matter is being measured on the criterion referenced test.

There is considerable debate presently as to how much should test results count as compared to portfolio content in appraising pupil achievement. Tests possess much subjectivity when subject matter is selected for inclusion. There certainly would not be agreement on which science content should go into a test. Objectivity occurs here when the results from pupil testing is being evaluated. If the result are scored accurately, there should be no subjectivity involved providing all scorers use the same scoring key. With portfolios, subjectivity is involved when who or three raters appraise any one portfolio. It will be difficult for these raters to come up with same results when evaluating each person's progress. Kane and Khaturi (1995) wrote the following:

Some questions related to performance assessment remain to be answered by future research. They have to do with basic and secondary issues in educational reform... . What knowledge and skills are pupils to demonstrate after a certain period of schooling? What other systemic reforms must be undertaken in order for assessment reforms to be effective? What assessment formats are most useful for which specific purposes? The greatest challenge ahead lies in designing systems of reform that synergistically support the core educational functions of teaching and learning for which teachers are the most powerful 'engine.'

CONFERENCES WITH PUPILS

The conference method can be an excellent way of assisting the teacher to determine what pupils have learned in science. Ediger (1996) wrote:

The teacher may conduct conferences with pupils individually or in a group setting. If a pupil, for example, has completed reading a library book directly related to the ongoing unit of study, the teacher may conduct an informal conference to determine attitudes and comprehension of the involved learner. The teacher might also conduct a conference with a small group of pupils who have read library books on the following topics relating to the present unit being studied in science:

1. The Seasons, Plants, and Animals;
2. Plants and Animals of Prehistoric Times;
3. The Uses of Nuclear Energy;
4. Uses of Magnets and Electricity;
5. Constellations and the Universe.

Pupils may reveal learnings such as the following in a conference setting pertaining to content gained from reading selected library books:

1. obtaining skills in reading critically and creatively;
2. acquiring selected facts, main ideas, and generalisations;
3. selecting ideas which come in a certain sequence;
4. reading to solve problems;
5. wishing to engage in reading for recreational purposes.

Conference methods of evaluating pupil achievement may be used along with other appraisal procedures. A conference may take a very short period of teacher time. Others may take longer depending upon the agenda of the science teacher. We believe conferences are a marvelous way of getting to know pupils better as individuals as well as guiding learners to achieve more optimally. In conferences with pupils as well as with any facet of the science curriculum, we believe teachers need to think about four questions pertaining to science lessons and units of study that Ralph Tyler (1949) raised:

1. Which objectives should pupils achieve?
2. Which learning activities should be chosen to assist pupils to achieve the stated objectives?
3. How should these learning activities be organised?
4. How should we evaluate to know if the objectives have been achieved?

These four questions might well provide for a framework for planning and implementing a quality science curriculum.

DISCUSSIONS AND PUPIL ACHIEVEMENT

Pupils with teacher leadership should have ample opportunities to discuss content acquired in science. Learners need to understand and attach meaning to what has been learned. Rote learning and memorisation of subject matter is not adequate. Pupils also need to comprehend and use what has been learned. Discussions can be lively and engaging. They certainly do not need to be dull. We have observed teachers lead discussions in classrooms whereby each pupil was truly involved wholeheartedly. If discussions seem to be boring and lead nowhere, pupils with teacher assistance need to determine causes for these occurrences. Science is a fascinating curriculum area in which pupils may truly ponder over questions and problems as well as being actively involved in each learning opportunity. Pertaining to discussions, Ediger (1977) wrote the following:

In discussion settings, feeback from learners is obtained in terms of relevant concepts and generalisations gained in a specific unit of study. Thus, learners may reveal the following understandings in a discussion:

1. What causes earthquakes, cyclones, and hurricanes?
2. What causes diverse kinds of weather on the earth's surface?
3. How gasoline and electrical engines operate in terms of involved scientific principles?

Using discussions as a technique to appraise learner progress, pupils also indicate:

1. if they can stay on the topic being pursued;
2. if they can communicate ideas orally in an effective manner;
3. if they respect the thinking of others.

By listening to oral reports given by pupils, the teacher may notice learner growth in the following ways:

1. Has the report been carefully planned and prepared?
2. Is there appropriate sequence of content being presented?
3. Does the reporter really understand the content being presented to listeners? Thus if a pupil is reporting on cirrus clouds, does he/she understand how these clouds are formed as well as have accurate perceptions on their physical appearances?
4. Does the learner speak clearly enough so listeners can clearly understand the contents being presented?

There should be ample time given after the oral report for listeners to ask questions and make comments in an atmosphere of respect. It is very important for pupils to learn to accept and respect each other. In an atmosphere of acceptance and belonging, pupils probably will learn more subject matter content than would otherwise be the case.

Conclusion

The development and use of portfolios should be a way for pupils to reflect upon their strengths and weaknesses in working toward higher achievement levels. Bimes-Michalak (1995) believes that a major reason for developing portfolios is for pupils and teachers to reflect upon what has been taught and learned. There is a motivating ingredient in portfolio development and that is active involvement by learners in compiling a truly excellent device to inform others of personal progress in science. The pupil is involved in a hands on approach in determining what should go into a portfolio and why. Gilman and Rafferty list the following advantages of using portfolios to appraise pupil achievement:

1. they evaluate both process and product;
2. they allow an integration of learning and assessment;
3. evaluation is not limited to a single score;
4. provide more information about a student's progress;
5. they encourage students to take charge of their own learning;
6. students feel they are a part of the assessment process;
7. they help develop the skills for lifelong learning;
8. they may actually reduce the daily burden of grading papers;
9. the information gained from portfolios is meaningful and substantial;
10. they provide a continuous example of a child's work in a context that is relevant and understandable;

11. They assess global understanding and thinking skills;
12. it is a form of evaluation that is bound to have parental approval.

Wolf (1996) suggests teachers also develop their own portfolios. He wrote the following:

Why this interest in portfolios? Although portfolios can be time consuming to construct and cumbersome to review, they also capture the complexities of professional practices in ways that no other approach can. Not only are they an effective way to assess teaching quality, but they also provide teachers opportunities for self reflection and collegial interactions based on documented episodes of their own teaching.

Essentially, a teaching portfolio is a collection of information such as lesson plans, student assignments, teacher's written descriptions and videotapes of their instruction, and formal evaluations by supervisors... .

Teachers and administrators need to look for better means of evaluation of pupil progress than what was used previously. Changes need to be made when moving from what is to what should be. What should be is based on the best thinking possible in education. Using test scores largely to reveal learner progress and achievement was weighed and found wanting. Norm and Criterion referenced tests provided some data on pupil achievement, but the scope was very narrow in showing what a pupil knows and can do. Test results show numerical data scores, such as norm referenced results indicating how well a pupil compares with others in taking the same test. Percentile ranks, standard deviations, grade equivalents, and quartile deviations are given to show how well a pupil is doing in the curriculum. Or in the case of criterion referenced tests, information is given if a pupil has or has not achieved predetermined objectives. Numerical test results do not indicate how well a person communicates orally or in writing in a contextual situation. The tests also are taken outside the framework of the ongoing lesson or unit of study being presented. Pupils then lack ownership of indicating how well they are doing in the curriculum area science.

References

Bimes-Michalak, Beverly (1995), 'The Portfolio Zone,' *Education Digest*. 60: 53-57.

Collins, A., and T. M. Dana 1993), 'Using Portfolios with Middle Grade Students,' *Middle School Journal*, 25: 14-19.

Cuniff, Patricia A., and Janet L. McMillen (1996), 'Field Studies,' *The Science Teacher*, 63: 51.

Ediger, Marlow (1998), 'Computers in the Science Curriculum' *School Science*, 36 (4), 62-71.

Ediger, Marlow (1995), *Philosophy in Curriculum Development* Kirksville, Missouri: Simpson Publishing Company, pages 114-115.

Ediger, Marlow (1996), *Elementary Education (A Collection of Essays)*. Kirksville, Missouri: Simpson Publishing Company, page 149.

Ediger, Marlow (1977), *The Elementary Curriculum. A Handbook*. Kirksville, Missouri: Simpson Publishing Company, pages 215-216.

Ediger, Marlow and Digumarti Bhaskara Rao (2001). *Teaching Social Studies Successfully*. New Delhi, India: Discovery Publishing House.

Ediger, Marlow and D. Bhaskara Rao (2000), Teaching Mathematics Successfully. New Delhi: Discovery Publishing House.

Gilman, David Alan, and Cathleen D. Rafferty. (no data given). 'Portfolios: They're Just Not Work Folders Anymore,' School of Education, Indiana State University, Terre Haute: Curriculum and Research Center.

Isele, Frederick (199), 'Performance Based Portfolios.' Paper presented at the National Council Social Studies Convention, Chicago.

Kane, Michael, and Nidh Khatri (1995), Assessment Reform,' *Phi Delta Kappan*, 77 : 32.

Shepherd, Gene D., and William B. Ragan, *Modern Elementary Curriculum*. New York: Holt, Rinehart and Winston, pages 109-110.

Tyler, Ralph (1949), *Basic Principles of Curriculum and Instruction*. Chicago: University of Chicago Press.

Wolf, Kenneth (1996), 'Developing an Effective Teaching Portfolio,' *Educational Leadership*, 53 : 34.

17

When Pupils Fail, Then What?

(Implications for Science)

Much is written about avoiding pupil failure in school and having an increased number graduate from high school, than the present seventy-five per cent rate. There probably is no other institution, other than the public schools, whereby so many pupils are to attend the same institution and go through a similar curriculum, especially the elementary and middle school years of schooling. The high school level provides more opportunities for pupils to differentiate in terms of courses taken, such as electives in the curriculum as compared to the elementary school. Or a pupil on the secondary level may go the vocational rather than the academic route. It appears, however, that the academic route is considered much superior as compared to the vocational route. We do not believe that it should be perceived this way. Rather, Individuals are different from each other in many ways and selected pupils will feel more empowered in vocational as compared to academic classes. Society certainly does need its vocational people to do carpenter work, repair automobiles, prepare food in restaurants, do plumbing, and the myriads of needed employment in society.

VOUCHER SYSTEMS

There are educators and people from the business world who advocate that schools which fail pupils should provide vouchers to parents to choose a receiving school for their child. Here, Parents need to be very receptive in studying what different schools have to offer in meeting individual needs of pupils. Receiving schools need to publish brochures to indicate what they have to offer incoming pupils. They should make known what it is that would assist pupils to do well in school. Dissatisfied parents may have behaviourally disordered children and need a school for their children that can offer a necessary curriculum. We would venture to speculate that pupils who do not do well in school, according to parental expectations, may have special needs. These pupils have not done well in the sending schools and now are looking for greener pastures where all is well. This may or may not follow when a pupil under the voucher system changes schools. Then too, if there are many vouchers available, will receiving schools be able to provide for pupils whose needs were not met in the sending school? If there truly is an outstanding teacher, known to many that he/she can help many pupils to be successful, how many new pupils can he/she take from receiving schools? Will the receiving school have adequate assistance of this excellent teacher to handle the new pupils? Or will the new pupils provide a burden to the outstanding teacher so that he/she can no longer do an excellent job of teaching. It takes one child who has many emotional problems to disrupt an entire classroom continuously. Then too, if the parents of this child are highly verbal in voicing dissatisfactions in the receiving school, what is the next alternatives? A highly vocal parents can do much to hinder teachers in providing for individual pupils. In the US, if pupils do not achieve up to what news reporters or the lay public wants in terms of test results, teachers are to blame in whole. It almost appears as if pupils have no responsibilities for achieving unless they have an inward desire to do so.

What if parents do not have the money to pay for differences between what the receiving school asks for in terms of money and what the sending school offers? There can be quite a gap between the two in dollars. Then too, transportation can be a real problem in sending a pupil to a different school. Will parents have the money and time to take their child to a different school? Schools also need to be chosen on the basis of what will truly assist a child to do better. This can be a major problem in selecting a new school for a pupil to attend under the voucher system. This opens the doors to a touchy situation in that some parents would choose parochial schools for their children. Would it be constitutional to send a child to a parochial school from voucher moneys? If too many pupils with parental approval decide to attend parochial schools and if this were legal, the parochial system of instruction would change much. Special services for the handicapped would need to be provided. All pupils who wished to do so may have to be admitted to the chosen parochial school. The role of the state might involve supervising parochial schools in terms of teachers hired and the quality of the curriculum offered. Parochial schools might then need to be enlarged with a problem arising as to who would pay for these costs.

We have the following questions to ask about the voucher system of parental choice of schools for their children, in addition to the problems raised above:

1. Will the quality of education really improve for the pupil with the voucher system?
2. Why not spend the voucher money, instead, in improving all public schools in the US?
3. How are brochures developed by receiving schools presenting their data in terms of honesty, objectivity, and integrity?
4. What happens to receiving schools when receiving vouchers to admit pupils in terms of school size, class size, and quality of instruction?
5. What happens to a pupil who no longer attends the neighbourhood school in terms of feelings and friendships left behind?

OPEN ENROLMENT

There are several states, such as Minnesota and Iowa, that have open enrolment. With open enrolment, parents may choose which school in the state their child is to attend. The neighbourhood school might, of course, then be bypassed. The local school is not as certain how many pupils they will have at the beginning of the school year since the option is open in terms of which school the pupil will be attending. Parents may then select a school based on the kind of curriculum which will be offered to their child. There is no money available in terms of vouchers to pay for changing from one public school to another. Parents need to find out then which school might offer a curriculum that would be of benefit to their children.

Feelings of insecurity may be there when a public school does not know how many pupils will be at the beginning of a school year. The same would be true of any receiving school. A problem then of space for pupils and adequate teachers need to be considered by the receiving schools. Many times, educators and the lay public argue that poor quality schools will be eliminated with open enrolment plans. Thus schools offering poor quality education may eventually have too few pupils to operate an educational system.

We have the following questions to raise about open enrolment:

1. Do parents select schools based on quality or rather on slogans presented? In other words are there ulterior motives in making choices of schools such as a boy or girl desiring to play on a basketball/football team which is known for its winning record and possible scholarships? Perhaps, there is nothing wrong in wanting to be on a top team in competitive athletics in order to obtain a scholarship. For example, we do have the theory of multiple intelligences which includes bodily/kinesthetic intelligence?

2. Why not attempt to improve all improve all public schools so that diverse curricula are offered within each school to provide for individual differences among pupils?

3. How can parents know which school will meet the needs of their children best?
4. Does a receiving school with a good track record want to accept numerous other pupils and perhaps ruin their good reputation due to having too many pupils or to many disruptive pupils?
5. Is it best for a local district to know approximately how many pupils there will be at the beginning of a school year in order to make quality plans for instruction?

MEASURING PUPIL ACHIEVEMENT

There are many ways to measure pupil achievement including standardised norm referenced tests, criterion referenced tests, district wide tests, state mandated tests, tests which accompany a basal reading or mathematics series, Education 2000 goals with diverse states developing tests to measure pupil achievement in attainment of stated objectives, national tests such as the National Assessment of Educational Progress (NAEP), and international tests which makes comparisons of pupil achievement among nations on the planet earth. We do not think educators and the lay public understand how each test is devised why there is so much controversy about how to measure pupil achievement and progress.

A. Standardised Tests. There are many rules which need to be followed before a test is standardised. A standardised test has the same directions to follow for all taking the test. The time limits are the same for all regardless of ability and achievement levels of pupils involved, scoring procedures of the results are the same, among other standardisations. The results of our pupils having taken the test are compared with those of the group the test was standardised on in numerous pilot studies. The manual section of the standardised test will state which categories of pupils were included in the standardisation group.

We see the following as major weaknesses of standardised testing to indicate pupil progress:

1. there are no objectives that go along with theses kinds of tests. The teacher then cannot teach so that pupils

might achieve objectives. Guesswork is involved in terms of what the test is to measure. What the teacher teaches is then not valid in terms of content in test items on the standardised test;

2. pupils lack security in not knowing what they will be tested on. What has been studied might be completely unrelated to content in the test items;

3. a test such as standardised tests may have high reliability and yet validity is difficult to determine. To be valid a test must measure what it purports to measure and that is pupil achievement in the different curriculum or academic areas. What is taught by teachers varies much from school to school. In a national curriculum, pupils could studying similar things in each of the different curriculum areas. That is something, however, that would not be prized in the US, at least not now. Thus there are no common objectives in and on standardised tests that teachers should teach for so that pupils might be successful in goal attainment. In addition to validity, reliability is an important term in testing and evaluation. It is much easier in pilot studies to obtain statistical figures on reliability. Reliability stresses consistency of test results for pupils when a retest or split-half reliability is used. Thus the chances are if a test item is written clearly, the pupil will respond consistently when the same test is being given such as in test-retest reliability. From pilot studies in standardising a test, weak items can be eliminated or modified so that consistency in terms of pupils' responses is obtained.

B. Criterion referenced tests. Here, the teacher has relatively easy access to the objectives that need emphasis in teaching so that he/she may stress selected subject matter in teaching learners. The test items then might be quite valid for pupils if the teacher has aligned instruction with the stated objectives. The content taught may then be valid since it aligns with the objectives. Reliability might also be good if the results from the CRT are the same/similar from pupils in a test/retest situation.

Our reservations about CRTs include the following:

1. the developers of the CRTs did not run pilot studies on test results of pupils; thus there is no data to show the validity and reliability of the CRT. In fact, this has happened in selected states in the US. The governor of a state then wished to hurry with implementing a new CRT and did not have educators do statistical analysis of pupil test results;
2. CRTs tend to have too many factual test items rather then stressing pupils engaging in critical and creative thinking as well as problem solving. Generally with multiple choice test items, the trend would be for factual knowledge to dominate content in and on the test.

C. District wide tests. These tests are developed in the same way as is true of CRTs. District wide tests, however, are written by teachers and administrators on the local school district level as compared to the state level as was true of CRTs. Unless carefully developed district wide tests might have the same weaknesses as do CRTs. It costs money and takes time to run tests of validity and reliability in pilot studies. However unless these pilot studies are run, the tests might well have weak and unclear test items. There are ample opportunities in district wide tests to align with content taught by teachers within that district.

D. Test which accompany a basal mathematics textbook series or other academic area. Here we will discuss mathematics only and accompanying tests with the basal text. There are several series that have tests inside the basal which the teacher can give to pupils. The tests seem to be well aligned, in most cases, with content covered for each unit of study in the basal. Authors of the text and the accompanying tests advocate pupils be given the test prior to teaching the first unit, for example. If a pupil obtains a score of eighty per cent or higher on the unit being pretested, he/she need not study that unit, but can take the pretest for the next unit of study in the basal. Again, if a score of eighty per cent or higher is secured by the pupil taking the pretest, he/she need not study or do the work in that unit of study. This approach of passing out of a unit continues until a pupil does not get eighty per cent or higher of the test items correct on a pretest.

We see the following weaknesses on a basal textbook test to measure pupil achievement:

1. these tests seemingly are not that valid and reliable to have pupils test out of studying and doing the work within a unit of study. We have heard most teachers of mathematics in my graduate classes as well as cooperating teachers whom we supervise in the public schools make statements that doubt the strengths of using these tests to measure if pupils can test out of a unit of study. However, teachers do say pretests such as those related directly to a textbook have their strengths to offer assistance to teachers in teaching pupils. Thus what pupils miss on these pretests may become a part of objective to achieve in the mathematics curriculum;

2. mathematics contains more exact and precise knowledge as compared to such curriculum areas as reading the literature, art, music, physical education, and social studies when ascertaining learner progress. We believe that mathematics tests due to their objective content can do a better job of measuring pupil progress as compared to other academic disciplines. There still as a problem as to what to emphasise on these tests such as products versus processes, the practical as compared to the theoretical in mathematics;

3. face validity may be fairly strong in subject matter tests since the writers of the tests look at content taught and then arrange items therefrom for the test. However, predictive validity is desired since the results form a learner in having taken the test is to predict how well he/she will do on the next ensuing unit of study.

E. Education 2000. The year 2000 is near and goals need to be looked at continuously for purposes of improving the curriculum as well as new trends are entering into the arena. At the 1989 National Governor's Conference, major broad objectives were identified at this meeting. We will mention two here for comment. We realise the Conference statements are very general in terms of objectives for pupil attainment, namely US pupils are to be first in test results in international comparisons among pupils in science and mathematics. US pupils have not done well in international comparisons on test results. There are and can be numerous reasons for achievement levels of US pupils when comparisons are made. We will raise several questions pertaining to these occurrences:

1. Are the objectives of US schools aligned with the tests of international comparisons?
2. Much stress is placed upon US pupil using what has been learned such as in science and mathematics. Do the test items on international comparisons also stress application of content learned or are more theoretical objectives being emphasised?
3. Do pupil reveal what has been learned through testing or are there better ways such as hands on approaches to indicate achievement in mathematics with the use of real objects?
4. Are there selected countries in the world whose pupils do better on international tests of comparison due to classroom work in mathematics stressing more of what is covered on these tests?
5. Which pupils are tested in the different nations when international comparisons are made? For example, US educates all pupils regardless of handicaps possessed such as mental retardation and those with behavioural disorders. Are these pupils a part of US pupils being tested and compared with other nations who do not have these kinds of learners in the comparison pool? US pupils stay in school until the senor year of high school when about 80 per cent of this age group graduate. How does this compare with other nations in holding power of schools. If more of the cream of the crop of pupils are tested in a nation, then higher achievement is possible here;

6. Are there too many variables among nations when making comparisons in science and mathematics achievement? For example, it is very difficult to make comparisons among nations as to how money earmarked for school is spent. In the US much of school moneys goes to busing pupils from rural areas into school. A considerable amount of money is spent also on busing for integration of the races purposes. There are nations that do not even need to use school buses, such as Russia.

F. The National Assessment of Educational Progress (NAEP). This is a real puzzler to me when viewing test results from NAEP. NAEP tests a sample population of nine, eleven, and thirteen year olds in the US every year. When test results are not what editors and writers of commentaries want, there is much criticism of schools.

Writers of test items can write them at an easier as well as a more complex level. If we want to show that the public schools are failing, we would write very difficult test items so that pupils would indicate low achievement. Should we desire to indicate very high public school achievement, we would write exceedingly easy test items for pupils to respond to. NAESP results do not tell me anything. The most information we can receive from NAESP is what the writers and statisticians declare. One of our learned personalities jokingly says when he has finished glancing at NAEP results—'Ten per cent of seventeen year olds did not know who the first president of the US was,' or 'Two per cent of the pupils tested could not identify what a verb is.' Generally, the statements given here in a humorous way state the very low pupil achievement, never in a way that 'Ninety-five per cent of thirteen year olds could write a meaningful paragraph.' We would like to see the test items on the NAEP and analyse them in terms of clarity and relevance. The test items on the NAEP are given outside of context. What worker in society is given a test to indicate how well he/she is doing his/her job? The answer is none. One shows proficiency by doing and applying, not from test results. We cannot become excited about the low test results as shown by NAEP. Constructivism is a philosophy of testing that stresses contextual situations for pupils to reveal what has been learned. People at the work place also indicate how well they are doing within a context, not within a testing framework.

CONSTRUCTIVISM AND EVALUATION

Constructivism emphasises pupils being evaluated in terms of the situations they are in. For example, if pupils write a get well card to an ill classmate, there is a need for a writing activity. When the get well card is written, then there should be efforts made to appraise the quality of the card that will be sent to the ill classmate. Or, if a committee of pupils is doing a science experiment that relates directly to the ongoing unit, the quality of the experiment needs appraising in terms of desired criteria. It is very difficult, for example, to write a paper/pencil test item or items covering how well a science experiment was done.

Pertaining to two versions of constructivism, Alrasian and Walsh (1997) wrote:

These fundamental agreements among the constructivists are tempered by some important areas of difference about the process of constructing knowledge. These differences are reflected in two versions of cognition: developmental and socio-cultural.

Development theories, such as Piaget's, represent a more traditional constructivist framework. This major emphasis is on the universal forms of structures of knowledge (e.g., prelogical, concrete, and abstract operations) that guide the making of meaning. These universal cognitive structures are assumed to be developed and organised, so that prelogical thinking occurs prior to concrete logical thinking in a developmental sequence. Within this framework, the individual student is considered to be the meaning maker, with the development of the individual's personal knowledge being the main goal of learning. Critics of developmental theories of cognition point out that this perspective does not take into account ' how issues such as the cultural and political nature of schooling and the race, class, and gender backgrounds of teachers and students, as well as their prior learning histories, influence the kinds of meaning that are made in the classrooms,' Cognitive developmental theories, it is claimed, divorce meaning from affect by focusing on isolating universal forms of knowledge and thus limiting consideration of the socio-cultural and contextual influence on the construction of knowledge.

Constructivism then stresses the following:

1. pupils being evaluated in terms of how well they perform within a specific ongoing learning activity;
2. pupils indicating they can apply what has been learned within a relevant task;
3. pupils indicating what has been learned in an intrinsic situation such as an experience that is being stressed presently, not in a formal testing situation extrinsic to the tasks being pursued;
4. pupils perceiving the value of the activity being pursued and revealing strengths and weaknesses therein.

ADDITIONAL TESTS BEING ADVOCATED

It appears that schools and education of pupils is criticised all over the world (The Educational Review, 1997), Kakkar wrote on 'Crisis in Education in India:'

What the school, of late, has been doing sometimes makes people talk of deschooling education and foreseeing a future in which there may be no school at all. This will not happen. But there is certainly ahead of us an interval of rethinking fundamentals, and of raising schools different from the ones we have.

Education is not only in a crisis just because the school is suddenly doing worse. In fact, It has done a terribly poor job all along. But what we have been tolerating in the past we can not longer tolerate today. It is a sheer delusion to think that school has been a place that children loved, that school years are years of happiness, or that students learned a great deal in school. School, in fact, has been a place of misery, of boredom of suffering, where, as every teacher knows, only one of every fifteen students learned anything, if at all. Even college students around the turn of the century cannot expect to learn much. They go to college because they have nothing else to do, or because it leads to a professional career, or because it is the socially accepted thing to do, to make valuable connections.

There have been very vocal critics of US education over the decades. Illich (1972) came out with his book on 'De-Schooling Society'. He recommended a thorough doing away with public education and offered a plan of schooling whereby arrangement would be made between a master in a field of specialisation and the pupil wanting to learn what the specialist had to offer. The specialist may offer classes in the following areas: music, art, drama, literature, geography, history, the sciences, and so on. Illich believed that compulsory school attendance made for mediocrity and dehumanised education. We well remember teaching and doing relief work on the West Bank of the Jordan from 1952-1954 and of the many refugees and bedouins that had very little formal schooling. When riding a bus from Jerusalem to Jericho, the bus would stop along the way to let selected passengers get off. There were several young bedouin boys that got off midway between Jerusalem and Jericho and followed a path to their tent at a distance. We truly felt for these young men and the lack of opportunities they had in life with, perhaps, no formal education. Poverty and the lack of education are two evils that one sees too frequently in societies around the world. Bedouins living in tents and herding sheep and goats as well as having camels for transportation in a nomadic setting do not have a changing environment to look forward for. We certainly could not buy the idea of deschooling society.

Too frequently, slogans in society are given to justify the thinking of the one presenting the diverse slogans (Ediger, 1997), such as in the following:

'let's have the business world teach pupils; the public schools are not doing the job.' Additional slogans here could be, 'The private sector has always been able to do things better than the public sector. Thus performance contracting has been emphasised in selected schools in which a certain level of achievement is guaranteed by the contractor in return for payment on a per pupil basis. Educational Alternatives of Minneapolis, Minnesota is involved in teaching pupils on a business basis. Performance contractors desire to make profits, large profits if possible for their ventures which is teaching in this case. Performance contracting was emphasised in selected school systems in the early 1970s.

Commentaries and reports on education can be quite critical. How accurate are these writings? It is hard to say. We believe a rational question might be raised about how much better other institutions in society are doing as compared to the educational arenas. There are many slogans which abound in American Society.

There are groups such as the National Alliance of Business (NAB) who have felt that public schools pupils definitely are not achieving adequately. They have offered to write tests which would demonstrate to the lay public what is lacking and needs to be changed in the public schools after viewing the test results. These approaches would involve a tremendous change in American school policy if this were done. Why? The business world of free enterprise might then determine what is of value and should be taught in the public schools. There are other segments of the population such as labour that would not be represented in such a venture. Questions that need to be raised here pertain to the following:

1. how can be business world now which content should appear on tests?
2. is there more to the education of children other than business interests?
3. what would be the rationale of having the business world be involved in testing pupils in the public schools?
4. how does the business world train their employees at the work place; is there a model for their advocacy in the educational arena?

In addition the business world and their plans of action, there and governmental leases who come up with ideas in education and the public schools. Thus President Bill Clinton in his 1997 State of the Union Address called upon the US to become first in the world in terms of quality education offered for public school age pupils. He advocated testing every fourth grader in reading achievement and every eighth grader in mathematics to ensure that high national standards in education are being met. Results from the tests would indicate what help a child needs to improve in reading and in mathematics. President Clinton advocated having the best teachers in the world if the best schools in the world are to come about. About one million volunteers will be needed in the public schools to provide assistance and ensure that pupils are reading independently by the end of the third grade (Bill Clinton, 1997).

Action by governmental leaders can be excellent in order to focus on the importance of education and the public schools. There are definite questions that might be raised here pertaining to additional testing and the writing of new tests such as testing fourth grades on reading achievement and eighth graders on mathematics progress:

1. are sufficient tests available already to measure pupil achievement academically without writing new tests?
2. how will new tests be developed to stress validity in reading? There are many issues involved in reading such as phonics versus the whole language approach.
3. how much testing of pupils should be emphasised to determine achievement? Here we come up with the debate of testing versus constructivism to indicate learner progress in teaching and learning situations.
4. how do test results of pupils in a single testing situation differ from learners revealing everyday progress in the classroom, as observed by teachers, in revealing reading achievement?
5. who will be involved in writing test items so that politics is minimised to indicate pupil achievement in the public schools?

Conclusion

If pupils fail, then what? There are so many alternatives here that may be discussed. First of all, is the result of failure internal in that the pupil does not care, nor put forth effort? Or, do pupils fail due to the numerous variables inherent in the public school system? Numerous approaches are used to assist pupils to do better in a receiving school such as would be true of the voucher system. Here, parents may choose which school their child is to attend, with the money available that would equal to what the sending school spends per pupil. The receiving school may spend more money per child and thus the parent needs to make up the difference plus transportation costs. Sending pupils at public expense to denominational schools is still not in evidence since church and state separation regulations apply in most case cases. Open enrolment is available in selected states in the US, such as Iowa and Minnesota, whereby parents may select the school within their state for the child to attend. Parents need to be aware of the curricular offerings in a new school chosen. The objectives, learning opportunities, and evaluation procedures need to harmonise with the pupil's very own style of learning. This would be true of all plans open to parent to assist the pupil to achieve and avoid failure. There may be problems involved when parents select a school away from home base for their child to attend. There may be room and board costs when the pupil is living away from home. Then too, the child may not be close to home when there is such a need to be near to parents/guardians.

Measuring up to predetermined standards can be difficult for many pupils. Standardised tests do not have these predetermined standards; however, different school districts may be using these kinds of tests to measure learner progress within a given school year. A slow learner may achieve at a low level on a standardised test and yet be achieving as well as can be expected. A gifted/talented pupil may achieve at a high level on the standardised test but is not really applying himself/herself in teaching and learning situations.

CRTs can be excellent if higher levels of cognition are being measured for pupils to attain. Learners may also progress as rapidly as possible on each of the sequential objectives with provisions then being made for individual differences. Slow learners here need additional assistance to achieve as optimally as possible. District wide achievement tests operate in a similar manner as do CRTs. Both need to be valid and measure in terms of what pupils have had opportunities to learn in the school curriculum. If the test items are vague and poorly written, learner achievement will not be indicated in an appropriate way.

Tests based on the basal textbook being used can be one way to appraise learner progress. That is true of all valid and reliable evaluation techniques in that each procedure is an approach to determine what a pupil has learned. There are no perfect ways nor panaceas to appraise pupil achievement. The teacher needs to use a variety of techniques of determine what pupils have learned.

The National Assessment of Educational Progress (NAEP) tests a random sampling of pupils in the US to ascertain what has been achieved. This is a complex venture in that the test items can not be valid for pupils to achieve. Thus there is no alignment between objectives of which there are none listed for pupils to achieve on the NAEP and the evaluation items for that test. It would indeed be difficult for test writers in writing items that are to represent that which pupils have learned and achieved. The following questions arise:

1. how difficult or how easy does one write each test item in terms of complexity?
2. what subject matter is to be covered on the test?
3. which is the most appropriate way for pupils to reveal what has been learned? Different ways of revealing learning may include paper/pencil tests such as is used in the NAEP tests; however, there are numerous additional ways such as experiments, demonstrations, hands on approaches, and art work, among others.
4. how much emphasis should be placed upon subject matter content in the tests as compared to skills and attitudes?
5. what meanings are to be given to test results of pupils?

If, for example, forty per cent of nine year olds cannot write a meaningful sentence, according to NAEP results, then the teacher needs to assist pupils in writing meaningful sentences. It is difficult to know what is meant by a meaningful sentence, according to NAEP workers and measurement specialists.

Constructivism has the most merit of all approaches in ascertaining what pupils have learned Why? The evaluation is not a one shot approach, but can be ongoing and continuous. Within a learning situation then, the teacher appraises how well a pupil is doing. The results may be obtained from teacher observation as well as test results. Feedback is then given to the pupil on what can be done to achieve sequentially.

Perhaps, all of the approaches mentioned above have some merit. However, the goal is to assist pupils to achieve more optimally, not to obtain test scores for comparisons to be made among pupils nor to minimise human values of individual learners. If pupils fail, teachers need to have information on guiding pupils individually to be successful learners.

References

Alrasian, Peter W., and Mary E. Walsh (1997), 'Cautions for Classroom Constructivists,' *Education Digest*, Vol. 62, No. 8, page 63, (condensed for *Phi Delta Kappa*, Vol. 78 No. 2, pages 444-449.

Clinton, Bill (1997), 'President Clinton's Call for Action,' *Education Digest,* Vol. 62, No. 8, pages 4-7.

Ediger, Marlow (1997), 'Slogans in Education and in Society, *Journal of Instructional Psychology*, Vol., 24, No. 1, pages 37-41.

Ediger, Marlow (1996), *Essays in School Administration.* Kirksville, Missouri: Simpson Publishing, pages 93 and 94.

Ediger, Marlow (1999), 'Problems in Teaching Science,' *Experiments in Education*, 27 (7), 112-117, published in India by the SITU Council for Educational Research.

Illich, Ivan (1972), *De-Schooling Society.* New York: Harper and Row.

Kakkar, S.B. (1997), Crisis in Education in India, *The Educational Review*, Vol. 102, No. 1 pages 1 and 2.

18

How Effective is Your School?

Teachers, administrators, and parents desire effective schools. They want pupils to learn as much as possible in attaining the schools' objectives. Learners are to do well intellectually, socially, emotionally, and physically. Later as adults, individuals will be trained and educated effectively to do well in the work place. In the work place, individuals hopefully, will experience self-fulfillment in terms of job or occupational satisfaction, economic efficiency, social development emotional adjustment, and physical health to pursue the tasks at hand. This is a difficult task for schools and others to perform. What makes for an effective school? This seems to be at the center of the debate on what should be in education.

EFFECTIVE SCHOOLS

Sizer (1986), through research in studying high schools, emphasised nine principles or criteria in stressing what is essential in the school curriculum. These are the following:

1. an intellectual focus is needed in the school curriculum;
2. the goals of the school should be stated clearly;
3. these goals should be applicable to all pupils in school;
4. the pupils is to be perceived as a worker;
5. pupils need to reveal what has been learned;
6. attitudes of learners is important in learning;
7. teachers are generalists first and specialists second;
8. personalised learning is needed in the classroom;
9. the school budget shows priorities in the process of education.

Schools have selected criteria here from which to evaluate their effectiveness. Among other items, improving pupil attitudes, learning being personal, and emphasising budgetary items are salient. Squires and others (1985), in summarising !eadership in effective schools research, posited four questions. These are the following:

1. Is there a purpose or reasons involved for the principal being involved in the school setting?
2. does the principal stress high academic standards?
3. does the principal provide support for school personnel, inservice education for staff members, and time for teachers to coordinate their efforts in school discipline, as well as in the instructional arena?
4. does the principal observe classroom instruction regularly and confer with teachers on instructional matters?

The school principal has always been perceived as being the leader in stressing curriculum improvement. Thus the principal has numerous responsibilities in guiding, directing, and leading teachers in moving from what is to what should be.

Rossow (1990) determines the following common findings that indicate a high correlation with increased student achievement:

1. a safe and orderly school environment;
2. high level of expectation for student success;
3. strong leadership;
4. clear and focused school mission;
5. schoolwide training for teachers and staff;
6. close monitoring of student progress;
7. considerable control by teachers and staff over instructional decisions.

Ediger (1988) stresses the use of workshops as one method of improving the curriculum. The theme of the workshop should be decided upon cooperatively by participants. The general session should have as a major goal the identification by participants of relevant problem areas that need solutions. Participants should volunteer to serve on a committee to solve an identified problem area. Teacher purpose needs to be involved when choosing a committee for participation. Time for individual study is also necessary since problems are unique to the teacher. Adequate consultant assistance should be available at the workshop. A professional library should be available to participants engaged in problem solving. What has been learned and accepted needs to be tried out in the classroom setting. Results may then be reported to all the participants in the workshop.

Jennings (1995) stresses a curriculum which has precise objectives, predetermined, for pupils to achieve. Teachers then teach toward the objectives using a variety of learning activities. Pupil progress is measured against the precise objectives. The objectives, learning opportunities, and evaluation procedures are closely related. In the process; validity and reliability are strongly emphasised here.

Toward the other end of the continuum, Eisner (1995) advocates that teachers look at individual differences in developing the curriculum. The curriculum incorporates pupil interest and purpose. Pupils should have ample opportunities to plan the curriculum with teachers since they will be involved in learning.

Learners then are engaged in decision making when being actively involved in selecting learning opportunities and evaluation procedures; the teacher serves as one who encourages and motivates pupils.

Evanciew (1994) estimates that approximately 25 per cent of individuals below age 29 have baccalaureate degrees from a collage or university. This leaves a large number that need a different kind of education than the academic. Thus many pupils need a quality vocational education curriculum. Vocational training should largely be emphasised at a place of business which stresses the kind of education needed by the apprentice. The apprentice in vocational education experiences the following learning opportunities from the instructor:

Modelling (demonstrating a task so students can observe and build a conceptual model of the processes required to accomplish it);

Coaching (observing students performing a task and assisting when necessary;

Scaffolding (supporting a student in a given task);

Articulation (assisting students to articulate their knowledge);

Reflection (enabling students to compare their processes with those of other students;

Exploration (encouraging students to develop their own methods).

MOTIVATION OF TEACHERS

Effective schools should have highly motivated teachers. Motivated teachers have a high energy level for achieving, growing, and developing. Wentworth (1990) suggests that low moral comes for teachers who do not perceive meaning in their professional lives. These teachers feel frustrated at not being able to affect needed change in the curriculum. The demands upon scarce materials of instruction may be great on the part of teachers. Wentworth emphasises that principals respond to the concerns of teachers. Principals should recognise good teaching.

Staff meetings, shared leadership, and quality communication aid in the professional development of teachers.

Weller (1982) advocates that principals use Maslow's hierarchy of needs criteria in working with teachers. These needs or motivators are physiological, safety and security, love and affiliation, esteem, knowledge and understanding, and self actualisation. Generally, the simplest need is taken care of first such as physiological, e.g. adequate nutrition, rest and sleep, proper clothing and temperature readings; safety and security needs must then be fulfilled, followed in sequence by the other needs listed above.

Walker (1990) indicates essential skills that principals need to possess in order to motivate teachers. These are the following qualities: being able to analyse problems, effective judgment, organisational skills, decisiveness, leadership, sensitivity, stress tolerance, oral communication, written communication, wide ranging interests, personal motivation, and positive educational values.

Schlansker (1987) emphasises the importance of principles helping teachers deal with stress. In her research, there are selected ways of assisting teachers. These are the following, involving teachers and principals:

1. sharing personal experiences;
2. getting administrative support on policy;
3. access to support personnel;
4. receiving feedback from the principal on teaching performance;
5. the principal showing actions of sharing, caring, and interacting;
6. job security;
7. provision of adequate physical facilities.

Selected educators, since the early twentieth century, have advocated using merit pay to encourage and motivate teachers to improve teaching. To be sure teachers need adequate remuneration for their professional services; however, there are few schools where merit pay has worked successfully to motivate teachers to do a better job of teaching

Ornstein (1998) indicates some of the reasons for the lack of support for merit pay. Politics and patronage may be involved in rewarding teachers with merit pay. Teachers may be less creative due to strict adherence to bureaucratic mandates which determine standards for merit pay. The unit of teachers might be threatened when competition for merit pay is stressed, rather than cooperation among teachers.

Jorde-Bloom believes that a quality school environment may be a positive motivator to teachers. This environment would emphasise collegiality, professional growth, supervisor support, clarity of roles and practices, a reward system, decision-making structure, goal consensus task orientation, physical setting, and innovativeness.

Rallis (1990) emphasised the importance of the following areas when professionalising the area of teaching: increasing communication among staff; improving sensitivity to individual student needs; establishing priorities in the list of necessary curriculum and material options; encouraging flexibility in programming, assessment, and use of instructional techniques; increasing teacher confidence, providing leadership roles for teachers; formalising and documenting previously informal conversations between teachers such as talk over coffee; recognising and remediating teacher isolation; demonstrating teacher needs for discussion of common issues; raising the overall level of professionalism in the building; and engaging teachers to talk about students in a positive way.

Dunn and Dunn (1979) have done much work in the areas of diagnosing learning styles for pupils. They identified four broad styles of learning possessed by pupils. These are environmental elements in the classroom such as musical recordings played in the classroom as compared to absolute silence in guiding pupils to achieve more. Second, emotional forces such as intrinsic versus extrinsic motivation. Third, sociological elements such as pupils working together with others on an activity as compared to individual endeavours. Fourth, pupils learning best through the use of one or more senses as compared to more abstract forms of learning. Physical factors could also stress eating/drinking while learning as compared to strict adherence to learning while abstaining from eating/drinking. If the teacher could truly know the kind of learning style possessed by a pupil, he/she could do a better job of selecting materials from which pupils are to learn. These materials could be concrete (real objects and items), semi-concrete material (pictorial forms of learning), and the abstract form (reading, listening, speaking, and writing) with not concrete or semi-concrete materials.

Bruner (1977) emphasises the following sequence in assisting pupils to learn: concrete materials (manipulative in nature): semi-concrete materials such as videotapes, slides, films, software containing pictorial items, video disks containing drawings as well as illustrations and snapshot reproductions; and symbolic materials of instruction such as learning through listening, speaking, reading, and writing. Bruner lists the materials of instruction to be used in order or sequence rather than as a particular learning style.

Cogan (1973) advocates using a clinical approach in supervising teachers in the classroom. There is a four step cycle involved in this model. The first step stresses having a preconference with the teacher involved. Here, the supervisor and the teacher cooperatively view the goals for instruction established by the latter. Goals may be modified or changed as the need may indicate. Second, observation of the teacher's teaching is made by the supervisor. The supervisor needs to observe which pupils are successful in goal attainment. Pupils need identification who do not pay attention nor appear to be interested in the ongoing lesson. The supervisor's goal is to aid all pupils to attain as optimally as possible. Third, analysis is in evidence. Here, the teacher and the supervisor discuss the completed lesson. The discussion zeros in on guiding each pupil to learn and achieve the stated goals. Rapport must exist between the supervisor and the teacher who was observed in teaching pupils. Fourth, the postconference stresses what can be done to assist pupils individually to achieve at a better rate. There needs to be agreement between the supervisor and the teacher as to which course of action the teacher should follow in future presentations.

The clinical method of supervision offers opportunities for teachers to gain inservice education assistance in a contextual situation.

Ediger (1994) advocates teachers being able to demonstrate to others different philosophies of education in contextual situations. The teacher should indicate how idealism as a philosophy of education may be implemented. A subject centered curriculum would then be in evidence. Pupils would attain abstract content using higher levels of cognition. The concrete and semi-concrete facets of learning would be stressed only to the degree that pupils are aided in attaining vital facts, concepts, generalisations, main ideas, and relevant thinking skills. Developing well mentally is the major objective for pupil achievement when stressing idealism as a philosophy of education. Second, the teacher should be able to model problem solving skills in teaching. Experimentalism as a philosophy of education emphasises problem solving activities. The problems should be real and lifelike. In context pupils with teacher guidance identify one or more problems. An hypothesis or answer to the problem is emphasised. Each hypothesis is tentative and subject to change and modification Data or information in context is gathered to test each hypothesis. Thus an hypothesis may need to undergo reconstruction. Experimentalists tend to stress pupils working on committees to solve problems since in society problems arise and in committees are solved to the best possible. Third, the teacher should be able to stress pupil decision making and teacher/pupil planning in the curriculum. This may or may not involve problem solving. Generally pupils individually choose which activities to participate in. Here, the teacher models, contextually, existentialism as a philosophy of education. Existentialists emphasise the subjectivity of knowledge. Pupils then construct their own knowledge. Fourth, teachers should be able to stress realism as a philosophy of education. With realism, specific objectives are chosen by the teacher prior to instruction. The chosen objectives are announced to pupils before a lesson is implemented. Pupils need to be clear on what is expected of them. The objectives and expectations are stated in measurable terms. After instruction, the teacher measures if pupils have/have not been successful in goal attainment. A different teaching strategy needs to be used to assist pupils to attain objectives, if they had been unsuccessful learners in goal attainment.

Specific psychologies may also be emphasised by a competent teacher in demonstration teaching. Thus to emphasise stimulus/response psychology of teaching and learning, the teacher rewards correct responses given by pupils to questions raised by the teacher. The reward may be verbal or physical. Generally, physical prizes will be given to learners for responding correctly. A ratio approach can be implemented in which a prize, for example, is given the pupil for every five correct responses made. Other ratios might also be used. An interval approach would reward a pupil with a physical prize for working and responding correctly every five minutes. The interval is a prize for five minutes of work performed correctly by the pupil. Other sized intervals may be used. Reinforcement theory stresses rewarding what is done correctly, using ratios or intervals of time. A token economy or prizes immediately given for correct responses may be emphasised in teaching and learning (Skinner 1979). Each response to a stimulus is measurable if it has or has not occurred. A logical sequence is in evidence since the teacher orders what pupils are to learn.

Eisner (1995) believes that pupils should take a leading role in ascertaining what should be learned. With learning centers, cooperatively developed involving pupils with teacher guidance, the learner may choose what to learn and what to omit. There are an adequate number of tasks available so that the pupil may sequence and omit with time on task. Here, the pupil sequences his/her own learning with tasks selected from the diverse centers. What tasks do not have perceived purpose may be omitted. A psychological sequence is in evidence since the pupil order his/her own experiences.

Piaget (1952) emphasises a development approach to teaching pupils. Learners go through sequential stages of development which the teacher needs to take notice of in planning the curriculum. These stages are sensorimotor, ages birth to two years; preoperational, two years to seven years of age; concrete operations, seven to eleven years of age; and symbolic thought or formal operations, beyond eleven years of age.

Teacher and administrators need to become thoroughly familiar with diverse psychologies of learning so that each may be used to assist pupils to attain optimally in the curriculum.

Conclusion

Pupils need to experience quality in the curriculum. The best objectives, learning opportunities, and evaluation procedures should be used to guide each pupil to achieve as optimally as possible. Teachers and administrators must be knowledgable as possible about the act of teaching and learning. Principals and teachers should be leaders in the school and serve as change agents to modify what is and change to what should be in the curriculum. Quality leadership is necessary to select the kind of philosophy and psychology needed to guide optimal learner achievement.

References

Bruner, Jerome (1977), *The Process of Education.* Cambridge, Massachusetts, p 33.

Cogan, M. (1973), *Clinical Supervision.* Boston: Houghton Mifflin.

Dunn, Rita, and Kenneth Dunn (1979), Learning Styles/Teaching Styles: Should They—Can They—Be Matched? *Educational Leadership.* 36, 238-244.

Ediger, Marlow (1988), *The Elementary Curriculum.* Kirksville, Missouri: Simpson Printing, Chapter Fifteen..

Eisner, Elliot (1995), Standards for American Schools: Help or Hindrance? *Phi Delta Kappan.* 76, 758-765.

Evanciew Cheryl (1994). Maximising Learning Through Apprenticeship Training. *Clearing House*, 6, 111-113.

Ediger, Marlow (1994), Early Field Experiences in Teacher Education. *College Student Journal.* pp. 302-306.

Eisner, Elliot (1995), Standards for American Schools: Help or Hindrance? *Phi Delta Kappen,* 76, 758-765.

Jennings, John (1995), School Reform Based on what is Taught and Learned. *Phi Delta Kappan*, 76, 765-770

Jorde-Bloom, P. (1988), Teachers Need 'TLC' too. *Young Children.* 43, 4-8.

Ornstein, Allen (1988), The Changing Status of the Teacher Profession. *Urban Education.* 23, 260-269.

Piaget, Jean (1952), *The Moral Judgment of the Child.* New York: Humanities Press, Inc.

Rossow, Lawrence F. (1990), *The Principalship.* Englewood Cliffs, New Jersey: Prentice Hall, Inc., p. 5.

Rallis, Sharon F. (1990), Professional Teachers and Restructured Schools: Leadership Challenges. *NSSE Yearbook.* Chicago, Illinois: National Society for the Study of Education, p. 197-198.

Rathaiah, Lavu and Digumarti Bhaskara Rao, eds. (1997), *International Innovations in Education.* New Delhi, India: Discovery Publishing House.

Sizer, T. R. (1986), Rebuilding: First Steps by the Coalition of Essential Schools. *Phi Delta Kappan,* September, 1986.

Squires and others (1985), *Effective Schools and Classrooms. A Research Based Perspective.* Akexandria, Virginia: Association for Supervision and Curriculum Development, p. 55.

Schlansker, B. (1987). A Principal's Guide to Teacher Stress, *Principal.* 66, 32-34.

Skinner, B. F. (1979), *Beyond Freedom and Dignity.* New York: Alfred A. Knopf.

Wentworth, M. (1990), Developing Staff Moral. *The Practitioner.* 16, 4.

Weller, L. D. (1982), Principals, Meet Maslow: A Prescription for Teacher Retention, *NASSP Bulletin.* 6, 32-36.

Walker, J. E. (1990), The Skills off Exemplorary Principals. *NASSP Bulletin.* 74, 48-55.

19

Bureaucracies and Schools

Much is written about the evils of a bureaucracy. Bureaucracies, according to many educators and lay persons, keep teachers from doing a better job of teaching. Thus, it is believed that there are too many rules, regulations, and mandates for a school system to fulfill. These requirements, along with central office expectations and wants, burden the teacher. School achievement then goes downdhill, according to critics. In these cases, teachers feel a lack of ownership of the curriculum.

Toward the other end of the continuum pertaining to bureaucracies, rules and regulations could be minimised. Complete elimination of rules and regulations would make for anarchy in that each teacher would do what seemed right 'in his/her eyes.'

BUREAUCRACIES AND EDUCATION

Bureaucracies in education take their lead from those who advocate stating objectives ahead of time, prior to instruction.

There are experts in the field who, in general, advocate with certainty what should be taught. The works of experts may be studied to determine, in part, what is relevant for pupils to learn.

Bobbitt (1934) was an early advocate of specifically pinpointing objectives that pupils should achieve. These objective were to be highly precise so that teachers might measure if pupils have successfully achieved objectives. An either/or situation was involved. Thus a pupil, after instruction, had or had not attained the stated objective(s). Objectives needed to be carefully chosen based on what experts did well, according to Bobbitt. Pupils would then emulate the expert in the school curriculum. Here, guesswork was not involved in determining what pupils should learn. Rather the expert was noted and studied to ascertain how he/she did things in the world of work. The positive observations made became objectives for learner attainment. The teacher taught so that pupils were to achieve the stated objectives. The teacher taught with certainty due to the stated objectives being written in measurable terms. After instruction, the teacher might measure how well a person had achieved due to precisions being involved in determining that which any one pupil had achieved. By observing the adult who specialised in a given endeavour, by interviewing people who excelled, by reading research results and by consensus, specialists determine what pupils are to attain.

Implications for Bobbitt's thinking were the following:

1. pupil input in curriculum development would be irrelevant since he/she lacked the expertise to do so;
2. a science of education is possible since the goals of instruction can be determined objectively;
3. teachers need to teach so that pupils may achieve each precise objective of instruction;
4. objectivity in evaluating pupil achievement is possible since learner processes and products can be measured against the standards of the expert upon which the original goals were established;
5. subjective factors in curriculum development can be eliminated or at least minimised.

Werrett Wallace Charters (1923), a predecessor of Bobbitt, stressed the determination of what should be taught through the use of 'job analysis' rather than Bobbitt's activity analysis.' By observing specialists on the job, a trained observer could ascertain what it is that any one person needs to learn. What was observed translated into highly precise objectives for pupils to achieve in terms of stated objectives. Doing away with subjectivity and irrelevant goals made for a science of education, according to the thinking of both Charters and Bobbitt.

The measurement movement was further extended into classroom teaching by E. L. Thorndike (1874-1949) with specific applications made for the school curriculum. Thorndike made the famous statement that 'whatever exists, exists in some amount, and if it exists in some amount it can be measured.' He believed strongly in objective knowledge which is verifiable if achieved by learners. Knowledge, objective in nature, is external to the individual regardless if there is an observer or not. The knowledge then is and exists independently regardless of any single perception by a pupil or person. The objective knowledge, is carefully chosen for implementation in teaching and learning, The philosophy and psychology of realism was strongly emphasised by E. L. Thorndike. Thorndike advocated an objective, verifiable psychology of instruction. The psychology of behaviourism was an end result. Behaviourism stressed connections made between the Stimulus and the Response when pupils acquired knowledge and skills. The bonds in the learner are strengthened as a result of the Stimulus connecting with the Response (Butts and Cremin, 1953). Connections or associations between the Stimulus and the Response (S-R theory of learning) were emphasised by E. L. Thorndike. Behaviourism emphasises that objectives be written and stated prior to instruction. This leaves little if any room for cooperative teacher-pupil planning of the curriculum. Today, state mandated objectives strongly emphasise the use of predetermined objective for pupils to achieve. The stated objectives have been developed on the state, not local levels. Most classroom teachers have had little or no input in writing these stated mandated objectives. Since 1985, the state of Missouri has emphasised the Missouri Mastery and Achievement Tests (MMAT) whereby objectives are developed on the state level and then made available to teachers. State developed criterion referenced tests (CRT's) are given at intervals to measure pupil achievement in attaining MMAT objectives of instruction. Prior to 1985, each district developed measurably stated objectives in what was called an Instructional Management System (IMS). The local district also developed the CRT's to measure how well pupils had achieved the stated objectives in IMS.

State mandated objectives have made for a bureaucracy in education. Thus there are layers of administration above and beyond that of classroom teachers. Objectives for instruction as well as measurement devices to ascertain learner achievement have been developed at the state level, not locally. If districts mandate objectives, such as IMS, local teachers might have had a much better opportunity to provide input into the selected objectives. However, IMS still remains removed from teachers selecting those objectives they deem relevant and salient for learners. Teacher empowerment is not there is these kinds of situations.

NATIONAL GOALS IN EDUCATION

At the National Governors Conference in 1989, USA there was agreement that a national set of objectives should be written and implemented in the public schools. Broad goals were identified for teachers to emphasise in teaching. It was voluntary if school systems/teachers desired to implement these goals in the curriculum. Selected states developed more specific objectives from these broad national goals.

Should the national goals, Education 2000, have become mandatory, those who determined the objectives would be even further removed from the local level as compared to state mandated objectives. Selected states have been involved in implementing these national goals even though it is voluntary to do so. These states have developed more specificity of goals than those written initially in Education 2000. Certainly, another level of bureaucracy, if Education 2000 had become compulsory, would have been in evidence as compared to state mandated objectives.

There are educators who have recommended a national curriculum. Reasons given for these advantages are the following:

1. a more uniform curriculum would be in evidence for all pupils;
2. a basic level of education might then be guaranteed to all pupils and that level would be learner attainment of the national Education 2000 goals;
3. specialists would be involved in developing these objectives for pupil achievement; the best minds possible would be involved here;
4. trivia and the irrelevant would be eliminated from the curriculum;
5. more unity in what is to be achieved in school in a nation would be involved when having pupils achieve national goals rather than state or locally developed objectives.

At issue here is how much of a bureaucracy or lack thereof should there be in education. There appears to be much disagreement among educators as well as lay people on the hierarchical arrangement of selecting objectives for pupil attainment. Should the objectives be formulated on the local district level such as in IMS? Or should the objectives for pupil achievement be chosen on the state or even the federal level of hierarchy? Compare these bureaucracies with my selecting objectives for pupil achievement in the early 1950's at home and abroad. When speakers and writers in education talk about cutting the red tape and doing away with bureaucratic structures, how far should state and federal standards go in this direction?

Acker-Hocevar (1996) wrote the following pertaining to getting ready for change:

The Education Quality Benchmark System holds promise for many superintendents and principals who are searching for models to transform existing school cultures built on quality principles and systems thinking. The thirteen school districts that helped to construct the EQBS were interested in mental models to guide their restructuring efforts within a systems framework.

They believed that educators must be freed from the bureaucratic constraints that limit innovation and improvement to restructure existing practices in schools.

These educators recognised that although schools will operate with some bureaucratic red tape, the aim of the project was to design as framework that developed skills of individuals and built organisational capacity for learning. Thus greater control and autonomy could be achieved by educators as authority, accountability, and responsibility for managing continual improvement shifted to schools, minimising the oversight function of the Auditor General.

Essential to this shift was the identification of dysfunctional bureaucratic practices and barriers to cultivating quality cultures such as top-down communication, turf battles, discrete and narrowly defined jobs, autocratic leadership, and fear of reprisal for questioning existing systems. Barrier removal was perceived to be highly symbolic of organisations committed to quality.

SCHOOL SIGHT MANAGEMENT

Much is emphasised pertaining to decentralising administration until school site management (SSM) is in evidence. SSM will vary somewhat from state and school system to school system. For example, the Chicago, Illinois school system has SSM whereby each school has a principal, two teachers, and four parents on a team that administer and operate a school. This team is in charge of curriculum, supervision, managing a budget, and, among other items, develop standards for school discipline. The SSM team then is responsible for operating the local school. Input from the lay public is a must. Rossow (1990) when comparing the district wide approach as compared to SSM wrote the following:

There are a number of advantages tot he district wide approach. First, it can provide greater coordination among the offerings throughout the district. This makes curriculum monitoring more efficient. Second, bringing together representatives from around the district can foster greater unity.

There are disadvantages. Because the decisions are being

made at the district level, there is a risk that building identity will be sacrificed. Because they feel removed from the curriculum development process, teacher apathy can develop.

The school site approach has gained much popularity in recent years with the rise of effective schools research. This approach is from the bottom tot he top, as opposed to form the top, down. The ideas for change and improvement come form the individual classrooms of each building rather than from the central office. The advantage of the school-site approach is that teachers can feel much more a part of the curriculum development process. In addition, the unique community served by each school can be taken into account when planning for a curricular change.

SSM may truly cut down on bureaucracies if the following conditions are met:

1. a democratic environment exists on the part of SSM team members and their lay public;
2. teachers may easily have input into the curriculum when the SSM team is at the apex of decision making;
3. decisions made are based on what helps each pupil to achieve as optimally as possible;
4. respect for the thinking of others is in evidence;
5. a caring and sharing philosophy prevails in the SSM concept of curriculum development.

With SSM, the movement has been away from decision making on the federal, state, and district levels of educational supervision and curriculum development. Those who advocate less of bureaucracies may well find SSM to their liking.

There are selected questions that need thought and action pertaining to SSM. These are the following:

1. Is it good to have a certain level of bureaucracy, such as the state level, to ensure the basics are agreed upon and all pupils are expected to attain competency therein?
2. Should there be agreement, in general, of the scope

and sequence in the curriculum at a higher level than the SSM level? Continuity may then be more prescribed in a mobile society of pupils.

3. Will there truly be more of democracy and less of bureaucracy in SSM as compared to state or national levels of curricular decision making? People could be highly autocratic on the SSM team level of decision making.

Educators and the lay public need to determine how much of a bureaucracy is needed to emphasise quality in the curriculum. Or should there be a return to individual decision making in terms of curriculum development? In fact, there were no measurable requirements. There seemingly was much trust between the local school system and the state/federal levels of administering the schools.

Conclusion

There are highly relevant questions to raise when educators and the lay public desire less of hierarchies and a leaner, thinner government.

Should there more of charter schools whereby there is less control exhibited by the central office in a school system even though the former is a part of the latter? With charter schools, advocates say that local teaches then have a change to improve the curriculum without the red tape that most schools so often face. Was there a reason for having the 'red tape' to begin with? It might be that certain rules and regulations are made for the sake of doing so. However, many legal restraints are there for definite reasons or purposes, such as minimal levels of achievement that pupils need to attain prior to graduation. We believe that teachers, administrators, and support personnel together with state and national legislators need to decide how much and what kind of bureaucracy to develop and maintain in education. A line may be drawn here pertaining to one end of the continuum showing complete freedom for teachers in developing the curriculum on an individual basis. Toward the other end of the continuum, state and federal levels of government might heavily prescribe all objectives for learners to attain. We are certain there are existentialist teachers who desire to plan all curricular experiences with heavy pupil involvement, be it individual or group endeavours. Then there are experimentalist teachers who believe in committees and groups that should be involved in determining lifelike problems for pupils to solve. The gap needs to be minimised/closed in curriculum. development between the two pints of view, hierarchical versus a non-hierarchical approach, using rational decision making strategies.

References

Acker-Hocevar, Michele (1996), 'Conceptual Models, Choices, and Benchmarks for Building Quality Work Cultures,' *National Association of Secondary School Principals Bulletin.* 80 : 79-80.

Bobbitt, Franklin (1934), *How to Make a Curriculum.* Boston: Houghton Mifflin Company.

Butts, R. Freeman, and Lawrence A. Cremin (1953), *A History of Education in American Culture.* New York: Holt, Rinehart and Winston, 335-337.

Bhaskara Rao, Digumarti, ed. (1998), *Reforming School Education.* New Delhi, India: Discovery Publishing House.

Charters, Wrrett Wallace (1923), *Curriculum Construction.* New York: The Macmillan Company.

Ediger, Marlow (1999), 'Portfolios, the Student, and the Teacher,' Technical and Vocational Education. Kirksville, Missouri: Simpson Publishing Company, 88-94.

Rossow, Lawrence F. (1990), *The Principalship.* Englewood Cliffs, New Jersey: Perntice Hall, 115-116.

INDEX